A Most Wondrous Babble

A Most Wondrous Babble
AMERICAN ART COMPOSERS, THEIR MUSIC, AND THE AMERICAN SCENE, 1950–1985

Nicholas E. Tawa

CONTRIBUTIONS TO THE STUDY OF
MUSIC AND DANCE, NUMBER 9

GREENWOOD PRESS
NEW YORK · WESTPORT, CONNECTICUT · LONDON

Library of Congress Cataloging-in-Publication Data

Tawa, Nicholas E.
  A most wondrous babble.

  (Contributions to the study of music and dance,
ISSN 0193-9041 ; no. 9)
  Discography: p.
  Bibliography: p.
  Includes index.
    1. Music—United States—20th century—History and
criticism.   2. Composers—United States.   I. Title.
II. Series.
ML200.5.T36   1987   780′.973   86-22728
ISBN 0-313-25692-6 (lib. bdg. : alk. paper)

Library of Congress Catalog Card Number: 86-22728
ISBN: 0-313-25692-6
ISSN: 0193-9041

First published in 1987

Greenwood Press, Inc.
88 Post Road West, Westport, Connecticut 06881

Printed in the United States of America

The paper used in this book complies with the
Permanent Paper Standard issued by the National
Information Standards Organization (Z39.48-1984).

10 9 8 7 6 5 4 3 2 1

Contents

Preface

A Most Wondrous Babble: American Art Composers, Their Music, and the American Scene, 1950–1985 is a study of musical creativity in the post–World War II decades. It takes up what these composers had to say about themselves, their aims, and their music and what critics and listeners had to say about them. The focus is not only on composers and their compositional styles, but also on the interaction of both with the larger American society.

I do not propose to concentrate only on technical and structural analyses and discussions. On the other hand, I am eager to examine each contemporary style's impact on the ear and how technique and structure contribute to that impact. This examination is necessary because what the composer says about his music and what the public experiences may have few correspondences.

Books on the postwar music scene are generally of two types. The first, an explanation of the technical innovations of the advanced composers, sometimes in terms difficult for the layman to understand; the second, interviews with the composers, which often exhibit little sense of unity or integration. The composer's viewpoint exclusively is of interest to the authors.

A Most Wondrous Babble is different in that it discusses all of the musical styles during the postwar decades, from highly experimental to the traditional, in terms that I hope are intelligible to the layman. Consideration is given to the general listener's interests, viewpoint, and technical limitations. No attempt is made to study every composer nor every work of the composers who are studied. To resort to the first would change this book into a dictionary of composers. To do the second would mean a redundant traversal of the same musical style over and over again to no purpose. Significant compositions that exemplify a particular style are discussed, as well as the reactions to them of music critics, professional musicians, and audiences.

I have listened to almost all of the compositions mentioned in these pages, either on disc and tape recordings or during performances. Since it is difficult to obtain recordings even of very important works—so little of the new music being available from commercial sources—I am grateful to the many people (performers, composers, and committed listeners) who have sent me dubs of otherwise unavailable performances.

Motivating my writing is a real concern for the health of art music in the United States and for the confusion of many listeners when confronted with the extraordinary profusion of contemporary musical styles, each of which is touted to be the direction that all music must take. Add to the listener's confusion a dislike of much of what he hears and his annoyance at some of the polemics issued against him, and one can bring to understand the reasons for the deep abyss separating contemporary composer and listener.

Because contemporary art music leads, at best, a fragile existence in the United States, the danger grows that a turned-off public, and the prominent figures in the aesthetic, political, and economic areas, who give the public heed, will together accomplish the demise of all new music—entirely refusing to hear it and to support it financially.

My conclusions about listeners' attitudes are based, first of all, on the reports and critiques volunteered by several hundred students, non–music majors and music majors, who have taken my course on American music. Direct discussion with and close observation of people at musical performances also have an important bearing on what I say. Insightful commentary has come from numerous colleagues in the Sonneck Society, an association dedicated to the study of music in America. Books, articles, and music reviews have also provided information.

Two more observations should be added. For every musical style discussed, however advanced it is, there exists a specialized audience of devotees. Whatever the attitude of listeners is claimed to be in these pages, it can change at some future time.

Today's art composers desperately need to come out of their isolation. Their music has to find a function within today's society. How do we accomplish both? This is also a topic of consideration in this book. Some composers, who once were modernists, are even now modifying their styles toward greater accessibility. Young composers are less apt to follow in the footsteps of their avant-garde teachers, instead looking for a meaningful way to approach the public. In short, there is hope.

Meanwhile, the contemporary mainstream composers, who are normally the respecters of Western tradition, occupy the sidelines. They remain ignored by the communications media. Some of them still await their turn in the sun. Assuredly, they have been responsible for at least a few excellent compositions—well crafted, communicative, and with exceptional content. Is it possible that the works of these composers, along with those of the former modernists and of the young composers already mentioned, can bring contemporary art music and audience together?

I pray that reconciliation will result. It will, if composers give some thought to the values that most listeners hold in common, and if listeners respect the composer's attempts at creating fresh and honest sounds. To facilitate this reconciliation, I summarize what these values are and suggest how composers and listeners can meet each other halfway. They must discover what is held in common between them, become sensitive to each other's imperatives and needs, and conjointly sponsor a new and mutually meaningful music.

A Most Wondrous Babble

1
Postwar Turbulence and Change

The end of World War II witnessed a divided American society within a divided world. Alongside the desire for peace grew the feeling of despondency brought on by the cold war waged between the United States and Soviet Russia. The Berlin blockade of 1948 and the formation of NATO strengthened this feeling. The testing of bombs, each successive one more powerful than the last, hung like the sword of Damocles over the heads of everyone. The thought that tomorrow we might all be dead haunted every mind. When our anticommunist stance drove us into the Korean War of 1950–53, the American dislike of communism changed into obsessive hatred. McCarthyism sought out and damned communist and innocent liberal alike. The Eisenhower administration, infected with a similar virus, confronted Russia with promises of massive retaliation for its perceived aggression. The hydrogen bomb exploded in 1952; Sputnik was launched in 1958; the Vietnam War tore America apart from 1961 to 1973; and the OPEC oil embargo of 1973 helped to weaken America's flourishing economy.

Add the disruptions brought on by Afro-American militancy against racism and the picture becomes more complicated. In 1954 the decision in the case of Brown vs. the Board of Education of Topeka struck a blow against discrimination in education. From 1955 to 1956 Martin Luther King, Jr., led Afro-Americans in

Montgomery against segregation in transportation. The next year, restaurants were integrated; a year later came the Freedom Riders.

Moreover, there were the traumas brought on by the assassination of President John F. Kennedy in 1963; his brother Robert in 1968; and Martin Luther King, Jr., in 1968. The afflictions affecting American society increased unbearably with the Watergate scandal and Richard Nixon's relinquishing of the presidency in 1974. The cement uniting American society dissolved, to be replaced by the divisiveness of rich against poor, conservative against liberal, youth against age, black against white, amoralist against traditionalist, and libertarian against the believer in the rule of law.

During the years when Americans felt these political and sociological shocks, they were also affected by the spirit of modernity. In his book *All That Is Solid Melts into Air*, Marshall Berman writes that certain modes of experience—one's relation to space, time, other people, and life's possibilities and perils—are common to all people today. These are modes of experience called "modernity." In its exhilarating aspect, modernity leads us to expect "adventure, power, joy, growth, transformation of ourselves and the world." In its depressing aspect, modernity "threatens to destroy everything we have, everything we know, everything we are." He continues by stating that most people "have probably experienced modernity as a radical threat to all their history and traditions."[1]

Americans felt the impact of scientific discoveries and technological advances that altered every feature of their ordinary lives. The accelerating tempos of living dizzied them. Increased urban growth, governmental regulation, might of corporations, and bureaucracies permeating all societal structures were concomitants of these discoveries and advances.

Berman uses a Faustian symbol for postwar humanity when he states that "the fate of 'all that is solid' in" life is "to 'melt into air' [Karl Marx's metaphor]." He writes of the dynamism of our economy and the culture growing from this economy, which destroys everything it creates—physical environments, social institutions, metaphysical ideas, artistic visions, moral values—in order to go on endlessly creating the world anew. This drive involves all humanity and forces us all to consider the question of what is essential, meaningful, and real "in the maelstrom in which we move and live."[2] Conflict was a predictable outcome of uncertainty and of individual searches for meaning. As a result a hunger for self-fulfillment and an urge to create novel lifestyles inevitably emerged out of the postwar confusion and the felt need to assert control over one's own life. The drive to satisfy these demands guaranteed the severe unsettlement of postwar American society.[3]

Contemporary composers attempted to cope with the societal and artistic disorganization as best they could. Some held on to what they saw as the proven past, feeling it was their only security. Others rejected the vulgar outside world and warded off its influence. They responded to their own sense of space and structure, which they hoped would be solidly built. Still others claimed one could not fight modern existence, even at its most vulgar and most chaotic; therefore, they embraced it. Those who felt the Western world was too much with them entered a different world: one of Zen, myth, magic, or a distant time gone by. They extracted their philosophical, artistic, and emotional guidelines from the experiences and thoughts of other peoples and eras. Finally, there were the reconcilers, synthesists, and humanists. They hoped to integrate the experience of modernism with what they saw as the universal roots of mankind.

Throughout the thirty-five years under investigation, these different groups often, though not always, remained antagonistic to each other. Witness, for example, what the composer Elie Siegmeister, a self-defined humanist, has to say about those other composers whom he saw as replacing a human orientation with one centered on technology, computers, and the cult of the machine ("the cold esthetic of scientism"). "Music," he says, "with an expressive, introspective, or humane quality, even the continued use of counterpoint, audible form, and melody were called 'old hat'. Abstruse calculation, cerebral patterns, machine-made sounds or, on the other hand, mystical throws of the dice were now touted as the new paths—in fact, the *only* paths for composition. Twelve-tone technology, then already 30 years old, became the escape route from a disturbed, hostile outer world. Soon the American note in music was pronounced out-of-date by those who had actively espoused it only a few years before."[4]

In the pages that follow, we will examine the causes of turbulence and change in America's postwar art music, among them the new internationalism, the demotion of tradition and older music, the espousal of original sounds often harsh and difficult to assimilate, the dismissal of the general music public as cowardly and vulgar, and the sway of fashion, ceaselessly pushing still adolescent styles into obscurity and newborn ones into the limelight.

FOREIGN INFLUENCES AND THE NEW YORK SCENE

America's history furnishes many instances of composers who spurned their own musical culture and looked to Europe for fresh directions. This was true of the generation that came to the fore in the decade after the end of World War II, "thus confirming the disturbing fact that the world of serious music here is still thought of as an outpost of that European world which Americans have so often found more attractive than the reality of what they have at home."[5] Elliott Carter, who made the above observation, concluded that these American composers felt a need to gain admission into the artistic world of Europe.

The tilt toward Europe was no less true for American musicologists. They, too, questioned the worth of America's cultural past and reflected European viewpoints in their valuation of our cultural present. Even into the 1980s, Joan Peyser claims, they believed in Europe's cultural supremacy and downgraded their own country's culture. Significantly, she suggests that one reason for the anti–American attitude was the training these scholars received either from European musicologists or from European-oriented American musicologists.[6] We will see that the anti-Americanism of many contemporary composers could also be attributed to training.

During the 1930s and 1940s, several of the most illustrious European composers migrated to the United States owing to the rise of totalitarianism in their countries followed by the upheavals of war. Among those who came to America were Schoenberg, Stravinsky, Bartók, Hindemith, Milhaud, and Krenek. Accompanying them on the transatlantic journey were noted architects, like Gropius and Breuer, and cubist and surrealist artists, like Leger, Mondrian, Modigliani, and Chagall. Most of these Europeans won important teaching positions in the United States and passed on to their American students not only their techniques, but also their European theories about art.[7] "By '36, '37, and '38," states Milton Babbitt, "suddenly the whole evolving process of contemporary music transplanted to this country. Bartók, Schoenberg, Hindemith, Stravinsky, Rathaus, Krenek—there was not a single European musical figure who was not functioning and teaching here. . . . So these people arrived here and changed our lives in fundamental ways. The whole intellectual atmosphere was altered. We were the reservoirs, we were the receptacles of this whole tradition which we had been standing outside of."[8]

In addition to the European emigrants, the American composer Roger Sessions, whose music was similar to the chromatic serial music of Schoenberg, became a sought-after teacher in the 1930s and 1940s. The young Babbitt, for example, studied with him for three years, after he had studied with Marion Bauer at New York University. While at New York University, Babbitt had discovered Martin Bernstein, an advocate of Schoenberg's music. Not surprisingly, when Schoenberg briefly resided in New York City, Babbitt was one of his students.[9]

Influencing American composers, too, were the works of Schoenberg's students, Berg and Webern, and those of younger Europeans, like Boulez, Stockhausen, and Berio. Their music was heard especially in New York City. The New York Philharmonic under Mitropoulos, the programs of the Chamber Music Society, the performances of the Juilliard and the Pro Arte Quartets, the concerts sponsored by the I.S.C.M. and the Fromm Music Foundation, and the musical evenings at the New School all showcased the advanced Europeans.[10]

When European composers visited the United States, they sometimes openly attacked American values, institutions, and culture. Behind the attacks was the assumption that America possessed a cheap civilization and the American public an ignorance of twentieth-century artistic works. They further hinted, occasionally in strong fashion, that American composers lacked the imagination and talent of their European counterparts. Curiously, even while some native composers were angered by this claim, they also cultivated styles akin to those of the visitors.

Paul Turok, in 1972, became irked with Luciano Berio, the "composer-mountebank." Turok wrote that when Berio came to

America, he was treated with respect and given a great deal of publicity. Moreover, he made more money from his music during the short while that he was in the United States than did most native art composers during their entire careers. Yet Berio did not hesitate to attack capitalism and point to its deleterious effect on American music. "In a not-very-subtle way," Turok states, "this is saying, it is safe to ignore American music, because the system . . . etc. In fact, the aggressive behavior Berio attributes to American composers best fits that of Boulez, also no friend of American music. European artists are for internationalism, so long as they come out on top."[11]

How then does one account for the imitative behavior of several important American composers? Here, Lionel Trilling provides an insight. Writing in 1956, Trilling observes that native artists felt alienated from the American way of life—its tempo, manners, and method for dealing with fundamental problems. They wanted to insist on their individuality within a society that seemed repellent and that refused to give them recognition as artists. He said that at such moments "the people of a foreign nation" could become attractive. American cultural history, he pointed out, contains many "romances with other cultures, or, sometimes, with other classes. Haunted . . . by unquiet dreams of peace and wholeness, we are eager and quick to find them embodied in another people."[12]

Certain native musicians of modernist inclination wished the approval of Europeans like Boulez or Stockhausen. Approval would advance their careers amongst cultivated Americans who took their lead from Europe. Performance at Darmstadt, Stockhausen's stronghold, or at Donaueschingen would be taken as strong commendation. American composers saw the European avant-garde as having powerful support from the music publishing houses, state-subsidized radio stations, and performing groups supported by public and private funds. For these and other reasons a place like Darmstadt loomed importantly as an originating source of modern Western musical thought. At first the stress was placed mostly on serialism, later on chance and other procedures.[13]

Following Schoenberg's and Webern's lead, the European avant-garde of the 1950s and its American disciples, sponsored serial composition that devalued tonal logic. The commonly accepted ways of making a vocal line appealing were usually neutralized through angular, nonlyrical leaps and through *Sprechstimme*. So dominant was this Central European viewpoint, that established composers like Stravinsky and Copland modified their own styles in order to espouse serialism.[14]

The principal entry point for the advanced European ideas was New York City, whose cultural orientation became international rather than national. This city was the center for concert management, radio, recording, music publishing, and television. American music periodicals and general magazines closely followed the current musical trends, especially as seen in New York City. So also did nationally read newspapers whose writers on music and performances had a broad impact.[15]

New York City also had painters, sculptors, architects, and literary writers of every description congregated within its municipal boundaries. Prior to World War II, they had usually led parallel lives and consciously shared few ideas. Nor had they taken any unusual interest in what creative people outside their own sphere were doing. If their attitudes and paths toward expression seemed similar, it was in response to the general condition of the world and the United States. After the war, creative people concentrated even more in Manhattan. They also began to take a great interest in what colleagues outside their own special field were doing. Propinquity facilitated interdisciplinary friendships and exchanges of ideas and the crossover of innovations from one medium to another. It also encouraged new works that amalgamated several mediums.

Moreover, the huge population of New York City could supply an audience for advanced music that, though minuscule in comparison with the millions of other residents, was sufficiently large to make concerts of modern music viable. In 1968, Harold Schonberg wrote that a special New York audience, numbering around 300 persons, existed for avant-garde concerts, and that it consisted mainly of music professionals, performers and composers. Half the people in the audience, he wrote, were going to have their own music played at a future date. The audience talked about "how interesting Milton's piece was, and how well Elliott's has stood up, and how clever Myron's ideas are, and did you hear that Arthur has a commission from Louisville."[16]

Schonberg's comment needs amplification. Although a steady

audience numbering around 300 did go to concerts of new music, the people attending were not always the same at each concert. An advocate of Babbitt's serialism or Carter's atonalism, for example, was rarely tempted to witness the no-holds-barred experimentation of Cage or Ashley. Furthermore, the audience contained the friends and family of the composer, as well as a number of music students, many of them his own. For a composer in the limelight, the audience increased, since many New Yorkers were on the watch for what was exciting current interest. Add a popular performer or conductor like Leonard Bernstein and the turnout could number a couple of thousand.

To live outside of New York, particularly during the 1950s and 1960s, might mean exclusion from serious consideration as a composer. For one, the New Yorkers who sought out contemporary music tended to favor the efforts of their fellow residents. The same was true of the writers for the influential magazines and newspapers published in the city. For another, the few other metropolitan areas and colleges and universities that did sponsor contemporary concerts suffered a major disadvantage. Their presentations were usually poorly advertised and ignored in most published reviews. The result was that serious young composers were "virtually unknown outside a few small circles of musicians," wrote William McClellan in 1965, when he was teaching at the University of Colorado.[17]

After the composer Ralph Shapey left New York to reside in Chicago, he went unnoticed. His music, if heard, was deemed of slight value. Wondering why Shapey was thus neglected, John Rockwell expressed the New Yorker's point of view when he decided it had mostly to do with "place and personality." Chicago was not New York. Shapey, "in choosing to live outside the nation's musical capital, inevitably delayed the reception of his new work and the honor accorded it." The composer, Rockwell added, embodied a contentious individuality, which contributed to his unpopularity. In contrast, Shapey said his neglect was owing to the New York music world being "made up of a bunch of cliques." If you existed outside of these cliques, you were "in trouble."[18]

Most writers concerned with the new-music events taking place in New York saw the danger in composers yielding to trend after trend in response to pressure from people eager only for the newest sound. Composers sapped their energies in this environment. Their music might sound overly slick and without substance.[19] Although speaking about painters, Nina Nielson, an art dealer both in New York and Boston, made an observation that could apply to composers. The avant-garde, she declared, was like "a herd of cows." Elsewhere, the creative impetus came from within; in New York, artists were "painting about their place in the art world rather than about their lives."[20]

Because New York's artistic world consisted of several rather exclusive circles, the composer usually had to make an effort to gain favor with one of them, then singlemindedly pursue his own interest, especially in getting performances. Some composers became "monsters," adept at playing the New York game, "where you are out to get people, out to survive and make the right maneuvers, and you don't really consider people as people but as pawns in your game of operating on the scene."[21]

Among other defensive actions, the composer might wish to win over one or more of New York's music critics, especially those writing for the *New York Times*. For one, most critics outside of New York regularly read what the *Times* had to say about music; for another, New York's critics were "the most powerful single factor in the making or breaking of an artist," according to Michael Caracappa. What makes the statement significant is that Caracappa was the *New York Times* editor on the cultural news copy desk. John English confirms Caracappa's observation, citing a national survey of critics, conducted in 1974, and then the results of a Harris Poll taken in 1970.[22]

A news item in *Musical America*, May 1979, indicates how important to music a *Times* review was considered: "Nobility was not obliging, last February 2, when an opening night audience . . . had to wait ten minutes while the *New York Times* critic bestirred himself to walk five short blocks to the theater."

OUSTING THE OLD

Many older beliefs and values were abandoned in the postwar period. The former notion of beauty, to give an instance, was now disfavored. It seemed freighted with Romantic baggage. When admiring a performance of new music, writers were cautious about

praising the music's "beauty." Nor were modern composers inclined to use the term in talking about their own music. Indeed,
the word disquieted many of them. It seemed to connote a facile
pleasantness and an annoying blandness.[23]

In addition to this term, other terms like "morality," "uplift,"
and "spirituality," says the composer Jacob Druckman, were
scrubbed out of contemporary vocabularies. Sacred music in the
old sense, declares the composer Virgil Thomson, was dead after
the war. If a composer wrote such music at all, it was "music for
a play" or "for a show." He admits to composing liturgical music, both Catholic and Protestant, "as for a play," and adds: "I
enjoy best writing for the theater."[24] To this, Leonard Bernstein
would certainly have agreed, for when he composed his *Mass*, in
1971, he made clear it was intended as a "theater piece for singers,
players, and dancers."

Prominent postwar composers declared triadic harmony and
traditional genres, like the symphony and concerto, to be dead. A
Concord Quartet member says that several composers were so
dominated by this sort of thinking that they turned down commissions to write string quartets. Roger Sessions confirms several
of the observations just made when he writes that traditional procedures were now defined as clichés.[25]

Alongside the rejection of past values and practices was the rejection of composers identified with them, especially nineteenth-
century composers. "You might think that Brahms would be a
favorite of the post-Webern 'pure music' school," Donal Henahan
wryly writes. "You would be wrong." Because of his popularity,
"Brahms has been made a symbol of all that is conventional, re-
spectable and safe in commercial music-making. In militantly
modernist circles, therefore, he can be safely shrugged off."[26]
Possibly, by denying the worth of Romantic composers, modernists were also reacting to their own powerlessness and guilt feelings when confronted with the criticisms hurled at them by people in power. They defended themselves "by declaring the
illegitimacy of the masters." By insisting on the past's illegitimacy, they could continue along their own way "without being
vulnerable."[27]

At any rate, Lukas Foss admits he learned from Schoenberg to
forgo tradition and from Stockhausen never to look back: "If one

has nothing to 'not look back to,' one plunges headlong into a would-be future. Anarchism, book-burning. One can hide in a would-be future, a cardboard future, even better than one can hide in the past. What Boulez so aptly called '*la fuite en avant*'—escape forward. Many of us who belong to that club with the nasty military name avant-garde are 'forward-escapists.' " Burning the past, Foss says, was playing it safe for the atonalists. It allowed them to continue their intellectual experimentation with tonally unrelated dissonant sounds. Chance musicians who made the same declaration felt safest of all because it smoothed the path for the approval of whatever they wrote, which they denominated as "nature having its own way." If choice was given the performer, it did not matter what he did; nor could the composer be blamed for any performance "error." John Cage "made silence safe by making it virtuous." Program notes and other writing about the new music being presented added to the safeness, if couched in a pseudoscientific jargon that concealed rather than revealed.[28]

Whenever a part of the past seemed susceptible to rehabilitation, modernists made it over in their own image. Because some electronic composers claimed noise to be proper to music, they asserted that Lully, Handel, Hanson, and Mozart had once been damned for making noise. They forgot that whatever noise these composers were responsible for was embedded in tonality and took on meaning through a widely recognized tradition. Mozart is unlikely to have stated, as does Herbert Russcol: "The argument of noise is always irrelevant. The true question is: does this noise, when familiar, fall into intelligible forms and convey notable content?"[29]

Instructive is how Michael Tilson Thomas, an American conductor attracted by modern music, rehabilitated Brahms for himself. During youth, he loved Brahms, but later hated him because of what he saw as bourgeois and self-congratulatory in the music. Yet, the more he examined Brahms's scores, the more he saw the "dichotomy between the thematic material, which is extremely Romantic, almost folkloric and cabaret-like, and the structure, which is of a rigorousness exceeded by no one. A tempered discipline" is needed when performing Brahms.[30]

What is curious about the admission is the intellectual valuation of structure over the warm expressive content of the music. By applying a "tempered discipline" to Brahms's music, the conductor might well falsify Brahms's intentions and siphon off the emotional impact that the general music public treasured.

Some older music was rehabilitated by reclothing it in modern dress. Ben Johnston's Fourth String Quartet, to give a mild example, makes use of the hymn "Amazing Grace." It is not, however, a straight restatement of the tune. Johnston subjects the melody to dramatic manipulations and to polyphony that considerably alters the natural simplicity of the original.[31]

The downgrading of older art music compounded a problem endemic in the United States. No strong tradition existed for listening to art music, nor for educating youngsters to it. Babbitt, for example, complained that musical illiterates entered the universities, unable to read, hear, or remember music.[32] Leon Kirchner agrees, saying that young people know neither Mozart nor Beethoven; therefore, rejection of the past demobilizes them.[33] On the other hand, several commentators on the current scene took an opposite stand, claiming such ignorance gave youngsters confidence and a greater certainty of what needs elimination or correction, although with less assurance about permanent replacements.[34] As will be seen, beginning in the early 1960s, many younger composers showed little inclination to examine older composers and questioned the systematic study of traditional musical theory. They would write works that exhibited novel, even outrageous, ideas. Frequently, however, their art cried out for a disciplining hand and a rational mind. In addition, the corrective of tradition was absent.

Added to the unfamiliarity with and rejection of the past was the fruitless search for cultural consensus in contemporary musical matters. It was one more reason why the fledgling composer might be tempted to decide it was up to him alone to carve out his own place in the creative world. Like a supermarket shopper, he looked over the many items offered for his delectation, making up his mind to try now this, now that, or to go all out on a single product. He heard several versions of rock music, Broadway ballads and dance songs, blues, mainstream jazz, bop in its hot and cool versions, experimental jazz, folk songs, folk-inspired protest songs, contemporary art music still working the traditional vein, dissonant and atonal compositions, strictly serial constructions, electronic bleeps, noise, silence, uncontrolled chance operations, and endless repetitions of a tiny sound cell. After a degree of self-searching, the young composer chose what particular creative procedures he would follow. He also had to assign a private significance to his activities, if only to reassure himself that what he was doing had some meaning. Unfortunately, when a composition was couched in the obscure language of atonality or the non-language of chance, the meaning assigned it by the composer rarely had a widely accepted significance. Neither the syntax nor the expressive content of the work conformed to the commonly held assumptions and expectations of most music lovers. Even highly musical people might find the meaning impossibly hidden, the syntax completely confusing, and the expressive content nil. As Sergui Comissiana said in 1977, when he was conductor of the Baltimore Symphony: "I feel many of the [new] scores are just an imitation of noise, of sound, and I don't think that *all* sound is music. Sound producing is not music making."[35]

The devaluation of the past also included the accessible American composers of the immediate past, many of whom were continuing their creative careers in the postwar years. Throughout the 1950s, these older composers—romantics, Americanists, and neoclassicists—were still creating what was held to be a viable music. Witness Howard Taubman's listing, in 1960, of pieces indispensable to the understanding of the contemporary spirit. He cites four conservative compositions: Barber's Second Symphony and String Quartet, and Menotti's operas *The Medium* and *The Consul*; four more advanced but mainstream works: Copland's Third Symphony and Piano Variations, Schuman's Third Symphony, and Harris's Third Symphony; and three works hovering between tonality and atonality, between what might become accessible to more than a tiny handful of listeners and what might remain incomprehensible: Sessions's Violin Concerto, Kirchner's Second Quartet, and Carter's Second Quartet.[36]

Raymond Ericson offers a similar list dating from 1959. He cites one conservative work: Hanson's *Romantic* Symphony; seven more advanced but mainstream works: Barber's *Medea's Meditation and Dance of Vengeance*, Carter's *The Minotaur* Suite, Copland's *Appalachian Spring*, Harris's Third Symphony, Ives's *Three Places in New England*, Mennin's Sixth Symphony, and Piston's Sixth Symphony; and one work that flirts with atonality: Riegger's Third Symphony. Ericson inserts this list in order to compare it with another made up in 1974, which was intended to promote the performance of American works in the United States and abroad. In compiling the second list, Igor Buketoff, director of the International Contemporary Music Exchange, asked ten composers, ten conductors, ten critics, and ten "leading media people" to recommend ten jurors familiar with American music. The selected jurors included people who composed, wrote about, or performed modern music. Some works from the listings of ten years before continue in favor: Copland's *Appalachian Spring*, Harris's Third Symphony, Schuman's Sixth Symphony, and Session's Third Symphony. The larger part of the list, however, is made up of aggressively dissonant works from the past: Ives's Fourth Symphony and Ruggles's *Sun Treader*, and atonal or experimental works of contemporary composers: Brown's *Available Forms II*, Cage's Concerto for Prepared Piano, Crumb's *Ancient Voices of Children*, and Foss's *Time Cycle*.[37]

As the 1950s and 1960s went by, sounds that utilized Americanisms grew passé, and those that suggested nineteenth-century romanticism grew vulgar in the writings of up-to-date critics, in spite of audiences' enthusiasm for them.[38] Alfred Frankenstein, an advocate for the most novel styles, reviewed the jazzy Copland Piano Concerto as "an appalling piece of trash, drivel, and *Kitsch*." Hanson's emotional *Nordic* Symphony was to him "a monumental piece of *Kitsch*." Barber's elegantly romantic Violin Concerto was at best amusing. It also contained an easygoing sentimentality that reduced it to mediocrity.[39]

Samuel Barber was often the target for criticism. His conservative idiom, genuine lyrical gift, and popularity with concertgoers irked defenders of the new. One defender, Alan Rich, found Barber's appealing Piano Concerto to be nothing but "organization music" and without "distinctive melodic substance." Carl Apone heard Barber's *Fadograph of a Yestern Scene* as "more like a man doodling than digging. The language is hardly in the twentieth-century vocabulary."[40]

The danger existed that yesterday's modernists might themselves be relegated to the trash heap. Otto Luening, for example, was deeply hurt when a brash younger generation of composers brushed both his music and his contributions to advanced experimentation in sound to one side. Despite his having been a pioneer in the use of electronic music, he writes: "There were the professional avant-gardists who thought we had invented music only for that week. Now *they* would move into the fray and show how to do it perfectly."[41]

John Rockwell, who remarked in the *New York Times* on Luening's bitterness, would, in turn, represent another new wave that would reject a great deal of the music that had come before. Atonality and serialism, including their electronic manifestations, were out in 1980, as far as he and "young postmodernists" were concerned. Serialism was a "didactic stultification of human emotion, its once revolutionary expressive gestures frozen by overuse into cliché."[42] One unhappy result of modernists' biting at each other was the weapon it handed the conductors and performers making them lukewarm about exploring any contemporary styles; they felt it safe to ignore both those criticized and the recommendations of the criticizers.

VIEWING A DIFFERENT SOUNDSCAPE

The new musical art in its several guises developed with remarkable speed during the twentieth century. As it did so, parallel innovations took place in literature, dance, painting, sculpture, and noncommercial motion pictures. Writing about this parallelism, Marshall Berman points to the brilliant creativity of artists like Günter Grass, Merce Cunningham, Twyla Tharp, and Jackson Pollock. Nevertheless, Berman warns: "We have mostly lost the art of putting ourselves into the picture, of recognizing ourselves as participants and protagonists in the art and thought of our time. Our century has nourished a spectacular modern art; but we seem to have forgotten how to grasp the modern life from which this art springs."[43] Audiences unquestionably found it difficult "to grasp the modern life from which this [music] springs." The composers had laden their works with impediments to understanding. The elimination of the well-known sounds and symbols of tradition caused confusion. The delight in abstract constructional operations, the treatment of music simply as unemotional sound material, and the curtailment of those qualities that seemed peculiarly human made the rapprochement of listener and modern composer hard to carry out.[44]

Another impediment was the often stated necessity for contemporary music to reflect its own time. In translation this meant a combination of sounds that were harsh, percussive, overly loud or overly soft, athematic, lurching between unstable pitches or abjuring pitch altogether, structures controlled by the iron grip of the composer or thrown like straws into the wind to settle where they might.[45] This rigorous "honesty" of sound required no connection with the mellifluous, said some writers. Somehow the music had to have undergone a sea change making it unique. Such a doctrine made it easier to relegate into limbo the more conservative contemporary composers, like Menotti, Dello Joio, Moore, and Bernstein.[46] In this context, Lee Hoiby's protest over his unfair treatment is informative: "I thought I would have a pretty easy time of it. My music was accessible. Audiences loved it. But I had a rude awakening. Critics did not like it; I was definitely out of step with the 1950's."[47]

The views mentioned were directly stated or implied in the books and articles reputed to be the most knowledgeable and insightful about American musical history. As might be expected some authors were also composers dedicated to the modern cause— Eric Salzman, David Cope, John Cage, Joan La Barbara, Charles Wuorinen, to name five. Predictably, readers who valued the more traditional composers would be indignant at the exclusion of artists they thought significant and worthy of inclusion. They might react by ceasing to look at any writing on the contemporary scene. At the same time, readers who listened in good faith to modern works recommended by these writers frequently found the music disappointing. They would conclude that nothing interesting was being composed. Moreover, students taking courses in contemporary music and assigned such writings would learn a possibly distorted account of American music from the past through the present.

In the spring of 1982, I met a young man who had discovered Persichetti's and Creston's music and was delighted with it. He told me of his dismay at finding so little information on these two composers in the several recent books on American music he had read. "I have no way of learning the truth about our music and its real history," he complained. Shortly thereafter, he read Charles Hamm's *Music in the New World*. His comment: "Look, I'm Italian-American and I'm proud of it. So I relate to guys like Dello Joio and Creston and Persichetti and Giannini. Why the hell do they have to be Anglos or blacks or sound like Schoenberg or a crazy like Cage to get into a history book? Are those composers American or aren't they? Did they write music and get it played and recorded, or didn't they?" The young man had looked up his favorite composers, all Italian-American, in the index and found them missing. I could not get him to suspend judgment until he had read some parts of the volume.[48]

In truth, many of the composer-writers on the modern scene feared what they considered a commonplace American musical culture. They saw it manipulated by technology, subtle advertisement, and the blandishments of commercial interests bent on selling the nth version of Rachmaninoff's Second Piano Concerto executed by performers who had become public personalities. These writers kept elevated the concept of a higher modern art unsullied by commercialism. For some, the fact that the music they espoused was not readily assimilated into the mass culture and that it required considerable effort to absorb was proof of its worthiness. For others, the more different a modern sound was from that the general audience had always considered musical, the more vital it seemed.[49]

The middle class, which made up the largest part of the audience for traditional art music, was defined as bourgeois—addicted to sentimentalism, sensations of the moment, and beguiling representations of itself. This downgrading of the middle class's tastes first took hold around the late 1920s, then became virulent after World War II. "Popularity and art parted company," writes Donal Henahan, "and nobody has figured out how to reconcile them. Accessible came to stand for meretricious, simple as that. . . . Any suspicion of public acceptance was enough to bring banishment to a composer."[50]

A certain elitism ran through the accusations of bourgeois shallowness when applied to the unmodern twentieth-century works by composers like Bernstein, Menotti, and Barber. Fame of sorts accrued to works unloved by the majority of concertgoers, written by composers like Feldman, Wuorinen, and Carter. All three composers had music presented at an avant-garde festival at the State University of New York at Buffalo in 1978. Herman Trotter, of the *Buffalo Evening News*, expresses a narrow view when he writes that only "the most renowned composers" were invited for a performance of their works, and that a "large gathering of advanced [music] students" attended, excited by "the chance to hob-nob with the likes of Elliott Carter, Henry Brant, Charles Wuorinen."[51] Ironically, few members of the general audience would ever have heard the names of these "renowned composers" and even less would have heard any of their music.

The general audience, however, did not count. "Who the hell is the public to decide what is valid and what is not? To decide what is art and what is not?" asked a querulous Martin Gottfried. "It would be in tune with our age" wrote an irritated Andrew Porter, in the *New Yorker*, to have symphony orchestras specialize in Romantic music, since it would please their subscribers, "who stomp from the hall soon after any contemporary work has started." Orchestras played little contemporary music anyway, Porter stated, and that little was played badly, so the best thing to do was to write off orchestras and subscribers.[52]

Roger Sessions and others in the atonal camp, in particular, maintained that because subscribers were mired in the slough of Romanticism, they had no business judging contemporary music. Moreover, only the musical work itself counted and only in the work were found "the criteria by which ideas about music, as well as music itself, must finally stand or fall." If the work revealed elements that seemed to pander to popular taste, its composer was aiming low, and the music was degenerate.[53]

Once when André Previn was expounding in this vein before students at Tanglewood, a youthful auditor protested, saying that "certain criteria [are] not met by most modern composers. People want to hear something melodic, with a certain structure." Previn replied that melody was indefinable and something utterly personal. Furthermore, Previn adds: "A melody is just a succession of notes. I suspect you're saying that people like music to be relaxing, passive listening." (Of course, that was *not* what the student had said.) He continues: "Most audiences sit at a concert the way you sit in a warm bath. It's extremely pleasant. I'm glad they've come. But it's a passive experience, not an active one. If you *make* them listen, *make* them participate, they often grow tired very quickly." Again, Previn finds proof that the audience's judgment is suspect.[54]

To be honest, art music to many people increasingly means the sort of limited repertoire that idolized performers like Pavarotti or commercial "good music" radio stations disseminate. Heavy advertising by people in the music business and diverting articles written for the general public concentrate attention on the same few compositions and elevate colorful musicians to godlike status. Curiosity about a wider repertoire and eagerness to adventure into unknown territory is killed. One result is that less and less people can listen to contemporary works with sympathy and with a desire to hear a different approach to musicmaking. Nevertheless, to decide that the honorable course for a composer was to write compositions as different from those in this limited repertoire as possible meant that fewer and fewer performers would present such compositions to listeners. The products would be unsalable and, owing to the increasing costs for presenting concerts, might result in financial disasters.

Throughout the years under study, endless argumentation went on between artists and intellectuals supportive of the new artistic directions and those Americans concerned over the unmet though inchoate cultural needs of contemporary society. Not until the 1970s would there appear a more-than-token willingness to write music that could accommodate both parties in the debate.[55] Meanwhile, intractable modernists continued to dismiss Americans outside their circle with abusive commentaries.[56] A few deluded themselves with the thought that "an ever enlarging group of people . . . want and need contemporary music."[57]

An opposite argument is set forth in Charles-Pierre Baudelaire's advice to poets, contained in an essay titled "Loss of a Halo." By abandoning his halo, the French writer states, the poet will find that "the aura of artistic purity and sanctity is only incidental, not essential, to art, and that poetry can thrive just as well, and maybe even better, on the other side of the boulevard," where the poet becomes "more like ordinary men." On the other hand, the bad poet "hopes to keep his purity intact by keeping off the streets, free from the risks of traffic."[58] This "halo" is in evidence when Richard Norton writes in praise of the electronic composer Morton Subotnick. The extraordinary soundscapes of Subotnick often dispense with performers altogether and can be heard only by means of recordings. Norton suggests that small groups of individuals should gather in intimate surroundings to receive the composer's message from the loudspeakers. They must absorb Subotnick's underlying meaning without assistance from anything beyond the sound itself. If they fail to do so, then they are in the wrong and "will never understand anything."[59] What Norton found of consequence was the music's purportedly superior quality and its exploitation of the electronic medium. The sound did challenge and disturb those contented with the musical status quo. It had, therefore, the virtue of leaving listeners less complaisant about themselves and the world around them. It provoked them into changing their ways of thinking.

This curious thinking failed to take into account that the generally middle-class audience attending concerts and operatic presentations was neither monolithic in its tastes nor always adamant in its opposition to adventurous sounds. Most people, however, were put off by the repudiation of melody as they had known it. Rightly or wrongly, "modern" came to mean any sound in which a general audience discovered little that was appealing.[60] Whether modernity meant serialism or anti-art and Dada–Zen experimentalism, writes Daniel Kingman, its tendency was to push things to extremes. It negated human imagination, memory, and intuition, and occupied an untenable position, separate from the bourgeois, but without meaningful relation to society.[61]

The long-honored symbols for communication were no more. Whatever new symbols in a single work were proposed by one modern composer were contradicted by those in other works of his and in works written by other modern composers.[62] The general listener was rarely willing to go through the labor of trying to understand a novel symbolism that struck him as unlovable. The music public's separation from the modern composer soon was measured in light-years. Its object of devotion focused more and more on the performer who dazzled it with immediately satisfying music. The contemporary composer had become a nonperson.[63]

Not until the end of the period under study, around the late 1970s, did many composers begin to speak, as Philip Glass did, about an attempt at reconciliation: "There's a consciousness once again of continuing the high-art tradition and being entertaining as well. For a long time, we would ask, rather querulously I think, 'Is it art—Or is it just entertaining?' We're less self-conscious now. We're having to acknowledge that we're in a period when things are being produced by serious artists—instinctively, naturally—that are very likable, very accessible."[64]

THE ROLE OF FASHION

Everything solid had melted into the air, and into the void entered fashion. "Radical chic" Tom Wolfe called it in 1970, referring to certain open-minded individuals who romanticized and embraced one radical cause after another. Along with the rapid technological and other changes taking place in the United States came the rapid succession of fashions in modern music—each acquiring an avant-garde label at birth to which the trend watchers could relate; each sweeping away the last fashion and pushing itself to an extreme; and each quickly exhausting the interest of the "chic set" to melt away into the air.[65]

One composer saw the emptiness behind many of the much touted musical "experiments" measured by the rapidity with which they were dropped in favor of newer ones. The "contrived innovations" revealed a built-in obsolescence: "one titillation and they are finished."[66]

From 1950 to 1985, neoclassicism gave way to various forms of serialism, from expressionism to totally organized abstraction; then came various atonal and quasi-serial styles. Next was heard a bewildering number of percussive and electronic styles. Later indeterminacy was advocated as an ideal, followed by performance art or music that invoked magic, mystery, and the philosophies of Asia. There was music for meditation, for psychedelic experience, and for the representation of contemporary chaos. In the late 1970s, the new directions were minimalism, neoromanticism, and a proliferation of eclectic styles that juxtaposed tonality with atonality, traditional melody with tone row, and collages of old musical compositions with those of the twentieth century. It was this constant proliferation of avant-garde styles, along with the simultaneous existence of many radically different approaches to musical composition that produced the "most wondrous babble" referred to in this book's title.

Some composers, perhaps fearful of their compositions becoming examples of yesterday's style, hesitated about completing a composition and set up another fashion, the presentation of a work in progress.[67]

Pertinent is the question Ferruccio Busoni was asking around 1921, when he saw novel compositional techniques becoming faddish and some passé even before they were thoroughly explored. Don't ask, he said, if one or another novelty is different from the old, but rather if it is as good or better than the old.[68]

The chic audience for avant-garde music saw itself as taste-maker for the majority. Whenever a presentation of advanced music took place, provided the offerings were representative of the latest trends, it came to express its excitement, aroused more by preconceived notions about what was proper than by the substance of the music.[69] Years back, when Babbitt was admired, I attended a concert of Babbitt's serial works where some 400 men and women, all correctly dressed and apparently intellectual types, came to indicate their approval in rather decorous fashion. In 1983, I again attended an all-Babbitt concert with the composer present. The same types appeared but they numbered less than half a hundred and gave perfunctory applause. Around 1970, I witnessed a George Crumb concert in a small hall packed with an assortment of young and old people, informally dressed or business-suited. Their reaction to the magical evocations of the music was one of worshipful silence, as if they were witnessing a mystery. George Crumb was then on the lips of most members of the avant-garde. In 1983, I spoke up for a concert of Crumb's music, and was told by the manager of a new-music performance group: "There's not that much interest around to warrant the trouble of reviving it.". He would "think about it," however, if Crumb came out with something new that might "get the modern crowd back."

The publications aimed at the general public also contributed to the launching of new fashions and the demise of old ones. Newspapers and magazines constantly looked for anything newsworthy, the more sensational, the better—anything to catch and hold a reader's attention. Yesterday's fashion was yesterday's news; tomorrow's possible fashion was today's news. Readers scanned the printed page for reports on the events occurring around them. Because busy with their own concerns and unable or unwilling to attend every new event involving the avant-garde, they depended on these reports to tell them what was happening and to winnow out the insignificant from the significant. Thus, the news story, the symbol of a music event, could easily become more important than the event itself, and the readership's concepts about a phase of new music more important than the music itself. In this way, readers on the alert for the new might become partisans of a music without completely understanding it, and gratify a felt need to behave responsibly in artistic matters without accountability for what happened.[70]

Owing to little understood styles and circumspect lives lead in isolation, the atonal and serial composers rarely commanded public attention and notice in the media. Their windows to the outside world had to be musicological journals like the *Musical Quarterly*, specialized house periodicals like the *Perspectives of New Music*, and a few reviewers sympathetic to the atonal and serial sound, like Andrew Porter of the *New Yorker*.

With the arrival of electronic sound and, coincidentally, the coming to light of the uninhibited experimentation of Cage and his associates, the news media did take notice. By 1968, David Hamilton was able to observe that this newer avant-garde had "caught on in a big way." Its latest extremisms were reported on "with a celerity approaching that previously reserved for Broadway musicals and contest-winning virtuosos." Its "articulate spokesmen" were "dragged hither and yon over the landscape to deliver oracular pronouncements and bestow jaundiced blessings in (often inadequate) 'festivals' of their music."[71]

To give one example of the newsworthy, Lejaren Hiller startled the media in 1957 by programming a computer to compose music, resulting in the *Iliac Suite*. Hiller said the event "hit the headlines—quite literally. All of a sudden I went from a nobody to somebody who was actually on the front page of many newspapers—usually in the most absurd kind of news article."[72]

Quite a few modernists quickly realized that producing a commotion worked to their benefit, especially if they were as yet unknown. To be booed and denounced caught attention and gave them a cachet that could prepare the way for future commissions, grants, and performances. At the same time, it forced hesitant critics who wished to be perceived as au courant and not among the reactionaries to join the current trend, like "nice little pooches," as Harold C. Schonberg once pointed out.[73]

Composers had to watch out constantly for what was coming in and what was going out as a medium of expression. In 1980, Morton Feldman was asked what he thought about the publicity given Philip Glass and Steve Reich, and whether their music constituted a new trend. Feldman replied: "In some ways the message is a little shocking in the Reich phenomenon. . . . I'm already in my mid-fifties, I'm supposed to have a developed language, and if you think I can sit down and write a piece and not be worried about Steve Reich, John Cage, Pierre Boulez, and Xenakis, you're nuts. I worry about these people. I worry about strong alternatives. . . . It *is* a contest."[74] The need to excite attention and the lack of strong personal convictions, said Morton Gould, encouraged the production of outlandish "sound-effects" music in order to reach bored critics and conductors ever in search for the new.[75]

The inconsistency of writers on the contemporary music scene increased even as the rate of stylistic change accelerated after 1960. Charles Wuorinen, irked when his serial music became passé, stated: "When I started out, my music was always characterized as being 'explosive,' 'chaotic,' 'barbaric,' 'angry,' etc. Which makes you wonder about the status of these reporters who now characterize the same music as 'academic,' 'grim,' 'dry,' 'freezing,' 'austere.' " Also note Ned Rorem's complaint about a reviewer "who knows what he hates" and who "has on four occasions reviewed my cycle *War Scenes* with four conflicting verdicts: memorable, bad, good, forgettable."[76]

When the New York City Opera went on tour with Carlisle Floyd's *Susannah*, in the 1959–60 season, the reviews were indeed contradictory. In Huntington, West Virginia, the work was found to be "among the true greats of contemporary music." Yet the Chicago reviewers wrote it was "put together with a do-it-your-self opera kit," the score was "embarrassingly derivative," and the composition was "not a great opera, nor even a very good one." When the opera was presented in Boston and in Philadelphia, the reviewers again promoted it to greatness. Finally, in Washington, the *Washington Post* reviewer found he couldn't stand the music, which lacked "the quality of melodic genius" and also the "genuine grandeur, or expressiveness to elevate us above the crushing tawdriness of it all."[77]

Writers sympathetic with contemporary experimentation, sometimes replaced contradiction with unintelligibility. Note Herbert Russcol's statement about electronic composers: "The artist is the witness of his time. . . . More and more we turn to the artist's vision for answers to our troubling questions [about poverty, social injustice, and political corruption]. He has been restored to his central tribal role as seer."[78]

Alvin Toffler once helped to conduct a survey among the nation's leading artists on the meaning and purpose of the arts, in conjunction with the building of the John F. Kennedy Cultural Center. He received depressing replies made up of "confusing, contradictory, philosophically meaningless, and unverified assertions." The arts, he was told, formed our characters, helped us to love each other, provided spiritual adventures, established moments of truth, and nourished us with the creative spirit, without which no country has achieved major importance.[79]

When modern composers tried to explain their own music, their language often continued murky. Milton Babbitt, for example, was noted for his unintelligible prose writings. Other composers stated the obvious. When Ralph Shapey in 1962 spoke on his *Dimensions* for soprano and twenty-three instruments, he described it "as an object in Time and Space," an "aggregate of sounds structured into concrete sculptured forms," and as a music of "images existing as a totality from their inception, each a self-involved unit of individual proportions."[80]

Bernard Holland in 1982 grew impatient with composers' explanations of their works on concert programs. He wondered why one composer had to remind the audience that his piece dealt with the repetition of materials of long and short duration. After all, so do most music works. Another composer, Holland reports, said she was singlemindedly pursuing aesthetic immediacy in her work. But don't most composers hope for immediate communication? A third composer elaborately analyzed his work in terms of statement, change, and repetition—hardly a novel scheme.[81]

When critics wrote about the performance of new works, whether reviewing them in newspapers, magazines, or other periodicals, the information they conveyed frequently left much to be desired. They at times forgot that they acted as deputies for the public. Furthermore, their opinions were hardly objective truths. First, the public wanted to know if the performance had been technically competent and the interpretation a fair rendition of the score. Second, if the piece was new, the public wanted to know its style and how it related to other pieces in a similar style. Third, who was the audience at the performance; how did it react to the piece? And fourth, what was the critic's personal reaction to the work, stated in clear, simple, and direct language.[82]

Regrettably few critics bothered with all of these points. A new work was apt to be discussed with little reference to its style and with none to the critic's own biases. To cite two reviewers, we could be certain that Andrew Porter, in the *New Yorker*, would praise almost every knotty composition of Elliott Carter; and that Joan La Barbara, in *Musical America*, would love many of the curious happenings at The Kitchen in New York City.

Rarely was the general music public taken into account when reviewing a new work. If the publication had the resources, it found a reviewer sympathetic to a given modern style and had him or her always review that particular area in music, with predictable results. It was in fashion, if only one reviewer was to be employed, to appoint somebody open-minded about what was current in music circles. (This certainly happened when Winthrop Sargeant left the *New Yorker* and Andrew Porter was appointed to replace him.) Unfortunately, when that reviewer's favorite new music went out of favor, he sometimes held to his now passé views and the value of his criticisms were discounted by the more up-to-date reviewers. Certainly this has happened to Porter and to several of his views about the serial and atonal composers.

Leo Steinberg was aware of the critical pitfalls. When confronted with the new, he asked himself questions that he could not answer: did it tally with his experience, was it art, did he find his knowledge of past art a hindrance, did anything teach him to evaluate the work aesthetically, was what he and what the artist experienced the same? "I am alone with this thing, and it is up to me to evaluate it." However, he felt humility and uncertainty. He concluded "I have little confidence in people who habitually, when exposed to new works of art, know what is great and what will last."[83]

Lack of confidence did not affect partisans of one or another of the modernist groups. They knew what was great and would last. Masterpieces demonstrating the extraordinary brilliance and skill of their favorite composers were uncovered every year. They said that these works were of infinite worth and priceless value to all people and for all time. The "masterpiece" disease also affected composers, especially those affianced to serial and atonal procedures. They felt it their responsibility to turn out pieces of seriousness and complexity. Such pieces, they thought, had to be accepted as *prima facie* masterpieces. "One curse," writes Peter G. Davis, "that beset composers in the 1950's and 1960's was the masterpiece syndrome—an ironic residue from the Romantic age when every note had to be of cosmic significance."[84]

In this regard, Lionel Trilling's comments on the demand for only first-rate works of art and literature are valuable. He claims that in the post–World War II years, Americans actively interested in the new wanted "only the Very Best." They wished to subscribe only to art "having a top rating for spirituality, apocalypticality, and permanence." Creators of such works were either great or nothing. Owing to the rule of fashion, they were usually "great for a season . . . and then sacrificed on the alter of our outraged . . . conscience, then possibly 'revived' again, only to be again interred. . . ."[85]

Enmeshed in this sort of thinking, it was not enough for the music reviewer Royal S. Brown to like Alden Ashforth's *Byzantia* for tenor, organ, and synthesizer. He found it "utterly amazing." The work made "consummate, sensitive, and profound use of a particular medium," and evoked moods that entered "into a dark, visceral universe of pure feeling." In short, it was "a masterpiece."[86]

Admittedly, not all composers have exhibited the masterpiece symptoms. Cage, for one, insists the attitude falsely stresses the consequences of compositional activity instead of what is more significant, the process itself. Yet, even here, when Cage repudiates the valuation of masterpieces as a consequence of their contents, he may be postulating instead that the concept and process

of composition is of overwhelming significance. Herein may hide
another formulation of the masterpiece syndrome.

Though aware of objections like that of Cage to the designation
masterpiece, writers continued to use the term. Alan Rich, in 1964,
found Andrew Imbrie's Violin Concerto to be one of the "few
real orchestral masterpieces of this century," though it demanded
"careful attention," owing to its intricate and difficult atonal procedures. Two years later, Alfred Frankenstein said David Diamond's Fourth String Quartet was a masterpiece, with its impressively complex structure. Ten months later, after finding the simple
and accessible *Music for a Great City*, by Aaron Copland, to be
"obvious and trashy," he exalted the forbidding sound in Elliott
Carter's Piano Sonata. Ten years later writers took note of the
burgeoning women's movement in music. Extremely sympathetic
reviews of compositions by women composers proliferated. This
new trend, at least in part, had an impact on Alfred Frankenstein's
appreciation of Joyce Mekeel's *Corridors of Dream*, another "masterpiece" and "one of the most dramatic American concert pieces
of recent years."[87]

During the 1970s, other styles undermined the lofty position of
atonality. A different breed of writer came to the fore, appreciative of the musics now becoming prominent. Richard Norton felt
delirium when he heard Morton Subotnick's otherworldly electronic noises, contained in the Nonesuch recording of *Silver Apples of the Moon* and *The Wild Bull*. "The public," he enthused,
"can now trace in Subotnick's music what will be treated in music
texts years from today as his *early style period*."[88]

Finally, John Rockwell, looking back over the decade of the
1960s from the vantage of the year 1980, found one expressionist
work to be masterly, Stefan Wolpe's String Quartet, in addition
to the works representative of the trends gaining dominance in
the 1970s: Pauline Oliveros's *Bye Bye Butterfly*, Steve Reich's *Come
Out*, and Terry Riley's *In C*. When Rockwell examined the music
of the 1970s, he again singled out one work in the atonal, expressionist style, Carter's Third String Quartet. The seven other masterpieces represented more recent trends: Morton Feldman's *Rothko
Chapel*, David Behrman's *On the Other Ocean*, Charles Dodge's
Earth's Magnetic Field, Steve Reich's *Music for Eighteen Musicians*,
Philip Glass's *Einstein on the Beach*, and Robert Ashley's *Private*

Parts. He claimed these compositions were great works that the general music public did not and probably would never like. But they had a potential to be admired in the world of generally cultivated people.[89]

Only an occasional voice was raised against the habit of announcing the arrival of countless masterpieces every year. Gunther Schuller warned that every new work was not "an irresistible masterpiece," pointing out that most music lovers were not convinced of this fact; nor had they asked the composer to compose the piece. Yet it was they who held "the trump card"; and it was they who ultimately decided the issue, whether composers liked it or not. Ten years later, Ned Rorem noted that writers were still discovering masterpieces aplenty. He also wondered why nobody had questioned the concept of greatness as absolute and irreversible. Besides, he found many of the socalled masterpieces to be monumentally boring.[90]

THE AUDIENCE FOR NEW MUSIC

Like all forward-looking activities, the several music movements, which had self-consciously broken with the past and attempted to achieve novel forms of expression, were entangled in a struggle between two seemingly irreconcilable forces. The artistic imperative to follow one's own vision clashed with the need to avoid extremes if the waverers in the audience were to be won over. Adding to the problem were the antagonistic views of the out-and-out traditionalists, which were appearing in print. Regrettably, at the same time that the Babbitt circle and the Cage circle excited their followers to intensify their fight against the old ways of doing things, they also evoked negative feelings among potential supporters weary of the war-horse mentality of the established performing groups. Babbitt and Cage were more successful as leaders of revolution sermonizing to the already convinced than that as conciliators hoping to attract the reluctant.

Depressed by what they saw around them, the music modernists felt they had to face the situation honestly—to realize that few men and women had ever exhibited discernment in the arts or treasured profundity of any sort. Those who favored serialism and atonalism, especially, reached this conclusion. For this reason, the best in music had to remain the property of a select minority. Whatever snobbism appeared was a necessary consequence of the mass public's inability to join in the appreciation of the new.

This kind of thinking had a long history. If we begin with Voltaire, Diderot, Rousseau, the Encyclopedists, and other forward thinkers of late–eighteenth-century France, we find that these men had lived in an inflexible and stratified society. Critical of what they saw, they helped bring on the French Revolution whose residue of violence and totalitarianism would remain until present times. Recognized as intellectuals in their own day, they occupied a fringe position, welcome in the more enlightened salons of Paris, neglected by everybody else.

They were Frenchmen in opposition to the traditions and institutions of their society, strong advocates of progressivism, and members of what Lionel Trilling calls "the adversary culture." Irving Kristol writes that their notion of progress coupled with revolution was of paramount importance during the twentieth century, especially amongst intellectuals and artists.

One result of such thinking was the idea that progress is uniquely the domain of a select group liberated from ignorance and exhibiting an intense curiosity about what was going on around it. Moreover, this select group had a duty to push for progress and, when resistance was encountered, to force it on society, however unwilling that society might be.[91]

Many contemporary composers subscribed to this idea. Some of them were more democratically inclined than composers like Milton Babbitt. Their objective was the spiritual improvement of the few amongst the mass public who might be saved, even though they denied these few the privilege of making judgments about what they heard.

Here and there was found a worried writer. He warned that the battle to improve the general audience's taste was being lost and that a weakening avant-garde continued to aim at final victory. Eric Larrabee, for instance, saw the problems of aesthetic democracy as not yet solved. The evidence to prove the majority of Americans merited distrust was everywhere at hand. The effort at democratization was about to sink all art music into the pit of degenerate mass taste. Paradoxically, Larrabee also expressed unhappiness over the idea of training taste, since the elitism behind it hinted at artistic fascism.[92]

From the American general audience's point of view, an argument could be made that musical life in the second half of the twentieth century was superior to that in the first half of the century. A larger percentage of the population lived comfortably and with secure incomes. More Americans could afford to purchase music instruments and recordings and to attend concerts. From this perspective, the America of post–World War II was not entirely the Dark Age claimed by the modernists. Nor were most Americans ready to submit to the cultural subjugation claimed to be good for their souls, however vulgar their tastes. What they were offered they neither needed nor wanted.[93]

Milton Babbitt admitted his music was rarely played, his recorded music rarely purchased, and his audience "virtually nonexistent." Christopher Small sorrowed over the undeniable fact that serious composers were addressing "a smaller and smaller proportion of the population." The audience for art music was a minority "within the general population, but the contemporary composer is able to engage the attention of only a small minority of that minority."[94]

I hasten to add, however, that many in this small minority did like what they heard and did sincerely embrace one or more of the newer styles and their composers. To them, the freshness of the contemporary sounds was preferable to the tiresome repetition of the limited number of works from the past.

Recalling Small's statement about the audience for all art music being a fraction of the total population, and the audience for avant-garde music being minuscule, it was to be expected that most American newspapers would take mild or no interest in regularly covering the events in the art-music world. A few years ago, John English wrote about a study conducted in the late 1960s by the University of Minnesota. The study summarized the arts reporting of sixty-seven newspapers, all randomly selected. Only 1.2 percent of their contents related to any of the arts, and the arts items were mostly in the form of straight news reports. About four-tenths of a percent of the contents were arts reviews. English could single out only three newspapers to praise for their reportage in the arts: the *New York Times*, the *Los Angeles Times*, and the *Boston Globe*. Under the best of conditions, writes English, even the urban newspapers most well disposed toward the arts assigned them less staff than they did sports. The *Atlanta Journal*, for example, had a sports staff of thirteen full-time reporters, while only four people reviewed all of the arts. At the height of its commitment to the arts, the *New York Times* employed thirty-two writers on cultural subjects, seventeen of these writers being critics. Yet at the same time the sports staff numbered forty-one people.[95]

Regrettably, during the 1970s and into the 1980s, the total number of newspapers in the United States shrank, as did the coverage of musical events. The surviving newspapers that heretofore had covered them increasingly overlooked the solo recitals and chamber music. As for the performances of modern music, their novelty, even when shocking, had become old hat and aroused less and less curiosity. Events in the real world were far more shocking, and these events were not make-believe. Besides, people had become satiated with what they perceived as the antics of the avant-garde. They rarely took notice of what its representatives said and its composers created.

The very small audience for contemporary music came to depend on only three or four daily newspapers and about the same number of weeklies (chiefly the *Village Voice*, the *New York Magazine, Musical America*, and the *New Yorker*) to let it know what was taking place in advanced artistic circles, and what was coming into or going out of fashion.[96] In the 1980s, only when an American composer achieved international acclaim and had a large devoted American following (as did Philip Glass, in 1983 and 1984) did he receive fairly widespread coverage.

NOTES

1. Marshall Berman, *All That Is Solid Melts into Air: The Experience of Modernity* (New York: Simon & Schuster, 1982), 15–16.

2. Ibid., p. 288.

3. Daniel Yankelovich, *New Rules: Searching for Self–Fulfillment in a World Turned Upside Down.* (New York: Bantam, 1982), 4.

4. Elie Siegmeister, "A New Day Is Dawning for American Composers," *New York Times*, 23 January 1977, sec. 2, 20.

5. Benjamin Boretz and Edward T. Cone, eds., *Perspectives on American Composers* (New York: Norton, 1971), 217. Carter's statement dates from 1964.

6. Joan Peyser, review of *The New Grove*, in *Musical Quarterly* 68, (1982): 284.

7. Charles Hamm, *Music in the New World* (New York: Norton, 1983), 555.

8. See Tom Wolfe, *From Bauhaus to Our House* (New York: Simon & Schuster, 1981), 41. Babbitt's statements come from an interview that took place in 1975. It may be found in Cole Gagne and Tracy Caras, *Soundpieces: Interviews with American Composers* (Metuchen, N.J.: Scarecrow, 1982), 44.

9. Gagne and Caras, *Soundpieces*, 44–45.

10. Robert Sabin, "Chamber Music," *Musical America* (1 January 1951): 5; Richard Franko Goldman, "Current Chronicle, New York," *Musical Quarterly* 47, (1961): 233.

11. Paul Turo, in the *Music Journal* 32 (November 1974): 4. See also Harold C. Schonberg, *Facing the Music* (New York: Summit, 1981), 362.

12. Lionel Trilling, *A Gathering of Fugitives* (Boston: Beacon, 1956), 61.

13. Donal Henahan, "The Evangelical Avant-Garde at a Dead End," *New York Times*, 25 June 1978, sec. 2, 19; David Schiff, *The Music of Elliott Carter* (London: Eulenburg, 1983), 134.

14. Paul Henry Lang, ed. *Problems of Modern Music* (New York: Norton, 1962), 10–11; Sidney Finkelstein, *Composer and Nation* (New York: International, 1960), 218.

15. Ernst Bacon, *Words on Music* (Syracuse: Syracuse University Press, 1960), 45.

16. Harold C. Schonberg, "Audiences Hot, Audiences Cold," *New York Times*, 11 February 1968, sec. 2, 15.

17. William McClellan, "Recordings and New American Music," *Music Journal* 23 (December 1965): 40.

18. John Rockwell, "Ralph Shapey at 60—He Defied Neglect," *New York Times*, 10 May 1981, sec. 2, 17. Between 1969 and 1971, Shapey contributed to his own neglect by refusing to make his compositions available for performance.

19. John Rockwell, *All American Music* (New York: Knopf, 1983), 69; Christine Temin, "NYC Plays the Pied Piper and Boston Artists Follow," *Boston Globe*, 19 February 1984, 102.

20. Temin, "NYC Plays the Pied Piper," 102.

21. Morris Risenhover and Robert T. Blackburn, *Artists as Professors*

(Urbana: University of Illinois Press, 1976), 54; Rockwell, *All American Music*, 66.

22. Michael Caracappa, "What Are Critics Like?" *Music Journal* 28 (May 1970): 66, 77–78; John W. English, *Criticizing the Critics* (New York: Hastings House, 1979), 88–89.

23. Much the same thing is said by Trilling, in *A Gathering of Fugitives*, 133–34.

24. Shirley Fleming, "Jacob Druckman," *Musical America* (August 1972): 5; the Thomson quotation may be found in *Musical America* (February 1982): 38.

25. See, respectively, Paul Turok, "Witchful Thinking and New Music," *Musical Journal* 28 (March 1970): 49; Herbert Kuperberg, "The Concord Quartet Embarks upon Its Second Decade," *Ovation* 3 (December 1982): 36; Lang, ed. *Problems of Modern Music*, 27.

26. Donal Henahan, "Progressive or Not, Brahms Still Fascinates," *New York Times*, 1 May 1983, sec. 2, 21.

27. Richard Sennett, *Authority* (New York: Vintage, 1981), 446–48.

28. Lukas Foss, "Composition in the 1960s," *High Fidelity* 18 (September 1968): 42.

29. Herbert Russcol, *The Liberation of Sound* (Englewood Cliffs, N.J.: Prentice-Hall, 1972), xi.

30. Martin Bookspan, "Michael Tilson Thomas," *Ovation* 3 (July 1983): 19.

31. These criticisms were made by Andrew De Rhen, in *Musical America* (August 1974): 31. I reacted similarly on hearing the composition.

32. Gagne and Caras, *Soundpieces*, 39.

33. The Kirchner statement may be found in *Musical America* (January 1971): 5.

34. Martin Gottfried, *A Theater Divided* (Boston: Little, Brown, 1969), 25.

35. Sergui Comissiana is thus quoted in *Musical America* (July 1977): 54.

36. Howard Taubman, "But Not Farewell," *New York Times*, 17 July 1960, sec. 2, 7.

37. Raymond Ericson, "The Pick of Modern American Music," *New York Times*, 25 August 1974, sec. 2, 13.

38. Sigmund Spaeth, "In and Out of Tune" *Music Journal* 18 (February 1960): 55; see also Stephen Douglas Burton, "The Emperor's New Clothes, or, Contemporary Music Revisited" *Symphony Magazine* 34 (June/July, 1983): 61.

39. See Alfred Frankenstein's reviews of these works in *High Fidelity* 12 (March 1962), 78; (May 1965), 66; (June 1965), 70.

40. Alan Rich, *High Fidelity* 14 (December 1964): 80; Carl Apone, *Musical America* (January 1972): 25–26.

41. Otto Luening, *The Odyssey of an American Composer* (New York: Scribner's Sons, 1980), 518.

42. John Rockwell, "An Influential Musician at 80," *New York Times*, 15 June 1980, sec. 2, 30; Rockwell, *All American Music*, 21–22.

43. Berman, *All That Is Solid*, 23–24.

44. Walter Simmons, "Contemporary Music," *Fanfare* 4 (May/June 1981): 22; [Roger Sessions] *Roger Sessions on Music*, ed. Edward T. Cone (Princeton, N.J.: Princeton University Press, 1979), 63.

45. Epithets like these are sprinkled throughout Wilfrid Meller's book *Music in a New Found Land* (New York: Knopf, 1965). See also Winthrop Sargeant, "Musical Events: Lost in a New Found Land," *New Yorker* (23 April 1966) 186, 189, 190.

46. These composers, who had managed to please audiences, were excluded from Elliott Schwartz and Barney Childs, eds., *Contemporary Composers on Contemporary Music* (New York: Holt, Rinehart & Winston, 1967).

47. Walter Cavalieri, "Lee Hoiby," *Music Journal* (December 1980): 10.

48. The young man, a music major at the University of Massachusetts, had taken my course on musical ideas and literature. He had returned to take my course in American music.

49. Dore Ashton, *The New York School: A Cultural Reckoning* (New York: Penguin, 1979), 233; Leslie Fiedler, *What Was Literature? Class Culture and Mass Society* (New York: Simon & Schuster, 1982), 75.

50. Donal Henahan, "On Being an 'Accessible' Composer," *New York Times*, 7 June 1981, sec. 2, 21. See also Dore Ashton, *The Unknown Shore* (Boston: Little, Brown, 1962), 3–6.

51. Herman Trotter, "June in Buffalo," *Musical America*, (December 1978): 24.

52. Gottfried, *A Theater Divided*, 22; Andrew Porter, "Musical Events," *New Yorker* (7 February 1983): 110.

53. Lang, ed., *Problems of Modern Music*, 24; Andrew Porter, "Musical Events," *New Yorker* (16 August 1982): 67.

54. Helen D. Ruttnecutter, *New Yorker* (17 January 1983): 62.

55. Robert Brustein, *The Culture Watch: Essays on Theatre and Society, 1969–1974* (New York: Knopf, 1975), 19–20; Cecil Smith, "Building an Indigenous Musical Life," *Musical America* 15, (March 1950): 50; Andrew Porter, "Musical Events: Babbitt on Broadway," *New Yorker* (15 March 1982); 130.

56. Jon Appleton, "New Role for the Composer," *Music Journal* 26 (March 1969): 59; John Cage, *Silence* (Cambridge, Mass.: M.I.T. Press,

1966), 64; Charles Wuorinen, "The Composer and the Outside World," *New York Times*, 5 March 1967, sec. 2, 28.

57. Charles Wuorinen, in *New York Times*, 10 September 1972, sec. 2, 25.

58. Berman, *All That Is Solid*, 160.

59. Richard Norton, "The Vision of Morton Subotnick," *Music Journal* 28 (January 1970): 49.

60. Henri Temianka, *Facing the Music* (New York: McKay, 1973), 241–42; Walter Simmons, review of *Inner Space*, by David Stock, *Fanfare* 6 (September/October 1982): 237.

61. Daniel Kingman, *American Music* (New York: Schirmer, 1979), 524; see also Fiedler, *What Was Literature*, 92–93, for a discussion of the same attitude as related to modern poetry.

62. Temianka, *Facing the Music*, 242; Mark Lawrence, "Roger Sessions Flunked Me," *Music Journal Annual* 21 (1963): 49; Thomas Darter, Jr., "The Aim of Music," *Music Journal* 28 (April 1970): 37; Robert Scott Kellner, "Avant-Garde Meatballs: Are They Edible?" *Music Journal* 31 (March 1973): 16–17.

63. Hamm, *Music in the New World*, 558–59, 579; Dennison Nash, "The Role of the Composer (Part I)," *Ethnomusicology* 5, (1961): 90; Winthrop Sargeant, "Musical Events," *New Yorker* (7 June 1969): 138; Elie Siegmeister, "Beyond the Avant-Garde," *Musical America*, (December 1971): 14.

64. Jeff Mclaughlin, "New Music Making Waves," *Boston Globe*, 11 March 1984, sec. B, 1.

65. Ellen H. Johnson, ed., *American Artists on Art from 1940 to 1980* (New York: Harper & Row, 1982), quotes the painter Jasper Johns as making this sort of observation in 1964; Matthew Baigell, *Dictionary of American Art* (New York: Harper & Row, 1979), s.v. "De Kooning, William," also does so; as does William Insley, in *Esthetics Contemporary*, ed. Richard Kostelanetz (Buffalo, N.Y.: Prometheus, 1978), 218; and Winthrop Sargeant, *New Yorker* (22 March 1969): 109.

66. Siegmeister, "Beyond the Avant-Garde," 14.

67. Carl Dahlhaus, *Analysis and Value Judgment* (New York: Pendragon, 1983), 14–15.

68. Adrian Corleonis, "Ferruccio Busoni," *Fanfare* 7 (January/February 1984): 103.

69. Quite a few writers have testified to this phenomenon. See, for example, the letter of Albert V. Maurier, in the *Music Journal*, (March 1960): 152; the comments of James Wierzbicki about the annual Contemporary Music Festival sponsored by Indiana State University, in *Musical America* (January 1961): 34–35; Gagne and Caras, *Soundpieces*, 109, on

Copland and others admiring the "in" composers of 1975, Druckman and Del Tredici; and, finally, Darle J. Soria, "Steve Reich," *Musical America*, (December 1982): 6.

70. John A. Kouwenhoven, *Half a Truth Is Better Than None* (Chicago: University of Chicago Press, 1982), 6.

71. David Hamilton, "A Synoptic View of the New Music," *High Fidelity* 18 (September 1968): 44. See also Tom Wolfe, *The Kandy-Kolored Tangerine-Flake Streamline Baby* (New York: Farrar, Straus & Giroux, 1965), ix; Tom Wolfe, *The Purple Decades* (New York: Farrar, Straus & Giroux, 1982), 8.

72. Gagne and Caras, *Soundpieces*, 233.

73. Harold C. Schonberg, "A Critic Reflects on 44 Years in the Business," *New York Times*, 6 July 1980, sec. 2, 13–14.

74. Gagne and Caras, *Soundpieces*, 173. See also Harold C. Schonberg, "Where Are They?" *New York Times*, 14 January 1962, sec. 2, 11, and Leon Kirchner's commentary in David Ewen, *American Composers: A Biographical Dictionary* (New York: Putnam's 1982), s.v. "Kirchner, Leon."

75. Roy Hemming, "The Serious Side of Morton Gould," *Ovation* 3 (November 1982): 35.

76. Kenneth Terry, "Charles Wuorinen, Atonal Tonalities," *Downbeat* 50 (February 1981): 17; Ned Rorem, *Setting the Tone* (New York: Coward-McCann, 1983), 295.

77. Ronald Eyer, "Operation Vanguard," *Musical America* (May 1960): 18.

78. Russcol, *The Liberation of Sound*, xiii.

79. Alvin Toffler, "The Politics of the Impossible—Art and Society," in *A Great Society?* ed. Bertram M. Gross (New York: Basic Books, 1968), 252.

80. Harold C. Schonberg, "Words, Words," *New York Times*, 1 July 1962, sec. 2, 7.

81. Bernard Holland, "When Composer Offers Words about His Music," *New York Times*, 16 September 1982, sec. C, 26. For other instances of meaningless explanations by composers, see Adrian Corleonis's review of the CRI SD 401 recording, in *Fanfare* 3 (May/June 1980): 407.

82. A valuable article on criticism, its types and functions, by Brewster Rogerson and Laurence D. Lerner, can be found in the *Princeton Encyclopedia of Poetry and Poetics*, ed. Alex Preminger (Princeton, N.J.: Princeton University Press, 1965), s.v. "Criticism."

83. Leo Steinberg, *Other Criteria: Confrontations with Twentieth-Century Art* (New York: Oxford University Press, 1972), 15.

84. Peter G. Davis, "Pianos Still Stir Composers' Souls," *New York Times*, 7 June 1981, sec. 2, 26.

85. Trilling, *A Gathering of Fugitives*, 21.

86. Royal S. Brown, review of the recording Orion ORS 74164, *High Fidelity* 25 (October 1975): 70.

87. Alan Rich, review of Columbia 6597, *High Fidelity* 14 (October 1964): 137–38; Alfred Frankenstein, review of Epic BC 1307, *High Fidelity* 16 (January 1966): 8; of Dover 7265, *High Fidelity* 16 (November 1966): 110; and of Delos DEL 25405, *High Fidelity* 26 (January 1976): 80.

88. Norton, "The Vision of Morton Subotnick," 35.

89. John Rockwell, "Which Works of the 70's Were Significant?" *New York Times*, 27 July 1980, sec. 2, 19, 22.

90. Gunther Schuller, "Can Composer Divorce Public?" *New York Times*, 18 June 1967, sec. 2, 17; Ned Rorem, *I.S.A.M. Newsletter*, (November 1982): 7.

91. See Paul Johnson's review of the book *Reflections of a Neoconservative*, *New York Times Book Review*, 2 October 1983, 7, 25.

92. Eric Larrabee, "Artist and University," in *The Arts onCampus: The Necessity for Change*, ed. Margaret Mahoney (Greenwich, Conn.: New York Graphic Society, 1970), 47.

93. Max Kaplan, "Music and Mass Culture," *Music Journal* 18 (March 1960): 20; Joseph Kerman, " 'The Proper Study of Music': A Reply," *Perspectives of New Music* 2 (Fall 1963): 153.

94. Jeffrey G. Hirschfeld, "Milton Babbitt: A Not-So-Sanguine Interview," *Musical America* (June 1982): 18; Christopher Small, *Music, Society, Education* (London: Calder, 1977), 164.

95. English, *Criticizing the Critics*, 15–17.

96. Virgil Thomson, "A Drenching of Music, but a Drought of Critics," *New York Times*, 27 October 1974, sec. 2, 1; also see the report of Robert Jones, "An Outburst of Minimalism," *Musical America* (July 1975): 15.

2
The World of the Modern Composer

Unease over dictatorial aspects of the avant-garde also character-ized the postwar years. Faultfinders claimed that, despite its insis-tence upon removing all creative restrictions from the composer, the avant-garde, in whatever its several manifestations, held onto its own dogmatisms and exacted its own conformities. To refuse to assent to one or the other took courage. Whether or not the advanced composer agreed with the comment, this conclusion was reached by several writers as early as the 1950s. The novice was admitted to probationary membership in the avant-garde so long as he was willing to study "the secret code of an exclusive frater-nity," as one outside observer expressed it. "To gain acceptance in the rarified circles of the musical elite, he must claim to see the Emperor's new clothes. The very freedom that the radicals pur-port to defend is belied when composers feel "constrained from writing anything too beautiful lest it be labeled banal."[1]

A number of musicians have spoken of how reluctant several prominent composers were when it came to seeing artistic matters in their relation to the larger musical society. Nevertheless, we must keep in mind that these composers were sincere artists. They struggled to make sense out of the paradoxes of twentieth-century existence. Under optimum conditions, the incongruities they en-countered and the tautness of mind and spirit they felt were fun-daments for creative strength. Also to be detected were hints at inflexibility when viewing alternate solutions to creative problems and at infallibility when setting forth their own views. As a result, "open visions of modern life" were "supplanted by closed ones," and cultural polarization became a fact.[2]

Leonard Bernstein in 1961 wondered about the future of symphonic music and tonality in the face of the modernist onslaught. He worried about the outcome because "the revolutionaries of the avant-garde had no . . . doubts." On the contrary, they had "one-track minds," he claimed. Also, "They are . . . propelled down their one-way track by the bubbling intensity of their motivation, and they ruthlessly run down anything in their way." He stated later, they demand "passive obedience" from the music world. From whence did these revolutionaries stem? From Webern and his brand of serialism, on the one hand; from free choice with no limits, on the other. He had reservations about the neodada influence of Cage and feared the electronic wild card on the horizon. The avant-garde, Bernstein warned, would continue to remain a tiny group, about which most Americans and professional musicians cared nothing. For this reason, its members could only "live by taking in each other's washing, analyzing each other's compositions, and sneering" at everyone and everything beyond their circle.[3]

PREJUDICE, PRIDE, AND FRUSTRATION

Some composers active in the postwar years were aware of the problems attached to narrow advocacies. Earle Brown, assuredly not a conservative composer, warned in 1966 that each of the two farthest departures from the conventional, whether the serialist's total organization or its opposite, the anarchist's chance operations, contained the "bomb of absolutism," ready to explode and destroy all music. These oppositions demonstrated the extremes of complete order and complete disorder. Each, he said, was a confining and indulgent point of view that brought on its own destruction.[4] Interestingly, Brown himself was identified with a cross-discipline avant-garde circle, numbering among his colleagues the composer John Cage, the dancer Merce Cunningham, and the painter Jackson Pollock. The comment came from an insider secure in his standing amongst the modernists.

Such security was denied the independents, composers who

went their individual way, cultivating their own little musical patch without benefit of an artistic support system. Their speaking up against artistic abuses was therefore "extraordinarily courageous," wrote Winthrop Sargeant in 1965, because men who expected to make their living by composing flout "the avant-garde establishment" at their peril. Modern cliques exerted a strong influence on what was and was not performed by musicians sympathetic to contemporary music.[5]

Owing to their need for supportive colleagues, posttriadic composers did tend to identify, formally or informally, with one or another set of like-minded persons. This inclination had already been evident in the 1920s, when the then young American composers, faced with similar problems of nonacceptance, had belonged either to the International Composers' Guild or to the League of Composers. Because post–World War II styles were even more divorced from mainstream procedures and from each other than had been the case in the 1920s, the number of composers' sets increased. Commentators familiar with the modern-music scene, for example, spoke of the Princeton–Columbia coterie of serialists and atonalists, whose members included Sessions, Babbitt, Wuorinen, and Sollberger, or the coterie associated with Cage and the rejection of formal musical procedures, which included Feldman, Tudor, Wolff, and Brown. These last composers often shared interests with another association of musicians whose compositions favored electronics and mixed media; here were found experimenters like Ashley and Mumma. Another group was connected in the 1960s with the San Francisco Tape Music Center—Subotnick, Sender, and Oliveros. Then there was a looser circle identified with Eastern ideas and trance or minimal music—Young, Riley, Glass, and Reich. In the 1980s, John Rockwell and Gregory Sandow were making a distinction between New York City's "uptown" composers and "downtown" composers. At times, prominent individual artists had one or more disciples cluster around them—Elliott Carter and his acolyte David Schiff being one instance.

Furthermore, a set tried to have at least one performing group identified with it, which served as an outlet for its works. Frequently, the composers themselves were also the performers. Immediately coming to mind was the Princeton-Columbia set's connection with the Group for Contemporary Music; Ashley's collaboration with "Blue" Gene Tyranny and David Van Tieghem; and the special ensemble formed by Glass and another formed by Reich.

When composers of different persuasions came together for a conference, dissension was guaranteed. In 1981, the YMHA of New York City hosted a panel of composers who met to discuss music's direction in the 1980s. On the first day of the conference, George Rochberg described his turning away from the "academic gray" of serialism toward what he described as a new romanticism. Swiftly, a dedicated atonalist, Hugo Weisgall, interrupted in order to destroy Rochberg. The argumentation threatened to get out of hand, so Morton Subotnick (composer of electronic "ghost" scores intended to produce altered inner experiences) tried to calm the two with talk about letting every flower bloom. However, Jacob Druckman, though irked at the arguing, rejected Subotnick's soothing words. Yet Druckman did effectively change the subject when he struck out at the YMHA for paying out money for the conference instead of putting it to better use by performing the panelists' music.

The matter did not end there. Soon the conference appeared to belong in Alice's Wonderland. The *Village Voice* reviewer Gregory Sandow, speaking from the audience, barred all the panelists from serious consideration as composers. To him, they occupied the periphery of music making, whose center was rock, minimal music, and the uninhibited performances at The Kitchen. After Sandow had his say, a proponent of women's liberation criticized the male chauvinism prevalent among artists.

The next day of the conference, panelists and audience resumed their quarrels with each other. Some angrily left; others denounced the past and called history irrelevant to today's music. In short, the conference underlined the incompatibility of the several parties at the session.[6]

Every composers' circle wanted its spokespeople to address a forum larger than an isolated audience in an auditorium. Through articles and books extolling the special virtues of its music, it hoped to gain more support. This consideration surely had some influence on Kurt Stone when he reviewed Babbitt's *Vision and Prayer* in 1963. Stone was then editor in chief of Associated Music Publishers and one of Babbitt's music publishers. The Babbitt work, he tells readers, "has by now almost reached the status of a classic. . . . Apart from rigidly applied row techniques (one assumes) we hear the rather touching contrast of a very human, emotional, agonized soprano voice versus four speakers from which emanate stern, maddeningly correct, slickly infallible synthetic sounds."[7]

When electronics became celebrated in modernist circles, one advocate, Elliott Schwartz, issued an apologia, *Electronic Music*. Reviewing for the *Music Journal*, Paul Turok states that the electronic community would love the book, since Schwartz names all of its members and criticizes none of them. Adds Turok: "It certainly can't hurt *his* position in the circle."[8]

The more eloquent spokespeople for one or another of the new styles, especially if respected critics, also provided another valuable service. Since personnel and tenure committees at universities and grants committees advising foundations and state and federal governments took seriously what was written, the composer had an easier time winning a university appointment, foundation commission, or government subsidy.[9]

A word of caution is also necessary. A Harris poll, conducted in 1970, revealed how critics, particularly those writing about music and drama, thought that the arts public paid them close attention and was educated by what they had to say. Further investigation, however, showed that a majority of the critics polled considered many of their colleagues to represent one or another "in group," puffing it when they could. Their failure to evaluate the group's works "in broad terms for the general public" resulted in their being "out of touch with the public."[10] Advocates kept no aesthetic distance between themselves and the music they talked about. John Canady says he knew one critic who was an "enthusiastic proselytizer" for the more extreme artistic expressions. This critic insisted on "interested sympathy" as a "uniquely necessary qualification" for writing about the modern movement.[11]

This sort of partisanship needed a corrective force, if only to bring a sense of reality home to a few composers. However, composers were normally employees of universities that guaranteed them freedom of action and shielded them from adverse criticism. Nor was the necessary corrective forthcoming from the faceless foundations and governmental agencies. The same composers who occupied academic positions were usually the judges appointed by these artistically inexpert establishments to decide where the money to be disbursed should go.

The absence of an effective corrective had predictable consequences. As Donal Henahan correctly concluded in 1975, the young composer began life, typically, by receiving a grant or a fellowship, usually aided by his teacher's sponsorship. He then disappeared "into the scholastic labyrinth." His compositions generally were "designed as if meant only to be performed for a few friends and colleagues." The measurement of success was winning another grant or fellowship or "being elected to the next honorary institute."[12]

Another consequence was the apparent inability to see anybody's side except one's own. This was made clear when the serial composer Milton Babbitt announced the existence of two sorts of composers, his legitimate "academic" kind and the "theater" kind that wrote to attract an audience. The latter was merely a "show biz crowd" and therefore to be scorned.[13]

Presumably, Babbitt could have found Carter's atonal complexities to be legitimate music. However, he would never have uttered the enthusiasms expressed by a worshipful David Schiff. Schiff said Carter's First String Quartet equalled "the heroic scale of Schoenberg's First Quartet" and surpassed "even Berg's *Lyric Suite*." As if this were not enough, Schiff goes to greater excess with: "The First Quartet was probably the first musical composition of this century to rival the formal daring of Eliot, Joyce, Proust or Eisenstein." Schiff laments the lack of performances given Carter's Variations for Orchestra, which "served to deprive audiences of the most important orchestral work written in the United States during the '50s."[14]

Schiff's hyperbole irritated Babbitt's fellow serialist, Charles Wuorinen. Although much is admirable in Carter's music, he says, Schiff's "adoring panegyrics" substitute for objective criticism and illustrate "the depressingly low standards for contemporary discourses on music."[15]

Gregory Sandow, whose protest at the YMHA conference on music of the 1980s was noted, stood his own ground against Babbitt, Carter, Schiff, and Wuorinen. He disliked "academics" and "elitists" and loved the "show biz crowd." He said the academic types were responsible for dead music that nobody wanted to hear. When performed, their compositions drew a small, aging audience that applauded with little enthusiasm. The music sounded unimaginative and showed a basic fear of life. In contrast, Sandow cheered Philip Glass. Glass's compositions showed affinities to rock music and filled concert halls and opera houses. Glass was "almost a pop star"; Carter was definitely "*not* popular." Sandow went on to accuse academics of fearing competition from minimalists like Glass and Reich. Yet both men were artists and not mere entertainers, despite what the "uptown" types thought. Theirs was a musical style for everyday life. It sounded as if they "took walks," "went to movies," and "made love." On the other hand, Carter sounded "like he never did these things. From his songs you'd think he never heard of colloquial English speech."[16]

Inexperienced composers, recently out of school, imbibed their teachers' precepts. They wanted performances by the finest ensembles, without working their way up as journeymen—so said Howard Hanson. If a few gained prominence, they were tempted to take the view expressed by Virgil Thomson, that composers owned music and had a right to destroy it if they wished.[17]

As was earlier pointed out, John Cage did his share of destruction by dismissing any discussion of beauty in music as meaningless. By sweeping away old precepts he hoped to eliminate all of the limits on the imagination. Cage claimed the issue no longer was between consonance and dissonance, but one between "noise and so-called musical sounds." He gave no consideration to what others might think. At a concert attended by the faithful, Mel Powell heard some of his advanced electronic pieces played, then passionately defended his art for art's sake and damnation for the public viewpoint to loud applause. Charles Wuorinen, who insisted on going his own way, said the public deserved to be spat upon for neglecting him. William Kraft hastened to defend Wuorinen's statement, saying, whether the public liked it or not, all composers deserved support as professional artists. Because Wuorinen aimed at the profound and spiritual and did not stoop to entertainment, he represented the best in American civilization.[18]

In exoneration of the writers who made statements like the above,

we must consider the frustrations brought on by few performances of new music, usually played in slipshod manner by underrehearsed ensembles, mostly before hostile audiences. Earl Kim
has spoken movingly about composing as "a *terrible* taskmaster"
and about "the baffling problems, the sleepless nights and getting
yourself performed! I am *awful* at marketing. I don't have the *chutz-
pah*, I guess." An orchestral piece is completed; some group agrees
to perform it; the composer spends money to get parts copied;
and then he hears the work only once. Kim concluded: "One is
not above being bitter sometimes."[19]

We can feel sympathy for the irate Ralph Shapey when he spoke
of the fine American music available and the reluctance of conductors to perform it. Conductors, he said, "are jackasses: They
can't even read music."[20] He described orchestra players as "the
biggest bunch of babies alive." Once he was invited to conduct
his *Invocation* with the Chicago Symphony. The orchestra, under
Martinon, was also rehearsing Carter's Piano Concerto. The musicians, he explained, like neither piece: "So they told me that they
were going to give me a hard time—I was the guest conductor,
so they could let me have it; they couldn't let Martinon have it,
he was their boss! Well, at one point I got fed up and walked out
of the rehearsal. I said, 'OK, I'm canceling my piece. . . . I'm
not going to take this God damned crap!' " Martinon, however,
talked him into persevering.[21]

Allowing for some exaggeration on Shapey's part and recognizing that his piece was extremely complex and difficult to learn,
justice was on his side. After the commitment to perform the work
had been made, the players should have responded professionally
and attempted to learn the music, however unpleasant they found
the sound.

American composers also expressed disappointment with their
lot after they realized to what extent European governments sponsored new music and even paid composers liberally for performance rights. Philip Glass, for example, was delighted with his
receipt of 8 percent of the box office when an opera of his was
performed in Europe. This was not the case in the United States,
where "we don't give a shit and that's about it. To hell with composers, they're beatniks, right? If they don't want to teach school,
then fuck 'em. We don't do anything for them at all."[22]

The outside world balking them at every turn, composers angrily struck out with profanity, irrational outbursts, and self-defensive arrogance. They scrambled after the few resources at their disposal, elbowing each other aside for the sake of their own artistic survival. During the postwar decades this intense competition between frustrated composers can account for much of their intolerance and ruthlessness.

ARTISTIC NARCISSISM, EXISTENTIALISM, AND DECADENCE

American music culture had for some time been seen as divided into two parts: one, music primarily for entertainment and profit; two, music primarily for sensitive and imaginative expression from which no profit was expected. The latter, art music, depended on the support of patrons to help it survive and, it was said, to free it from the coercions of popular taste. Here was also art music's heel of Achilles. In the past, the composer, however individual his style, had worked within a tradition shared by patrons and large segments of the art audience. This was less true in the postwar years. The composer might develop a tunnel vision that excluded alternate, possibly more fruitful, approaches to music writing. The composer could lapse into insuperable ambiguity and excessive refinement.[23]

He might sport a self-consciousness verging on narcissism; that is to say, an immoderate valuation of one's own accomplishments. An occasional corollary was the attempt to gain personal recognition, sometimes through outlandish behavior and pronouncements or through bizarre creative work. As David Yankelovich states, self-denial is turned on its head. Instead of a concern with "obligations to others pursued at the cost of personal desire, we have the concept of duty to self pursued" without regard for others. "Personal desire achieves the status of an ethical norm."[24]

Christopher Lasch's *The Culture of Narcissism* describes the narcissistic person as obsessed and driven to *outré* activities, in order to find meaning and purpose in life, to find something to live for." Of moment to this study is Lasch's choice of the composer Cage as an example of the person he is writing about, a narcissistic artist who often resorts to arbitrariness and the renunciation of free choice in favor of the dictates of tossed dice, *I Ching* sticks, or coins. Lasch continues: "Whereas earlier ages sought to substitute reason for arbitrary dictation both from without and within, the twentieth century finds reason . . . a hard taskmaster; it seeks to revive earlier forms of enslavement. The prison life of the past looks in our own time like liberation itself."[25]

Note the narcissism in statements like Babbitt's "One writes for what one considers to be the first, most important, and most demanding audience—oneself . . . and there is no reason in the world for one to write for others." Note also Robert Ashley's statement about his *Perfect Lives (Private Parts)*. He says everybody he knows likes certain parts of the composition. Then he adds: "Actually, people have told me things they don't like, but I block those out. I can't remember what they were."[26]

A deterrent to rational criticism (which aimed at distinguishing the recondite from the ridiculous) was the fiction that all great composers had suffered from philistinism. Besides, to many composers such criticism had nothing to do with their music, especially when they sought to express philosophical ideas, mysticism, and spontaneous interaction with life.[27] It may have occurred to one or two of them that one way of succeeding as an artist was to make up your own rules of creativity, so that your music became its own finest example of a unique style. At the same time, it meant you had your own field to yourself, since according to your rules, others are scarcely in the running as competitors.

Under such conditions, how could composers easily talk to each other about their music? Regarding this matter, Glass states that when he has gathered with other composers, the talk was on the nitty-gritty of their profession—contracts, recordings, publishers, promoting concerts, and the like. Even to listen to each other's music when it was not politic to do so, or when not scouting rival territory, was a chore. Barbara Grizzuti Harrison also makes this observation when describing the composers she had known at the MacDowell Colony. She saw composers escaping out of windows when other composers' works were performed.[28]

Artists were battling almost every element of the music world—the performer, manager, publisher, and audience. In 1967, Gunther Schuller made a significant assessment of his fellow composers. They were tempted, he said, to insulate themselves from a "misunderstanding and apathetic public" and from colleagues seen as "obviously 'inferior.' " As a result, the composer's "only contact . . . consists of flaunting his superiority vis-à-vis the public, the critic, the performer," which allows him to repudiate obligation.[29]

Egocentrism and isolation encouraged a musician like Wuorinen to urge composers to "rise up and demand" an end to the attacks on them and their music, and an end to "inadequate compensation" for the act of composing. Revolt was necessary.[30]

The protest was pathetic and revolt meaningless, if the outside world took no notice. Referring specifically to composers like Wuorinen, Abram Chasins once remarked about the unwillingness to realize that noncommunication had left composers without any public. Unable to face reality or "to read a balance sheet" they lived "a fantasy life in limbo, sputtering bitter charges that have little validity."[31]

The decades after World War II saw the concept of existentialism take hold. In general, existentialism held men and women personally responsible for their lives. They existed in a world without external values. Therefore, the artist had to project his work "into a twilight zone where no values are fixed," writes Leo Steinberg. His composition transmits anxiety to the public, so that its "encounter with the work is—at least while the work is new— a genuine existential predicament. Like Kierkegaard's God, the work molests us with its aggressive absurdity" and requires a "leap of faith" to accept it.[32]

The leap of faith was required whether the work came from the serialist camp of Babbitt or the atonal one of Carter or the antiteleological one of Cage and Feldman. Members of the first two groups were overwhelmed by the thought of personal responsibility in a world without established values. They fixed their musical values within an elaborate system based on a tonal series or a Ur-harmony. The last group, as Leonard Meyer writes, had no goals and wished to arouse no expectations. The music was "simply *there*"—directionless and unkinetic, whether as contrived sound or as sound derived from indeterminacy. Although someone like Cage claimed a relationship to Zen Buddhism, the spirit behind the group had much in common with existentialism.[33]

Along with narcissism and existentialism, a third term was

sometimes heard in relation to postwar music—decadence. Writers used the term to describe artistic works that seem artificial and outside of convention, which made reference to private sensations and values. The characteristics of decadence could include a highly developed aestheticism (art for art's sake), contempt for one's society, never-resting curiosity, propensity for experimentation, subject matter that stresses eccentricity or exoticism or morbidity, reversion to occultism or mysticism or ritual or an alien religion, complex and difficult-to-grasp structural systems, emphasis on the overly rational or the overly irrational, and fondness for obscure utterance.[34] Another characteristic of the postwar artistic world was the formulation of theories that had to be understood and accepted before the listener could absorb the qualities of a creative work. This activity represented a preciousness akin to decadence. All too often the theories had more to do with what the mind encompasses than with what the ear hears. In other words, a hypothetical set of principles with slight relation to the phenomenon of actual sound directed the composer toward a composition's realization.

Each modern style had a theory behind it, whether affecting the structuring of the sound itself, or the philosophical mindset of the composer. This relation of theory to art had been verbalized in 1974 by Hilton Kramer while reviewing an art exhibit. Kramer complained that he could not take the realists seriously because they lacked a persuasive theory. The theory was crucial, since through it the experiencing of individual works was joined to an understanding of the values they signified. Tom Wolfe, in *The Painted Word*, lit into Kramer's insistence on theory coming before the experiencing of art. Wolfe described it as an extraordinary admission that "without a theory to go with it," a person "can't *see* a painting." With tongue in cheek, Wolfe speculated on future art historians teaching students about the postwar artistic era. They would marvel "over the fact that a whole generation of artists devoted their careers to getting the Word, internalizing it," and then "divesting themselves of whatever there was in their imagination and technical ability that did not fit the Word."[35]

Writing about the same time, John Kouwenhoven set forth as a major theme the pervasive danger to all of the arts that came with the acceptance of words as the equivalent of sensory reality.

Thinking similarly, Roger Sessions worried about how contemporary musicians were driven to theorizing about music. The era was one "of artistic upheaval," of "cultural pessimism," and of formulation of ideas in "aesthetics, theory, and syntax" that lack vitality but help musicians arrive at "working formulations of their own."[36] Other musicians warned that the resultant compositions were impossible to accept as sound.[37]

Wolfe's "painted Word" becomes the composed-music Word in Carl Dahlhaus's analysis of postwar compositions: "Decisive is not the significance of a work by itself . . . but rather the extent to which it enters influentially into the development of musical thought and methods of composition. And in the extreme case, works that do not matter become superfluous."[38]

A strong tendency existed in the United States to identify composers not simply by their compositions but by the theory on which their music was based. In addition, apologists for a style tended to explicate not just the music but the theory and processes it exemplified. In 1980, Shapey objected to the constant talk about what music compositions were all about: "I think the music has to speak for itself. . . . And if the music is played a hundred years from now, it's going to have to speak for itself. You're not going to have Babbitt, Cage, or anyone else telling you what to listen for."[39]

THE FRAGMENTED CREATIVE ACT

The American society during the first three postwar decades comprised distinctly different racial, religious, ethnic, and social groups. These groups reflected special interests when they participated in the total culture. Often the result was divisiveness. The artist operating within such a society, writes Paul Ramsey, responds in several major ways, all of which can be detected in the music of the period.[40] Eclectic appropriation of values from a different culture that is then expressed creatively is one response. Here, Lou Harrison and his attraction to Javanese gamelan music comes to mind. A syncretic union of two or more cultures is also found. Alan Hovhaness's combination of Armenian music with that of the European Baroque, Renaissance, or Middle Ages serves as an example.

Another composer might assume the existence of a mystical unity, such as the oneness of life and death or infancy with age. This kind of unity is assuredly found in the works of George Crumb. Or he could assume the existence of a body of people oppressed by a humanistically valueless society and express its longing for liberation. Frederic Rzewski's politically leftist compositions serve as excellent examples.

A favorite response to social fragmentation was the theme of individual isolation and anomie. The extraordinary *Philomel* of Milton Babbitt, with its live soprano voice, recorded soprano voice, and synthetic sounds, all operating in a kind of eery limbo, captures this sense of isolation and loneliness.

Some composers, disturbed by the uncertainty of values, resorted to the expression of regional ideas, traditions, and characteristic sounds. Certainly many of Carlisle Floyd's operas are very much of the American South in their themes, dialogue, and musical idiom.

Paul Ramsey also writes that artists do exist who can see the society, however fragmented it may be, in terms of permanent standards and realities, which exist beyond and make possible our civilization. He quotes a moving passage from Longinus: "What is it they saw, those godlike writers who in their work aim at what is greatest and overlook precision in every detail? This, among other things: that nature judged man to be no lowly or ignoble creature when she brought us into this life and into the whole universe as into a great celebration, to be spectators of her whole performance and most ambitious actors. She implanted at once into our souls an invincible love for all that is great and more divine than ourselves. That is why the universe gives insufficient scope to man's power of contemplation and reflection, but his thoughts often pass beyond the boundaries of the surrounding world. Anyone who looks at life in all its aspects will see how far the remarkable, the great, and the beautiful predominate in all things, and he will soon understand to what end we have been born." [41]

Could a composer see humankind in this fashion, and communicate his vision to more than a select circle? To claim vision without attendant communication, as happened with Ralph Shapey, helped to perpetuate the disconnectedness that everyone sensed. To claim humanistic orientation and ability to communicate with a large part of the music public, as does Elie Siegmeister, causes us to ask the question how large a public is deeply bound up with the music and how transcendent is the vision of the composer? This is meant not to detract from Siegmeister's music but to posit an overriding issue that requires examination.

The breakdown of the usual patterns of thought in American society has been attributed in some part to a country dominated by technology. Technical experts were everywhere during the years under study—in applied science, in economic planning, and in treating the social ills of the nation. One result had been the constant change and reconstitution of society by means of technical innovation.[42] A similar spirit of innovation grew in artists. To create something original by using new materials, tools, and techniques meant progress. When asked about their work, one of the first things artists referred to were their innovations, writes Carla Gottlieb. It was conclusive proof that "this facet of their art is important to them and/or their interviewers, as well as to the art community at large."[43]

As for music in particular, Hans Lenneberg blames Nicolas Slonimsky and his *Lexicon of Musical Invective* (1952) for accentuating the notion that great art is always progressive and that geniuses must overthrow tradition.[44] In truth, it was but a manifestation of a generally accepted viewpoint.[45]

The changeover in music critics, from those sympathetic to tonal music to those believing in innovation, began in the 1950s and was an accomplished fact by the end of the 1960s. The *New Yorker*, for example, had Winthrop Sargeant as its music critic until 1972. He was a skeptic with regard to the claimed greatness of the avant-garde and its ideal of innovation as progress. His taste and the taste of the educated middle class that attended musical performances had much in common.

Then the 1960s arrived. Lionel Trilling states: "The advanced culture began to press harder upon the middle-class consciousness than it had formerly done and the *New Yorker* bestirred itself to respond to this new exigency. The expression of its always liberal political views became more highly charged, and for its critical

columns and major articles it increasingly recruited serious writers
of note, many of whom had come to reputation as exponents of
left-wing views" in art.[46]

In music reviewers, the change was from Winthrop Sargeant to
Andrew Porter, an intelligent and capable writer. He, however,
thought little of contemporary music that failed to mirror the innovations introduced in the postwar years and had no interest in
middle-class tastes. If one kept track of what composers he ap-
proved during the 1970s, they all belonged to the progressivists—
George Crumb, Elliott Carter, Milton Babbitt, Roger Sessions,
Stefan Wolpe, Mario Davidovsky, and Jacob Druckman. These
would not have been Sargeant's favorites. Typically, Porter called
Session's opera *Montezuma* a masterpiece of legendary fame after
he heard it performed by the Boston Opera Company in 1976. He
was on slippery ground when he said that if *Montezuma* was found
too dense and complex, the charge was dismissable. Why? Because it was once brought against Mozart, Rossini, Wagner, and
Berlioz.[47] Yet I too attended the production in Boston and witnessed the unpopularity of the work with almost the entire audience, including musicians who were by no means conservative.
They spoke of the music's failure to evoke mood and drama, to
enliven the stage spectacle, and to move in the direction of sen-
suousness.

Two months after reviewing the Sessions opera, Porter wrote
an article about Menotti's new opera, *The Hero*. The opera, Porter
writes, "is a slight, feeble, philistine, and rather common work."
The composer was glib and banal, in despite of the "few tuneful
scraps of sub-Puccini melody."[48]

Whatever the quality of Menotti's music, its valuation as given
above was in some part based on preconceived ideas about innovation and progress. Porter would have agreed with the *Boston
Globe* reviewer who wrote: "Nothing is more important in the
musical year than the emergence of new works that challenge tradition even as they lengthen it."[49]

As for lengthening tradition, the claim on one level is a truism;
anything brought into existence becomes a part of the past and
"lengthens" its own narrow tradition. Whether it ever becomes a
part of the musical mainstream and its tradition is another question. Indeed, the composer as innovator is unique to modern

Western society. The composer in other societies and in all other periods of history has invariably created whatever is new while working within a traditional system.[50]

Nothing better demonstrates the attitude of the modernists toward innovation than a remark Elliott Carter made in 1984, when he interpreted the musical pendulum as swinging back again to the side of tradition. Carter said to an interviewer: "In the 20th century, there has been a period in which there are continual oscillations between two kinds of tendencies, between doing things that were very inventive with the material—radical departures from what traditional music did—and then a regression to more conventional, familiar patterns. I think there is, at the present time— just as there is in politics and everything else—a general regression to be mediocre."[51]

By the time Carter made these remarks, the American musical world had experienced over fifty years of innovation, some of it intemperate. Nothing shocked because everything was permitted. Music had become anything a composer said it was. And if music could be anything, it could be nothing. This returns us to Carter's worry about a renewed interest in the familiar. If nothing was left to revolt against then the only possible rebellion left for younger composers was against the avant-garde itself.

ELECTRONIC SOUND

The employment of electronics to generate sound can be traced back to Delaborde's electric harpsichord, demonstrated in Paris in 1761. More than a hundred years later, in 1876, Elisha Gray produced his "electroharmonic piano." In 1906, Thaddeus Cahill's "telharmonium" appeared. Also, early in the century, a few composers tried to manipulate the sound of disc recordings. During the 1920s several instruments producing electronically generated sound appeared, among them Jörg Mager's "spherophone" (1924), Leon Thérémin's "thérémin" (1927), and Maurice Martenot's "ondes martenot" (1928). In the next decade, the electric guitar, organ, and piano came on the market. Not suprisingly, several composers, among them Varése, Milhaud, and Hindemith, experimented with one or more of these instruments. Then, in 1939, came Cage's *Imaginary Landscape No. I*, realized through manipulation of variable-speed phonograph turntables.

The postwar history of electronic sound began in Europe with the French engineer Pierre Schaeffer in 1948 and his experiments with the electronic transformation of natural sounds, known as *musique concrète*. The next couple of years saw Pierre Henry associating with him, followed by Pierre Boulez, Olivier Messiaen, and Karlheinz Stockhausen. About this time, too, the first commercially available tape recorders appeared, thus making it possible to preserve the results of the experimentation. Finally, at the beginning of the 1950s, Karlheinz Stockhausen and Herbert Eimert established their influential electronic music studio at Cologne.

The longing for innovation found satisfaction in electronically generated sound. At first this sound was created through direct tampering with the tape itself. The computer, however, offered wider possibilities, since it was a programmable machine capable of storing materials of musical import, provided they were transformed into computerized language. It could then retrieve them and process them as data to be converted into music, usually placed on one or more tapes. The synthesizer did away with much of the tediousness associated with the computer. A computerized electronic machine, it afforded direct production and control of sound. Whether tape recorder, computer, or synthesizer, electronic equipment plugged modernists into the technological spirit of the postwar years, if only because these were both unexplored "musical instruments" and machines that had to be perpetually updated. Moreover, in keeping with the times, they were machine robots capable of replacing performers, even as robots in factories were replacing human labor.

It follows that there would be attempts, at least in part, to replace the composers themselves. Dr. M. V. Matthews, director of the Behavioral Research Laboratory at Bell Telephone, said in 1964 that the computer could produce any imaginable sound and could also function as a composer: "It can either compose pieces based entirely on random numbers or it can cooperate with a human composer. It can play its own compositions. I look forward to the future, to the time when the computer is itself the composer."[52] In 1957, Lejaren Hiller and Leonard Isaacson did program a computer to generate its own musical compositions in the form of a printed code, which could then be transcribed into musical score. The first result of this experimentation, the *Iliac Suite*, was significant because of the possibilities revealed, not because of musical quality.

The first effective public display in the United States of the potentials of the new sound took place in the spring of 1952, when Otto Luening asked Vladimir Ussachevsky to demonstrate his experiments with the manipulation of taped sound at Bennington College in Vermont. This led to the collaboration of the two men in further experiments. Orson Welles had them prepare a soundscore for his production of *King Lear*. The unexpectedness of the musical effects intrigued many people who attended. Another experiment of Luening and Ussachevsky was in response to a commission from the Louisville Symphony—the *Rhapsodic Variations* for taped sounds and orchestra of 1954.

Luening himself has written that those men and women in the audience who favored the music were attracted by its novelty and the surprise it generated. When he identified the people, Luening named several avant-garde composers, their students, engineers, and scientists: "Ours being an electronic age, scientists, engineers, and technologists were the ones who got on the bandwagon and cheered. For them we were definitely on the right wavelength."[53]

In the period 1955–56, RCA developed its first Electronic Music Synthesizer, which comprised a row of tone generators, a pitch capability of eight octaves, a number of devices for shaping tones, and a decoding system consisting of prepunched holes in a roll of paper. The machine was bulky and complicated. Therefore, various engineers attempted to develop miniaturized synthesizers, including portable ones. Two of the more successful of the developers were Robert Moog and Donald Buchla, who joined forces in 1966 to produce microsynthesizers on a commercial basis. Small synthesizers capable of live performance soon were available from several sources, identified by names like Moog, Buchla, Synket, and ARP.

An improved version of the RCA synthesizer was installed at the first American electronic studio, the Columbia-Princeton Electronic Center, in 1959. This ensured the ongoing production of musical compositions utilizing electronic sound composed by various academic composers, the chief of whom was Milton Babbitt. Ten years later around fifty electronic studios existed in the United States, according to Joan Peyser. Jon Appleton adds that by this time there were, internationally, 560 electronic studios, more than 5,000 electronic compositions, and 920 composers who had worked with electronic sound. Most American studios were located in colleges and universities for the benefit of resident composers and their students. What is more, some high schools had also installed studios.[54] Every description of music was subjected to electronic devices: serial, atonal, nonrational, theatrical, meditative, chaotic, and so forth.

How do we account for this proliferation? One reason, mentioned by some composers, among them Babbitt, was the elimination of the need for performers. Composers were driven to using electronic machines, owing to their lack of a sizable audience and their inability to secure performances from traditional sources. Pierre Boulez claimed it was also owing to the American composer's enslavement by fashion, electronic sound being the newest fad. Certainly, originality was easier to achieve. By utilizing a computer or synthesizer one could mix bewilderingly varied sounds selected from an unlimited number of possibilities. This gave some assurance that a composition would be unlike any other.[55] In short, several of the reasons for the switch to electronics include considerations already discussed—frustration, fashion, innovation, originality, and progress.[56]

Exaggerated claims for electronics followed. Salzman, for example, said that electronic sound was quite in harmony with the age: "Of course electronic music *is* written with machinery; but what is the piano but a very elaborate piece of machinery? And look at modern wind instruments with their valves and keys." Russcol insisted that young people were accustomed "to a fantastic sound spectrum of folk, classical, pop, rock music, and commercials. Their nervous systems are extended to receive messages from every corner of McLuhan's global village, and they groove with electronic music, the true voice of our 'technotronic' age." Young people Russcol asserted, sense that our age is rootless. The "impersonal sound of electronic music is . . . *right*" for them, because it is cool and emotionally neutral. Alfred Mayer proclaimed: "The handwriting is on the wall: electronic music is here to stay. . . . In electronic circles I've heard thoughts expressed on how they were going to wipe out all previously made music."[57]

Regrettably, when an electronic piece was placed on tape, every aspect of the performance was fixed for all time. "It's always the same," complained Aaron Copland. "It seems less exciting when you contemplate repeated performances. . . . You finally think, 'Oh, I've played that enough now, I'd like to hear somebody else's version." Virgil Thomson simply said: "It sounds 'canned.' "[58] As early as 1964, Ben Deutschman had noticed that numbers of people were "becoming convinced that strange beeps and unearthly noises coupled with monstrous groans and earthly rumblings are the sum total of Electronic Music," and one question was being asked, "Why bother?"[59] Roger Sessions commented on the mechanical and "dead" production of sound. In addition, he said, electronic music had produced its own boring sound clichés. Absent was the subtlety of expression afforded by traditional instruments. Missing also were human gesture and movement, which are essential to the musical experience. Few people, he concluded, cared for dehumanized sound.[60]

Composers, however, also tried to combine electronics with live performance on traditional instruments or with voices, a practice already in evidence in 1954, when Luening and Ussachevsky composed their *Rhapsodic Variations* for tape recorder and symphony orchestra. Or they combined a synthesizer for live performance with traditional instruments, as did John Eaton, in his *Concert Piece for Synket and Symphony Orchestra* (1967). Or electronic sound was used as part of a theatrical or mixed-media event, a famous example being John Cage's *HPSCHD* (1969). During the 1970s and into the 1980s, composers like Ashley, Behrman, and Glass would tie electronics to the sort of sound produced in rock music and attract a young, rock-educated crowd.[61]

SUPPORT SYSTEMS

Statistics proved that art composers could rarely support themselves through their music alone. For example, in 1961 the American Music Center surveyed composers through the mail, receiving a reply from 430 of them on their annual earnings. Of those reporting, 145 said they received no income from their music, 75 earned less than $100, 106 earned between $100 and $1,000, and 70 earned between $1,000 and $5,000. As for their main income, 345 respondents cited teaching; 92, performance; and 44, independent sources. Grants and fellowships gave significant support to 22 composers. Several said a wife's income kept them going.[62]

A majority of composers depended on teaching to exist. Asked what would happen if forced to live from his music, Babbitt replied: "Couldn't do it. I couldn't stay in music. I wrote a musical comedy which was never produced. I did write a film score and I would never be in show business. . . . To be a composer one must have a private income or a university."[63]

In 1981 Joan La Barbara reported on the trend among composers to organize themselves for the sake of greater influence. She cited, as an example, the Minnesota Composers Forum, one of whose functions was the administration of a Composers Commissioning Program, intended to stimulate new works by composers resident in Minnesota. Community groups were urged to prepare a commissioning proposal; then a local composer would be found to carry out the request. The New Music Alliance, formed in 1979 and at first named the New Music New York Conference, existed for a similar reason. It also tried to set up a touring network in order to help traveling composers. It hoped to compile a list of sponsoring organizations that would promise a composer performances in contiguous places, so as to provide him with a real tour. In addition, it wished to stimulate summer festivals throughout the United States, where current trends could be displayed and local talent encouraged.

La Barbara went on to mention the Pilot Music Touring Program of the California Arts Council. Next mentioned was the Meet the Composer organization, based in New York but active in three states and trying to go nationwide. It helped composers to attend performances of their music, and sponsored composition projects and concerts of its own. As a sign of the times, she wrote, the American Music Center was now trying to represent the entire country rather than mainly the New York area.[64]

Various efforts were made to subsidize performing ensembles specializing in the presentation of advanced music. The assumption was that the avant-garde needed all the help it could get, while composers of more conservative cast would be courted by the regularly established ensembles.

I have heard from enough of the nonadvanced composers to conclude that oftentimes new-music performing groups neglected their music, whether they lived far from New York City, as did the Arizona composer Robert Muczynski, or close to it, as did Elie Siegmeister. Siegmeister in 1984 remarked about the subsidies paid to new-music performance ensembles and their increase in number. He said that although he did receive performances elsewhere, New York performances eluded him. "Today more than 400 ensembles are devoted largely to the performance of post-serial and neo-dada works in this country, confined mainly to the university orbit. Between the 'Uptown' post-serial composers and the 'Downtown' neo-dada composers, 'midtown' or 'out-of-town' composers need not apply. Officially rebels against the 'Establishment,' the self-styled 'new music' leaders have become the new Establishment."[65]

The complaint that no regular group, whether symphony orchestra or opera company, served as a dependable outlet for any new music was unquestionably true. For this reason composers hoped to find someone to champion their music. The American conductor Christopher Keene was just such a champion for the music of Glass and of Corigliano. When Glass completed his opera *Satyagraha*, Keene conducted it. When Corigliano offered him *Three Hallucinations for Orchestra*, Keene premiered it, saying: "Whatever he composes I'll find a way to perform."[66] Robert Miller, the concert pianist, liked serial and atonal music and played it whenever he could. Not surprisingly, a number of the composers wrote for and dedicated compositions to him: Wuorinen's *Sonata, 1969*, Wolpe's *Form IV: Broken Sequences*, Perle's *Toccata*, and Wyner's *Three Short Fantasies*. These works were also recorded by Miller. Elliott Carter was fortunate in having several ensembles take up the cudgels on his behalf: Speculum Musicae, the Contemporary Chamber Ensemble, the American Brass Quintet, the Juilliard Quartet, and the Composers Quartet.

Ben Weber became an expert at manipulating others to work for him, patrons, friends, and musicians. Ned Rorem writes about Weber as follows: "I still recall Seymour Barab and Shirley Gabis, when I was a student at Curtis, in 1943, playing the cello music of Ben [Weber] . . . ; Eugene Istomen performing the *Bagatelles*; Patricia Neway singing the songs. Later it was Stokowski and Mitropoulis, and above all the invaluable William Masselos who, from the standpoint of living composers, was in the forties and fifties the most important pianist in the world. And Newell Jenkins, who commissioned the haunting *Dolmen* with those disconcerting string glissandos. And the New Music Group, which recorded his Second Quartet. . . . And Francis Thorne who helped him financially, as Alma Morgenthau (Barbara Tuchman's mother!) once had. And Oliver Daniel who procured him performances through the American Composers Alliance, as the I.S.C.M. once had. And the Ajemian sisters, and Frank O'Hara and Morris Golde." Lastly, he writes: "And me this morning with fingers guided by Ben's as I type these words."[67]

Grants, of course, helped pay the expenses of commissioning and performing new works. The wealthy Paul Fromm, to give an instance, wrote in 1960 that he realized how isolated young composers were. He therefore formed the Fromm Fellow Players, a group of eleven young performers at the Berkshire Music School of Tanglewood. This group helped composers by letting them hear their newest music. It performed weekly lecture-concerts honoring visiting and resident composers, presented student works to the public, and gave formal concerts.[68]

Although modern composers concentrated on writing for small ensembles (since the large ones were closed off to them), now and again a large performing group was created especially for their benefit. One such group was the American Composers Orchestra of New York. In the fall of 1975, the conductor Dennis Russell Davies and the composers Nicolas Roussakis and Francis Thorne (who had just been elected president of the American Composers Alliance) investigated the possibility of giving at least one concert devoted to new orchestral music. In February 1977, they and the Alliance sponsored a concert by the infant American Composers Orchestra. Concurrently, they sought more private and public funds in order to increase the annual concerts to three. In 1981 the American Composers Orchestra received a N.E.A. grant of more than $19,000 for the purpose of coordinating the efforts of an association of four orchestras. In accordance with the grant's provisions, it commissioned a work from John Adams; the Milwaukee Symphony, from Charles Wuorinen; the Tri-City Symphony, in Illinois and Iowa, from Nicolas Roussakis; and the Oakland Symphony from Lukas Foss. By the 1983–84 season, the orchestra's directors tried for five concerts annually. Yet the orchestra still had a major problem: never in the years of its operation had there been more than 250 regular-season subscribers. No solution was in sight. In order to help matters, a foundation in the early 1980s funded the purchase of 100 tickets for distribution to conservatories and schools of music.

By the early 1980s, it had performed ninety-five works, of which twenty-six were world premiers, thirty-one New York premiers, and many others revivals of worthy but neglected scores. It taped all concerts for broadcast over National Public Radio. Yet the orchestra, however important its contribution to avant-garde music, did not gain wide public support. Without funds provided by individuals, foundations, and governmental bodies, it would have foundered.[69] The same story was true for most other ensembles specializing in twentieth-century music. The most fortunate ones were also backed by some institution of higher learning.

Some large (therefore costly to maintain) music groups leavened their contemporary offerings with traditional works. The Kansas City Lyric Opera, under Russell Patterson, for example, had a reputation for hiring young American singers, doing operas in English, and mounting one contemporary work annually. To cite a second group, Robert Boudreau founded the American Wind Symphony Orchestra in Pittsburgh, in 1957, and tried as much as possible to commission new works, performing them on board a floating concert hall, the *Point Counterpoint II*.

Why do certain musicians like to perform contemporary works? John Reardon, a consistent participant in operas by living Americans, mentioned the stimulation in singing something different. He enjoyed creating characters where no precedents existed, so that he was listened to without preconceptions. He also performed in new works because he could not afford the luxury of turning down the money offered him. Because of his accuracy in traversing the most awkward intervals and his ability to remember modern musical passages, he was in demand for the performance of new compositions.[70]

Under normal circumstances, some rapport had to exist between performers and composer. Otherwise, the connection was severed. This was the case with Katherine Ciesinski, who sang comfortably in serial compositions. Her gift of absolute pitch and accurate memory, as with Reardon, created a constant demand for her services. Nevertheless, in 1979 she ceased singing works that utilized what she now considered nonmusical vocal sounds. She said that she tired of screeching and screaming and feeling she was in a circus act. She wished to sing contemporary works only when the vocal lines impressed her as lyrical.[71]

Joan Tower, a well-regarded composer in her own right and a pianist with the Da Capo Chamber Players, has spoken of seeing composers through a performer's eyes and thinking they often failed to understand the tradition of repertoire, which performers felt they needed to learn and preserve. Composers had to expect some time to elapse before new pieces entered the repertoire, she said. The unusual virtuosity called for in some works could be especially frustrating to musicians. This was one of many performance issues that a composer needed to take into consideration.[72] For her ensemble, a basic requirement for rapport with the music was established when the composer has so written the piece that it jumped off the page at the players and took on its own definite shape. If the way it was put together, or the pitch structure, remained unclear then players could not feel the music to their core or know intuitively whether they had played a wrong note. If the piece failed to speak to the performers, the excitement was missing, nothing happened expressively, and the work failed.[73]

The maximum in rapport, of course, resulted when the composers themselves were a part of the performing group. The Group for Contemporary Music provided its composer-members Charles Wuorinen, Nicolas Roussakis, and Harvey Sollberger with the optimum in sympathetic understanding of their complex and difficult styles. As might be expected, when the ensemble performed the works of other composers, they were usually in styles that paralleled those of the ensemble's members—the music of Babbitt, Carter, and Schoenberg, to name three.

When John Corigliano accused the ensemble of refusing his works because he was not radical enough a composer, Charles Wuorinen claimed the ensemble's discrimination was solely against music that lacked quality and confessed that this was a form of intolerance the players intended to continue cultivating.[74]

Wuorinen's music, in turn, would have seemed to lack quality to the ONCE Group, formed by Ashley in 1963. ONCE's interest lay in multimedia productions produced with as much spontaneity as possible, not in the academic works played by the Group for Contemporary Music. Ashley admitted the members had formed ONCE to play their own music. He expressed boredom at playing other people's compositions, since he never found them interesting.[75]

When we consider musicians who were not composers but who were dedicated to the performance of contemporary music in its several varieties, we discover people who have provided the most valuable services to new music. Among them were the pianist Ursula Oppens and the singers Bethany Beardslee and Jan De-Gaetani. I have heard Ursula Oppens perform with conviction pieces as diverse in style as the knotty pianisms of Carter and the melodically direct and invigorating writing of Rzewski. Jan DeGaetani has been wonderful both as a straight singer of modern works and as an actress-singer—at one moment, sex-driven; at another, innocent and childlike; at still another, mysterious and moody—her voice changing its character to adapt to different styles and personifications.

Ned Rorem, a specialist in song composition, marveled at how certain singers were "skilled to deal with current vocal concerts." They could "stress words as sound no less than as sense, and inevitably enmesh the voice in a jungle of instrumental hues." He cites Bethany Beardslee "who could always do anything, as can Julius Eastmann, Cathy Berberian, Jan DeGaetani and Phyllis Bryn-Julson."[76]

Not always were these musicians happy about being identified only with modern music. Phyllis Curtin once wrote of how discouraging it was for her to perform new works when reviewers persisted in reviewing mostly the composition she sang and not her singing. Nor did identity with the new help when she wished to perform standard compositions: "At first I had difficulty getting to do anything in the standard repertoire because everyone associated me with new music—and saved me for it."[77]

Jan DeGaetani made a similar protest, saying: "I really don't like to think of myself as a specialist in modern music. The truth is I do as much standard repertory as contemporary." Yet Jack Heimenz, in his article of 1974 on the singer, wondered how long she could continue to do older music, since the demand for her contemporary-music services was growing and foundations were asking her to designate composers for commissioning, whose compositions she would be willing to sing.[78]

Indeed, the performer as intermediary between commissioning agency and composer was a commonplace occurrence. As illustration, the members of the Concord String Quartet sought financial help from foundations and private individuals, and sometimes paid out of their own pockets, to commission works from composers they believed in. Again, Richard Cormier, conductor of the Chattanooga Symphony Orchestra, has praised the backing of Chattanooga's Lyndhurst Foundation, which, beginning in 1981, provided major commissions to composers linked to the southeast region of the country. A third example is provided by the pianist Jerome Lowenthal. He writes of how he searched for money in order to commission a piano concerto from Ned Rorem: "I consulted my benefactor of the past quarter of a century, U.S. Ambassador Fredric R. Mann, on the matter of a concerto commission. . . . The Ambassador gave me generously of his advice." Acting on Mann's advice, Lowenthal got the Aspen Festival to fee the composer, Boosey and Hawkes to publish the concerto, and William Steinberg to conduct the finished work. The premiere came in December 1970.[79]

Occasionally, prestigious but traditionally oriented ensembles and conductors gave commissions. For the most part, however, such commissions were token gestures directed toward composers who were currently fashionable. Carter has said that often the ensemble involved valued publicity more than the music. It underrehearsed the work and paid the composer an absurdly low fee, out of which had to come travel and copying expenses. In addition, some conductors had the habit of putting off a premiere for years after receiving the completed composition.[80] Be that as it may, composers, especially those who had limited recognition, could not afford to turn down the possibility of major exposure for themselves and their music and were usually inclined to accept commissions of the sort just described.

Composers were pleased when museums of art sponsored concerts of their music. One can point to the concerts of modern music at New York's Museum of Modern Art. I remember how the Whitney Museum of American Art in 1968 exhibited Harry Partch's instruments and performed his music. There was also the Boston Museum of Fine Art's sponsoring of an all-Cage concert and later an all-Oliveros concert. However, what concerts museums normally have given center on early rather than contemporary music. A much more reliable outlet for performances has been conservatories of music, colleges, and universities.

Already mentioned was the arrival in the United States during the 1930s and 1940s of several composers with international reputations. By winning teaching positions they reinforced the idea of the composer-professor and justified the inclusion of courses in music composition as academic offerings. Their high esteem encouraged young composers, who might otherwise have gone elsewhere, to attend colleges and universities. The young musicians, too, later became professors and taught the next wave of native composers, thus producing a new type of artist, the academic composer.[81] The composer Earl Kim, delighted with his light teaching load at Harvard, said: "I don't believe that starvation is conducive to creating music. The universities are the modern Esterhazys. You can count on one hand the twentieth-century composers who have lived by composing alone.[82]

Aaron Copland was less sanguine about a composer's affiliation with the university. He worried about the danger of too much intellectualization, an inevitable concomitant of the academic situation. He warned of isolation from the real world beyond the academic walls. He saw academic compositions becoming more complex, more difficult to understand, and more disliked by general audiences.[83] The bridges he and others had tried to build between composer and public were being dismantled.

The younger modernists were less worried. Alfred Frankenstein, for example, praised the American college as "a citadel of advanced experiment in music, analogous to the experimentation going on in its scientific laboratories. This new role strongly affects the musical climate everywhere."[84] Leslie Bassett was able to observe in the mid-seventies that every composer he knew held a professorship, was an artist in residence, or was a conductor at a university, "the patron of our day." He adds that only through his affiliation with a university (University of Michigan) has he been able to accomplish what he has. The school was a stimulus to his work; it helped him get a Fullbright to go to Paris; and it helped him financially after he won the Rome prize: "There have been grants. I've had lots of recognition and commissions which wouldn't have come to me if I hadn't been in the university."[85]

The amount of music, old and new, performed at the more affluent schools was astounding. As an official of Columbia Management explained, the cultural explosion as far as he was concerned did involve colleges and universities. Schools were the largest buyers of serious music, accounting for at least 75 percent of the professional performances in America. When we consider that Indiana University at Bloomington alone had over 600 concerts and recitals a year, plus eight or more new opera productions, we can get some notion of how extensive this activity could be.[86]

The number of school-affiliated string quartets burgeoned during the postwar years. To give a brief description of one ensemble, the Cleveland Quartet was formed in 1970, as a resident group at the Cleveland Institute of Music. Later, it moved to SUNY at Buffalo, then to the Eastman School of Music.

The Cleveland Quartet contained professionals expected to perform the most difficult music with a high degree of excellence. A similar excellence applied to many student instrumentalists and singers. In Boston, I have listened with pleasure to capable student orchestras at the New England Conservatory of Music, Boston University, Harvard University, and the Massachusetts Institute of Technology play difficult music from the past and of the present. To confirm this, I cite a review of the M.I.T. orchestra, when it played at Carnegie Hall in 1983. Noting that none of the players were conservatory trained, Edward Rothstein writes that the ensemble "hardly seems a student orchestra. . . . The group of musicians from the M.I.T. and Wellesley university communities are a refined and disciplined ensemble." Performed that night were Stravinsky's *Firebird*, Persichetti's Piano Concerto, and the premiere of John Harbison's Incidental Music for Shakespeare's *Merchant of Venice*, a program neither ordinary nor easy to execute.[87]

Alongside the artist in residence idea, where the musician performed and taught at a university and had freedom to concertize elsewhere as well, grew the idea of the composer in residence. The composer so designated was freed from a full teaching schedule so that he could create music. In turn, the production and performance or the music under academic auspices helped bring prestige to the institution. Some composers who by the mid-sixties had been engaged as composers in residence, were Lukas Foss at U.C.L.A., Ross Lee Finney at the University of Michigan, Gardner Read at Boston University, and Roger Sessions at Princeton.[88] Several institutions also instituted mini-residencies for composers, as did Bucknell University. During the course of one year, Hannay, Babbitt, Cage, and Amram came to lecture and supervise the performance of their music.

The hazard of seeing the university as comprising the world was one faced by both the abstract and cerebral composers and the nonrational and experimental ones. For example, Conrad Susa writes about a New Image of Sound concert at Hunter College in 1969. Featured were productions of Lucier, Ashley, Salzman, and Mumma. Presented were amplified brain waves, grotesque electronic noises, sexually explicit sounds, and the performer's unrobing to nakedness—all in the name of music. Susa says these composers, like most composers supported by universities, exemplified a strain of inbreeding often described by observers of the contemporary music scene. They remained separated from reality and from responsibility for their actions.[89]

Every now and again a composer heady over his own importance openly criticized his academic colleagues, scorning the principle of collegiality. I know of several composers who have operated thusly, some of whom were quietly invited to leave. Perhaps the most widely bruited instance of a composer who found himself dismissed because of his acerbic personality took place in 1971, when Columbia University fired Charles Wuorinen and ceased sponsoring the Group for Contemporary Music.

Wuorinen did not depart meekly. He lashed out at his critics in an article in the *New York Times*, published in August 1971. The

controversy is worth going into because it reveals the kind of un-
realistic attitude some composers had, in part owing to the nur-
turing of universities and in part to the lingering German-roman-
tic elevation of the composer to *Artist*. Wuorinen begins by claiming
that all compositional activities at Columbia were the result of
individual effort, not the university's encouragement. A music department dominated by musicologists interested only in the past,
whose sense of music had atrophied, plus the characteristically
American philistinism of the administration had contributed to his
fall.

Paul Henry Lang, the eminent music historian, wrote a reply to
the Wuorinen claim, saying that he himself was no longer connected with Columbia and had no hand in ousting the composer.
He adds that Jack Beeson, the department chairman, was also a
composer, not a musicologist, and had a reputation for impartial-
ity. Wuorinen and his group had received tremendous support from
the university—none of which the composer acknowledges. Though
Wuorinen was gifted, he was also temperamental, arrogant, ruth-
less, and contemptuous of "anything outside his bailiwick." Indeed, he could not stand people who saw things differently and
discovered an enemy "in everyone not of his persuasion."[90]

Other writers arose to rebut Wuorinen. A musicologist spoke
of his own firing by an all-composer tenure committee. Another
composer pointed out that Wuorinen had arranged the facts to suit
his argument, that whether in Columbia, Princeton, or other institutions, composers were well represented in the decision making. Still another wrote that neither society nor the university owed
a composer anything, especially since nobody except a few friends
really wanted to hear his music—"no one else does."[91]

Predictably, Wuorinen savaged everyone who disagreed with
him: "Often when you overturn a stone, you cause the little crea-
tures crawling beneath it to scurry around furiously in indignation
and alarm."[92] This was scarcely the way to win over critics, some
of them powerful.

The controversy, nevertheless, raises the question of the university's attitudes, those of administrative officers and faculty members, not composers, toward music. We find a tendency to view
American music as an element for objective study in order to reach

verifiable conclusions by means of verbalization. What is felt or otherwise experienced is of lesser importance. Knowledge is directly acquired through rational thought and logical inference. Music as communication, as a tripartite exchange between composer, performer, and audience, is deemphasized. Aesthetics means the dissection of expressive meaning and the querying of composer's intent in order to arrive at authoritative answers, which may or may not correspond to what composer or listener intuits.

The composer in such a setting, according to Carter, tends to be treated as a commodity whose assets are his reputation, verbal articulateness, production of novel ideas, and ability to stay close to the newest trends in composition. He is under suspicion of being overly subjective unless he sets out, as Babbitt did, to prove otherwise.[93]

To maintain his academic status, the composer has to avoid being perceived as an entertainer, somebody who merely pleases the public. Otherwise other faculty members, including musicologists, will not consider him a serious artist. Witness the rage of the Columbia musicologist Denis Stevens at Arthus Parris for suggesting a value in popular music. Parris, says Stevens, is "a traitor to his calling"; he once wrote a valuable study of the fifteenth-century composer Binchois; he now writes "bilge." The music that Parris praises "is written or improvised . . . by decomposers as part of their duties as corrupters of public taste and for the glory of the Almighty Dollar." Parris should not compare Binchois's nor any great composer's music "with the primitive vomiting noises wallowing in overamplified imbecility that typifies most 'commercial' nonmusic today."[94]

The French composer Boulez was surprised at the number of American composers who had adapted themselves to what he considered to be the stultifying atmosphere of universities. He called it an "American malady." In Europe, he said, music was not mostly connected with universities, nor did composers live as much in ivory towers. The condition of American composers was unhealthy. "I do not like this pedantic approach. I do not like scholars who bring only Death to music. The university situation is incestuous. . . . The university musician is in a self-made ghetto, and what is worse, he likes it there." Most significantly, though university composers sent angry letters to the *New York Times* (where the Boulez statement had appeared), the general music public seemed apathetic about the uproar.[95]

Behind Boulez's remarks was the condescension with which Europeans usually viewed American culture. It is true that throughout the thirty-five years examined in this study, the overwhelming majority of American composers continued to hold institutional positions. Yet, there was no place else they could go to make a living in America. That the relationship frequently influenced their art is clear. Although many works were indeed deadly, some were skillfully composed and highly rewarding to hear.

NOTES

1. Christine A. Murrow, "The 'New Music': A Reply," *American Music Teacher* (January 1983): 49.

2. Marshall Berman, *All That Is Solid Melts into Air: The Experience of Modernity* (New York: Simon & Schuster, 1982), 24.

3. Harold C. Schonberg, *Facing the Music* (New York: Summit, 1981), 203.

4. Earle Brown is quoted in *Breaking the Sound Barrier*, ed. Gregory Battcock (New York: Dutton, 1981), 99.

5. Winthrop Sargeant, "Musical Events: *Whither?*" *New Yorker* (4 December 1965: 200; Benjamin Lees, "The American Composer, His Audience and Critics," *Music Journal* 26 (March 1968): 86; Ned Rorem, *Setting the Tone* (New York: Coward-McCann, 1983), 296.

6. Patrick J. Smith, "YMHA Conference on Contemporary Music," *Musical America* (June 1981): 23.

7. Kurt Stone, "Current Chronicle, N.Y." *Musical Quarterly* 49 (1963): 374.

8. Paul Turok, review of *Electronic Music* by Elliott Schwartz, *Music Journal* 31 (May 1973): 44.

9. John Rockwell, *All American Music* (New York: Knopf, 1983), pp. 100–1.

10. John English, *Criticizing the Critics*, (New York: Hastings House, 1979), 109–13.

11. John Canady, *Embattled Critic* (New York: Farrar, Straus & Cudahy, 1962), 14; Samuel Hazo, in the *Princeton Encyclopedia of Poetry and Poetics*, ed. Alex Preminger (Princeton, N.J.: Princeton University Press, 1965), s.v. "Aesthetic."

12. Donal Henahan, *New York Times*, 9 November 1975, sec. 2, 11; John W. Gardner, *Self-Renewal* (New York: Harper & Row, 1965), 40.

13. John Peyser, "The Affair Proved Traumatic," *New York Times*, 12 January 1969, sec. 2, 17.

14. David Schiff, *The Music of Elliott Carter* (London: Eulenberg, 1983), 152, 174.

15. Charles Wuorinen, review of *The Music of Elliott Carter*, by David Schiff, *Musical Quarterly* 69 (1983), 606–7.

16. Gregory Sandow, "A Turning Point," *Village Voice*, 10 January 1984, 73; "Popular Music," *Village Voice*, 17 January 1984, 92–93.

17. Howard Hanson and Walter Sheppard, "Music in Our Age," *Music Journal Annual* 23 (1965): 51; Donal Henahan, "Can Musicians Really Isolate Themselves from the Public?" *New York Times*, 2 July 1978, sec. 2, 13; Winthrop Sargeant, "Musical Events: The Dead Hand of the Present," *New Yorker* (27 August 1966): 116.

18. John Cage, "The Future of Music," *Music Journal* 20 (January 1962): 45; Roland Leich, reporting on the Composers' Forum at Carnegie Tech, Pittsburgh, *Music Journal* 26 (March 1968): 80–81; William Kraft, "The Wuorinen Hassle," *Musical America* (August 1975): 3–4.

19. Eugene Cook, "Penderecki: The Polish Question—And Others," *Music Journal* 35 (February 1977): 8; Janet Tassel, "Golden Silences," *Boston Globe Magazine*, 27 February 1983, 39.

20. Cole Gagne and Tracy Caras, *Soundpieces: Interviews with American Composers* (Metuchen, N.J.: Scarecrow, 1982), 378.

21. Ibid.

22. Ibid., 223.

23. Alvin Toffler, "The Politics of the Impossible—Art and Society" in *A Great Society*, ed. Bertram M. Gross (New York: Basic Books, 1968), 268–69; Winthrop Sargeant, "Musical Events," *New Yorker* (2 March 1963): 94; Ned Rorem, *I.S.A.M. Newsletter* (November 1982): 7.

24. Daniel Yankelovich, *New Rules: Searching for Self-Fulfillment in a World Turned Upside Down* (New York: Bantam, 1982), 187.

25. Christopher Lasch, *The Culture of Narcissism* (New York: Warner, 1979), 178–79.

26. Jeffrey G. Hirschfeld, "Milton Babbitt: A Not–So–Sanguine Interview," *Musical America* (June 1982): 18; Gagne and Caras, *Soundpieces*, 29.

27. For a longer discussion of this topic, see E. H. Gombrich, *The Story of Art*, rev. ed. (London: Phaidon, 1972), 485–87.

28. Gagne and Caras, *Soundpieces*, 225; Barbara Grizzuti Harrison's comment on composers at the MacDowell Colony may be found in *New York Times Book Review*, 23 January 1983, 22.

29. Gunther Schuller, "Can Composer Divorce Public?" *New York Times*, 18 June 1967, 17.

30. Charles Wuorinen, "We Spit on the Dead," *Musical America* (December 1974): 16–17.

31. Abram Chasins, *Music at the Crossroads* (New York: Macmillan, 1972), 162–63.

32. Leo Steinberg, *Other Criteria: Confrontations with Twentieth-Century Art* (New York: Oxford University Press, 1972), 15.

33. Leonard B. Meyer, *Music, the Arts, and Ideas* (Chicago: University of Chicago Press, 1967), 72–73. For further discussion of the relation of existentialism to music of the postwar period, see also Robert Morgan, "The New Pluralism," *High Fidelity* 31 (March 1981): 56; Carla Gottlieb, *Beyond Modern Art* (New York: Dutton, 1976), 70–71; Anthony Everitt, *Abstract Expressionism* (Woodbury, N.Y.: Barron's, 1978), 5–6; and Dore Ashton, *The New York School: A Cultural Reckoning* (New York: Penguin, 1979), 181.

34. Alfred Garwin Engstrom, in the *Princeton Encyclopedia of Poetry and Poetics*, s.v. "Decadence."

35. Tom Wolfe, *The Painted Word* (New York: Bantam, 1976), 4–6, 119–20, 339–40.

36. John A. Kouwenhoven, *Half a Truth Is Better Than None* (Chicago: University of Chicago Press, 1982), x; Paul Henry Lang, ed., *Problems of Modern Music* (New York: Norton, 1962), 23.

37. Robert C. Ehle, "The Evolution of Musical Style," *American Music Teacher* (January 1983): 20.

38. Carl Dahlhaus, *Analysis and Value Judgment* (New York: Pendragon, 1983), 14.

39. Hubert Lamb, "The Avant Gardists," *Music Journal* 22 (January 1964): 99; Gagne and Caras, *Soundpieces*, 380.

40. Paul Ramsey, in the *Princeton Encyclopedia of Poetry and Poetics*, s.v. "Society and Poetry."

41. Ibid., 779.

42. Daniel Bell, in *The Harper Dictionary of Modern Thought*, ed. Alan Bullock and Oliver Stallybrass (New York: Harper & Row, 1977), s.v. "Technocracy."

43. Gottlieb, *Beyond Modern Art*, 119.

44. Hans Lenneberg, "The Myth of the Unappreciated (Musical) Genius," *Musical Quarterly* 66 (1980): 229–30.

45. Carolyn Reyer, "Why Perform American Music?" *Music Journal* 26 (April 1969): 28.

46. Lionel Trilling, *The Last Decade*, ed. Diane Trilling (New York: Harcourt Brace Jovanovich, 1979), 131–32.

47. Andrew Porter, *Music of Three Seasons: 1974–77* (New York: Farrar Straus Giroux, 1978), 341–43. The review was published in the *New Yorker* on 19 April 1976.

48. Ibid., 377–78.

49. Richard Dyer, "Music," *Boston Globe*, 25 December 1983, sec. A, 1.

50. For further reading on this matter, I highly recommend Dennison Nash, "The Role of the Composer (Part I)," *Ethnomusicology* 5 (1961): 81–94; and "(Part II)," (1961): 187–201.

51. David Sanders, "Elliott Carter Speaks about His Own Work and Directions of New Music." *The World at Boston University*, Supplement (14 March 1984): A, D.

52. Ben Deutschman, "Music from Mathematics," *Music Journal* 22 (October 1964): 54.

53. Otto Luening, *The Odyssey of an American Composer* (New York: Scribner's Sons, 1980), 518.

54. Joan Peyser's claim appeared in the *New York Times*, 3 May 1970, sec. 2, 21; that of Jon Appleton, in his article "New Role for the Composer," *Music Journal* 27 (March 1969): 60.

55. Howard Hanson, "The Music of 1967," *Music Journal Annual* 25 (1967): 28; Joan Peyser, *Boulez* (New York: Schirmer, 1976), 181; Peter G. Davis, "Electronic Music on Records," *High Fidelity* 17 (October 1967): 108; Appleton, "New Role for the Composer," 28.

56. Virgil Thomson, *American Music Since 1910* (New York: Holt, Rinehart & Winston, 1971), 11; Russcol, *The Liberation of Sound* (Englewood Cliffs, N.J.: Prentice-Hall, 1972), 180, 187; David Cope, *New Directions in Music*, 2d ed. (Dubuque, Iowa: Brown, 1976), 13.

57. Eric Salzman, "From Composer to Magnetron to You," *High Fidelity* 10 (August 1960): 90; Alfred Mayer, "Electronics Music, Like It or Not," *Music Journal* 31 (April 1973): 17; Russcol, *The Liberation of Sound*, xxiii–xxiv.

58. Alan Hershowitz, "Aaron Copland," *Music Journal* 39 (April 1981): 12; Gagne and Caras, *Soundpieces*, 108; Thomson, *American Music Since 1910*, 77.

59. Deutschman, "Music from Mathematics," 54.

60. Gagne and Caras, *Soundpieces*, 363–64; Lang, ed. *Problems of Modern Music*, 31–32.

61. Cope, *New Directions in Music*, 91; David Ewen, *Composers of Tomorrow's Music* (New York: Dodd, Mead, 1971), 133–35; Rockwell, *All American Music*, 135–39.

62. Eric Salzman, "The World of Music," *New York Times*, 1 October 1961, sec. 2, 11.

63. Hirschfeld, "Milton Babbitt," 17.

64. Joan La Barbara, "Organizing—It Makes a Difference," *Musical America* (April 1981): 21, 39.

65. Elie Siegmeister, "Humanism and Modernism," *Keynote* (January 1984): 9.

66. Lisa Marum, "Christopher Keene," *Ovation* 3 (October 1982): 46.

67. Rorem, *Setting the Tone*, 153–54.

68. Paul Fromm, "The Princeton Seminar—Its Purpose and Promise," *Musical Quarterly* 46 (1960): 155–56.

69. John Rockwell, "News of Music," *New York Times*, 8 October 1981, sec. C, 26; Allen Kozinn, "The American Composers Orchestra," *Symphony Magazine* 34 (June/July 1983): 23–24.

70. John Reardon, "The Challenge of Modern Opera," *Music Journal* 29 (April 1971): 28–30.

71. See the remarks made about her, written by Arthur Satz, in *Musical America* (July 1979): 5.

72. Laura Koplewitz, "Joan Tower: Building Bridges for New Music," *Symphony Magazine* (June/July 1983): p. 39.

73. Ibid., 37.

74. Mark Blechner, "The Group for Contemporary Music," *Musical America* (November 1977): 25.

75. Gagne and Caras, *Soundpieces*, 18.

76. Rorem, *Setting the Tone*, 231–32.

77. Phyllis Curtin, "Pioneering for New Music," *Music Journal* 19 (October 1961): 53.

78. Jack Hiemenz, "Jan DeGaetani," *Musical America* (April 1974): 6–7.

79. Herbert Kupferberg, "The Concord Quartet Embarks upon Its Second Decade," *Ovation* (December 1982): 36; the news report on Cormier and the Chattanooga Symphony may be found in *Symphony Magazine* 33 (June/July 1982): 16; Jerome Lowenthal, "Pianist's Diary: Birth of a Concerto," *Music Journal* 29 (January 1971): 23, 43.

80. Robert Stephen Hines, ed., *The Orchestral Composer's Point of View* (Norman: University of Oklahoma Press, 1970), 41–42.

81. Anthony Keller, "Composers on Campus," *High Fidelity* 16 (October 1966): 104.

82. Tassel, "Golden Silences," 39.

83. Aaron Copland, "Is the University Too Much with Us?" *New York Times*, 26 July 1970, sec. 2, 13.

84. Alfred Frankenstein, in *High Fidelity* 12 (January 1962): 37.

85. Morris Risenhoover and Robert Blackburn, *Artists as Professors* (Urbana: University of Illinois Press), 33–36.

86. Ibid., 43; Chasins, *Music at the Crossroads*, 81.

87. The review may be found in the *New York Times*, 27 April 1983, sec. C, 21.

88. Gardner Read, "The Year of the Artist-in-Residence, Part I," *Music Journal Annual* 25 (1967): 34.

89. Conrad Susa, "On the Off-Beat," *Musical America* (August 1969): 8–9.

90. Paul Henry Lang, "Music at Columbia Will Endure, Even Without Wuorinen," *New York Times*, 29 August 1971, sec. 2, 11.

91. Several of these letters were published in the *New York Times*, 29 August 1971, sec. 2, 11.

92. Wuorinen's letter in reply to his several critics may be found in the *New York Times*, 29 August 1971, sec. 2, 22.

93. *The Writings of Elliott Carter*, ed. Else and Kurt Stone (Bloomington: Indiana University Press, 1977), 280–81.

94. Denis Stevens, letter in the *New York Times*, 19 December 1971, sec. 2, 16.

95. Peyser, *Boulez*, 182–84.

3
The Music of Serialism and Atonality

At the end of the first decade of the twentieth century, various European composers were trying out new ways of writing music, among them Claude Debussy, Maurice Ravel, Igor Stravinsky, and Béla Bartók. From the nineteenth century they had inherited a music of increased dissonance, chromaticism, and instable tonality. The Austrian-born Arnold Schoenberg, in particular, continued this tendency in music. He freely altered tones and ceased using triadic harmonies. Recognizable relationships of pitch and key centers disappeared. Contrapuntal activity increased. The elimination of tonal references in his music was referred to as atonality. He was caught up in an artistic trend, known by the term Expressionism, that affected many creative people in the nonmusical arts, as well—Wassily Kandinsky and his abstract paintings and Franz Kafka and his nightmarish novels immediately come to mind. The music captured an expression strained to the utmost, verging on psychological disorder. Melody twisted from one unstable interval to another. Musicians' abilities were taxed. Seemingly nonrelated contrapuntal lines intertwined to elicit insuperable tension.

Troubled by the threatening chaos in his new musical procedures, Schoenberg arrived at a novel organizational principle, that of twelve-tone, or serialism. Any given order of the twelve tones of the chromatic scale was set up as a tone row, which then governed melodic and harmonic compositional procedures. Although

strictly defined modifications of the tone row were allowed (retrograde, inversion, retrograde-inversion, and transposition). The
repetition of a tone was carefully regulated. Until the end of World
War II, Schoenberg's two chief European followers were Alban
Berg and Anton Webern. In the United States, no prominent
composer subscribed entirely to Schoenberg's views, but three
musicians paralleled Schoenberg's activities—Carl Ruggles, Wallingford Riegger, and Roger Sessions. They, too, employed techniques akin to serialism.

When Schoenberg and other European atonal composers es-
caped from Nazism to the American shores, they taught their
posttriadic procedures to young Americans. After the war, Pierre
Boulez and Karlheinz Stockhausen, the new heads of the European avant-garde, for a time preached the virtues of serialism, especially as articulated in Webern's pointillistic compositions. They,
too, impressed the young American composers. Once relegated
to the sidelines, serialism and atonality in various guises became
the dominant modern styles of the 1950s, as practiced by composers like Milton Babbitt and Elliott Carter, respectively. This sort
of modernism entered the compositions of most progressively
minded American composers. Looking back at the 1950s, Harold
Schonberg, music reviewer for the *New York Times*, was able to
say that twelve-tone technique had "reached into virtually every
corner of contemporary composition, finally enwrapping such re-
calcitrants as Stravinsky and Copland. Any kind of romantic writing was hooted down." Once respected artists "like Howard Hanson or Douglas Moore were accepted only on sufferance—and never
by the intellectuals."[1]

During the years of their ascendancy, serial and atonal composers "dominated funding, prizes, academic hiring, and both the
public's and the music world's perception of what contemporary
'serious' music was all about—and at the same time isolated
[themselves] from the classical music world and from American
culture at large. . . . At the height of its power, the clique talked
as if other composers weren't legitimate or, in extreme moments,
even as if they didn't exist."[2]

THE NATURE OF EARLY POSTWAR MODERNITY

The new music was in an international idiom, without a place-able identity. It supplanted the national style of Copland, the personal romantic style of Barber, and the laconic-Yankee neoclassic style of Piston. Fortunately for this new music, the long-playing record became commercially feasible about the same time and helped it gain a foothold in America. Enough was recorded so that its sound could become familiar to musicians.

The Webern wave, writes an unsympathetic Donal Henahan, crested in the 1960s. One could believe that every academic professor was writing music by the numbers, constructing "terse, bloodless scores" written "to impress faculty tenure committees or foundation officials."[3] In 1962, Richard Franko Goldman attended a conference of the International Society of Musicology and listened to a concert featuring three composers then in the fore of the modern-music movement—Babbitt, Carter, and Kirchner. Goldman's comment: "It is a curious sidelight on the status of music these days that this concert of contemporary music . . . should have been given by and for musicologists, and that the three composers represented should have been, respectively, professors at Princeton, Yale, and Harvard."[4]

The composer Morton Feldman, who later established a style unlike the modernism being described, says that in the 1950s like other young composers, he was eager to explore the dominant new-music style and wrote in a Webern-cum-Babbitt serial style, citing as examples his *Composition for Four Instruments* (1948) and *Extensions 1* (1951).[5]

Speaking of his former serial writing, Jacob Druckman said: "Intellectual organization seemed to be the vital concern of that moment in history. Also, not being a serialist on the East Coast of the United States in the sixties was like not being a Catholic in Rome in the thirteenth century.[6]

The modern music of the 1950s fell into two broad categories. One, either atonal or loosely serial, stemmed directly from the Expressionism fostered by Schoenberg and Berg. It sounded restless and tense, as if driven by unstable inner states. Or two, it featured abstract lines and the juxtaposition of completely controlled tones and movement marked by complexity and mathematics. Behind this music was a historical and an aesthetic justification. The former spoke of atonality, and especially of totally controlled serialism, as a necessary and valid consequence of a historical process.[7] As for the aesthetic justification, the spokesmen for this music indicated that valid varieties of human expression might be captured through intellectual acts or transcendent ideas, resulting in music unrestricted by ordinary reality and one that yielded its meanings usually after effort on the part of the listener.[8] A periodical for explicating this style began in 1962, funded by the Fromm Foundation and edited by Arthur Berger and Benjamin Boretz, the *Perspectives of New Music*.

A complaint was raised concerning Babbitt, Wuorinen, Imbrie, and most of the other composers whose writings appeared in *Perspectives*. These men, the complaint went, demanded that "certain *arbitrarily* defined categories" alone be accepted as worthwhile contemporary music. They taught students a restricted view of what constituted cultural knowledge and wanted to define for everybody what should be counted as "good" music.[9]

Only rarely did any of them add a proviso voiced by Ralph Shapey: "Yes, I believe in an elitist society; I believe that great art is an elitist thing. But as far as I'm concerned, the doors are open to anybody. To me, great art is still the *Holy of Holies*—a very old-fashioned idea. You have a right to come to it; it does not come to you." (Note that art will not reach out to the listener; the listener must come to it.) Then Shapey makes a statement that most modernists described in this chapter would have accepted: "Music, art, do not make money. The old civilization knew it. The first elite that supported it was royalty. When they were finished, it went into the church and they supported it; the church was the new elite. Then the state took over. That's what we need in America, the same damned thing. But of course, in this so-called 'democracy' it'll never happen, not the way it should."[10]

Nevertheless, whether they understood the music or not (and it was admittedly too complex for most minds to understand), men and women should be obligated to support composers—so said Babbitt in 1958. Owing to the music's seriousness, the usual type of musician and the shallow public will never attempt to appreciate it. Or, as Wuorinen put it four years later, instrumentalists, like listeners, are contemptible. Nevertheless, "it is their duty to understand the composer."[11]

The men were apparently in earnest. Moreover, jesting was as absent from their music as from their words. The serialism in Wuorinen's opera *The W. of Babylon* (1975), for example, sounds craggy, disturbing, potentially tragic, but never whimsical or funny, writes Ned Rorem.[12]

As for understanding the composer, how could that happen? Babbitt frankly states that the music is impossibly complex in its construction. The expected repetitions of sound ("redundancy") are absent. Greatly increased "pitch simultanieties" and difficult to perceive relationships add to the problem.[13] Writing about atonal and especially serial music, Leonard Meyer comments that theoretically a listener could play a recording of a work over and over again to learn it. However, he would rarely have the interest to do so. Besides, after considerable effort to understand one piece, the listener would find no carryover to a new piece. He had to start the process of learning once more. The music showed an "absence of a stable stylistic syntax, archetypal schema, audible compositional order, and patent 'natural' patterning" that resulted "in a level of redundancy so low that communication" was virtually precluded. No one part of the structure was to be inferred from any other. To discuss the music as listening experience was impossible. "All one can do—and it is significant that this is what *has* been done—is to *exhibit* its systematic precompositional materials."[14]

The reaction of the generality of listeners was easy to predict. Books, articles, and letters to newspapers and periodicals expressed their dislike. To them, the music sounded dehumanized, severed from human feeling, unmelodic, and without a trace of charm or sense gratification.[15]

If the feeling of anxiety and inner tension was conveyed, it was not necessarily because the composer was writing to elicit such feeling. It was as likely to be the result of the compositional techniques used. Going from one work to another work employing similar techniques resulted in similar feeling. Witness Tim Page's review of a serial composition: "The first movement of Sheila Silber's string quartet (1975) was full of chromatic *angst*—why does this combination of instruments suddenly turn too many American composers into 'Alban von Schoenberg' weeping for lost Vienna?"[16]

As a part of his advocacy of twelve-tone music, Theodore Adorno described a hierarchy of listeners: one, the expert listener who knows the techniques used in the work, misses nothing, and remembers and connects up "spontaneously" all parts of the most complicated work. Two, the good listener, who may not be knowledgeable about the techniques used and the structural implications, but who also remembers and connects. Next came the culture consumer—bourgeois, a reactionary who likes gossip about music and remembers only themes or melodies, not the form of a work. At the bottom was the emotionalist, for whom music triggers feelings and becomes "a source of irrationality," thus proving he is naive and does not want to know anything.[17]

Who was likely to be the "expert" or "good" listener for serial and atonal music, whether today or in the future? According to Donal Henahan, the main hope of composers had to be the continuing interest of a small specialized audience. Most listeners would not take this music to heart. Despite seeming differences, the composers represented a "mandarin class of Western artists, composers whose works are not meant to concern the world outside the palace walls—or, at any rate, seldom do. That stultifying situation has long since been accepted as a reality by the musical public, which usually has been proved right about such matters over the long haul."[18]

In the pages that follow, I am concerned with the effect of the new music on this public. I will not cover all composers. Nor is extensive analysis of individual works considered desirable. Other books, dictionaries and encyclopedias of music aimed at the curious reader, and specialized books aimed at the musically trained do this adequately. What I do attempt is to delineate selected composers' works in various styles and listeners' reactions to their sounds. These listeners are members of the general audience and not necessarily musically specialized or technically trained.

SERIAL AND QUASI-SERIAL COMPOSITIONS: THE OLDER GENERATION

The older generation of composers included Stefan Wolpe (1902–72), Ross Lee Finney (b. 1906), George Perle (b. 1915), and Ben Weber (1916–79). Wolpe, born in Berlin, was taught musical composition by Webern. He arrived in America by way of Palestine in 1939. One reason for mentioning him in these pages is his importance as a teacher of younger American composers, including Ralph Shapey, Ezra Laderman, David Tudor, and Morton Feldman. He was not a strict serialist, and occasionally did hint at triadic constructions, synagogal cantillation, and jazz practices. What serialism he employed was limited to a set of less than twelve pitches, freely manipulated. The listener can detect rhapsodic expressiveness and dramatic strength in his best works. The performer can expect thorny technical difficulties. I recall Wolpe's First Symphony (1956), which Leonard Bernstein requested him to simplify and make more feasible for an orchestra to learn. Dense textures, fragmented ideas, incessant dissonance, and absence of recognizable melody characterize its two movements. Developmental-variation techniques are imposed upon a group of pitches to yield what sound like motives. Strong reminders of the atonal and expressionistic Schoenberg, before his arrival at twelve-tone, are frequently heard.

Finney turned to serialism in the 1950s. Asked why he changed directions, Finney replied: "I knew the technique and had been thinking about it for a long time. . . . Secondly, I was involved in the Second World War, and that was a devastating experience to me, as it was to a lot of people. I have such memories of the utter hopelessness of trying to express the feelings I had in the same way that I had done before the war. In other words, when I got back from this, I felt that I had to have more expressive stuff in my vocabulary. Then, in a certain work, I suddenly found myself writing twelve-tone techniques."[19]

Finney's compositions continued to have some tonal feeling. In addition, recognizably melodic phrases can be heard. Thus, he may sound tamer than the other serialists, as in his Piano Quintet (1953). Indeed, in its slow, effusive opening, its contrasting incidents, and during the longer interruptions of a nocturne and scherzo, one hears less the serial manipulation, more what sounds like traditional thematic material. One has the impression of definite themes and careful ordering of the twelve-tone row. Orthodox harmonic combinations, even consonances, are made possible in works like the Second Symphony (1959) and Third Symphony (1960). At least, they do not sound like a hundred other serial symphonies.

Perle, in a letter sent to Robert Whitney, conductor of the Louisville Orchestra, writes of how it is commonly assumed that the new begins when the old becomes too restrictive. He insists it should be the other way around. Within our system of music more and more possibilities have resulted so that "just about anything goes." Yet, infinite possibilities bring chaos. A composer cannot build a composition if "no principle of selection" operates. Herein is the reason for his resorting to twelve-tone writing as a way of organizing material through postulating functional relationships between the twelve tones.[20]

His music is not completely confined within the bounds of serialism. He allows some tonal feeling, especially through the stress placed on one or two tones, so that a substitution for traditional tonic and dominant functions is made possible. Moreover, some expressive variety is introduced. Writers have pointed to Perle's affinity to the preserial Schoenberg and to Berg. However, I hear a strong continuation of the sounds in Carl Ruggles's works, like his *Suntreader*, in Perle's compositions of the 1950s and 1960s, three of them being the *Rhapsody for Orchestra* (1954), the *Three Movements for Orchestra* (1963), and the Fifth String Quartet (1960, revised 1967). Like Ruggles's music, these works move between acerbic quietness and inflamed assertiveness, power leashed and unleashed.

The *Three Movements for Orchestra* begins with a Prelude featuring static harmonic blocks of sound. No melody in the usual sense is heard. The tones of one instrument or choir constantly overlap those of another instrument or choir. Angry, Ruggles-like dissonances assail the ear. Interestingly, the most appealing part of the movement is toward its end, where harp and clarinet play softly and are answered by a subdued woodwind choir. The second movement, Contrasts, does just that from section to section, which may be lyric, contrapuntal, involved with flashes of jazzlike percussion or vague and impressionistic. The last movement, Ostinato, is expressionistic with its sudden dense-textured outcries and twisting melodic phrases. At the close is a subtle flashback to the opening of the first movement. Technically, the work is built on a fixed twelve-tone "mode" that emphasizes two perfect-fifths separated by a semitone. Whether one can always hear these intervals, or their reshapings as two semitones separated by a perfect-fourth, or as a tritone within which is a major-third, is doubtful.

The same can be said of the Fifth String Quartet, although it at times has a charm that the orchestral piece lacks. Every now and again a Viennese lilt invests the music of all three movements. One is dimly aware of the thirds used in the work's construction. Welcome, too, is the reversion to more traditional development and recapitulation of motivic ideas. This does help orient the listener within each movement.

Alfred Frankenstein, in a *High Fidelity* review of CRI 148, discovers "profound musicianship" and "high integrity" in Perle's String Quintet of 1958.[21] To listeners, these phrases are codes signifying complexity and absence of pleasureful values.

The Seventh String Quartet (1973) demonstrates a departure from Perle's previous, more accessible style. Now heard are the disconnected sounds associated with post-Webern serialism. Tempos speed up and slow down for no discernible reason. At one moment, notes chipped out of the texture fly out like hard splinters; at another moment, they form a lyric line crooned over unstable or secundal intervals, producing a feeling of foreboding. There is a remoteness about the work that carries over into other compositions written around the same time, like the *Thirteen Dickenson Songs*.

In at least one of his late works, *Songs of Praise and Lamentation*, for chorus and orchestra, Perle heeds other current trends and makes use of early Renaissance music and Hebraic and Gregorian chants, incorporating them within his twelve-tone system. The increased reference to tonality is also noticeable. Perhaps one of his most immediately pleasureful compositions is a *Scherzo* for flute, clarinet, violin, and cello, possibly written in 1980. The music, compared with all of the other mentioned works is more sunny, tender, amiable, and with an attractive airiness.

Much of Ben Weber's musical education came through his own

efforts. For him, a twelve-tone row was intended to firm up the skeleton of a composition. It also contributed melodies he hoped were recognizable to the listener. His vertical combinations, rather than always sounding like haphazard aggregations of tones, do occasionally give the impression of late–nineteenth-century harmonies, but with no sense of functional movement one to the other. As for his overall formal structures, he used what tradition had handed down to him. In most of these respects he seems a descendent of Berg. A hope for making a wide appeal was possibly present. Witness his comment about his not being only an experimenter: "I feel more that I am an exponent of musical art with deep reference to the past, and with great respect for the best accomplishments of all those times."[22] A work like his *Sonata da Camera*, for violin and piano (1950), with its sarabandlike "Lento, con gran eleganza," freely altered passacaglia marked "Moderato," and rondo "Allegro con spirito," all based on one tone row, gives a nod to the past. The work is admirable for its craftsmanship, its less than eleven minutes of length, and for its introduction of bittersweet lyricism that some listeners may find enjoyable.

His Piano Concerto (1961) is perhaps more typical of his style. Throughout the work's twenty minutes of playing time, serial technique is modified to suit subjective needs. The first movement, a fantasy, contains a development and recapitulation of the opening ideas. Thematically, it is not as assimilable as its counterpart in the *Sonata de Camera*. It is also more discursive. The second movement sounds a dark elegy in memory of Dmitri Mitropoulos. Its middle section is a passacaglia with five variations and a coda. The Finale, a rondo, is the most rhythmic of the three movements, with a rhetoric like that of Bartók.

Weber did not write many works during his forty creative years. Among his most attractive ones are the two cited above, and the Two Pieces for String Orchestra of 1960. This last composition is not twelve-tone music.

None of the four composers taken up in this section completely abandoned the past. All of them hinted at tonality, fashioned recognizable motives out of their twelve-tone row, used some modified version of traditional formal structures, and adapted the serial system to their own personal requirements.

SERIAL AND QUASI-SERIAL COMPOSITIONS: THE MIDDLE GENERATION

Milton Babbitt (b. 1916) was a mathematician who decided on a musical career and came to teach at Princeton University. In the late 1940s he completed an exhaustive study of the theories and techniques of twelve-tone music. Eventually, he arrived at the concept of the total serialization of music. Each composition was to represent a set of interdependent empirical–rational choices out of a vast domain of possibility (according to the explanation given by Benjamin Boretz). Because of the absence of universals to guide creativity, it was necessary to stipulate a composition to be a "total structure" realized as a "multiple integrated set of determinate, particular relations among all its discernible components. Since no principles external to the work's contents could provide it with a musical identity, a comprehensive idea of musical structures alone had to account for the work's unique qualities. Babbitt's invention, on a conceptual level, comprehended the structure (the twelve-tone set, its transpositions, and its restatements in inversion, retrograde, and retrograde-inversion), the compositional resources available through this structure and the realization of structure and resources through compositional materials shaped for that particular piece.[23]

In effect what Babbitt did was to extend the serial principle. He organized and articulated the relations between not only the twelve tones, but also note values, dynamic levels, instrumental timbres, and intervals of time. This meant a foreordaining of all musical events in a work. The predetermination was easy to postulate but difficult to observe at every point in the creation of a musical piece. This is one reason why later he would work with an electronic synthesizer: the possibility of control was strengthened; aberrant behavior of the composer was kept at a minimum.

Babbitt never doubted any aspect of his theoretical system, although his former teacher, Roger Sessions, did. Sessions warned that "total organization" raised many questions. He did not see it as really organizing music, but "various facets of music, each independently and on its own terms or at best according to a set of arbitrarily conceived and ultimately irrelevant rules of association."[24]

Babbitt first set down his ideas in a monograph published in 1946, "The Function of a Set Structure in the Twelve-Tone System." His first compositions to realize (but only partly) his ideas were the *Three Compositions for Piano*, written in 1947 and 1948. Then came his important *Composition for Four Instruments*, for flute, clarinet, violin, and cello. Here, his system was completely in control.

John Cage said the piece reflected the music of Webern and Boulez (the Piano Sonata No. 2): "Timbre and amplitude . . . clarify the basic division of the twelve-tone row (which itself does not appear in any simple statement) into four groups of three notes each. The composer connects these notes (sometimes quite separated on the page) not by melodic means, but by their loudness and/or timbre." The music has "an effect on the ear as mixed-spottedness has on the eye." Furthermore, it should not be thought that knowing this one work helps to know others, because "he approaches each work as a new problem."[25]

Though Babbitt claims otherwise, most musicians perceive a far stronger connection with the abstractions of mathematical science. Mathematics influences both the music's organization and expression.[26] Paul Henry Lang, for example, says Babbitt's is "the music of the intellect, a happy abstract world where there is no need for a knowledge of life, for mathematics does not know the incomprehensible complications of life." Consider also what Herbert Russcol has to say about Babbitt's music—that it has a "mathematically determined kaleidoscopic quality," where nothing occurs arbitrarily.[27]

No matter what the theories and concepts behind a work, it must be dealt with for its impression on the listener's ear, whether its composer is Babbitt or his creative opposite, John Cage. Several writers, including Lang, have said the music raises questions of what is being communicated, if anything.[28] Virgil Thomson finds "the clarity of distilled water and just possibly the sterility. Certainly it leaves in the listener no appreciable deposit of emotion."[29] Consequently, the general listener and the performer shun his music. John Rockwell sees Babbitt's scientific position as romantic and Promethean, as that of an "independent artist who flies free of the earth and its compromises" to dwell in an unreal world.[30] Rockwell is not a Babbitt enthusiast. Nor is Cage. Babbitt is no seer, Cage states. He fashions objects that he thrusts upon others and that he then writes long articles about; and then has "that *Perspectives of New Music* and all that mathematical business in order to convince us that, if we didn't agree on an ear level, we will be obliged to agree on a mathematical level."[31]

Babbitt has also had defenders, although they usually defend him with reservations. Andrew Porter, for example, finds something to love in the piano music, calling it the "most vivid and attractive of our day." He describes the thirteen-minute *Canonical Form* as brilliant and charming; a set of "twice twelve variations" that are elegant, spare, and clear, like "a new Goldberg Variations." On the other hand, Porter admits the *Paraphrases*, for nine winds and piano, is difficult to take, being in Babbitt's "bitty or ejaculatory manner, which makes both lines and pulse hard to determine."[32]

On 4 August 1983, when I attended an all-Babbitt concert at Wellesley College, with the composer present, the audience was pitifully small, most of it apparently more than fifty years of age and from the academic community. Although Porter seemed to be able to distinguish between two different Babbitt manners, from conversations with members of the audience it was apparent that hardly anyone could make such distinctions. Just before the famous *Composition for Four Instruments* of 1948 was conducted by Mario Davidovsky, Babbitt announced that three of the four instrumentalists were "veteran players of the piece." After thirty-five years, it still sounded formal, overly sectionalized, and cryptic. And it was still difficult to play—a few minutes into the work, and the "veteran" players got so mixed up they had to start again from the beginning. The end of the concert produced sedate applause and one "bravo." The composer was called back once, then, as if on signal, the applause suddenly stopped. At the postconcert reception, I asked an academic musician how acquainted he was with Babbitt's music (I had seen him chatting with Babbitt). "As well as most people in tonight's audience." Did he hear any changes in style between 1948 and the present? "Its all cut from the same cloth. Nothing's too different," he replied. "I'm still puzzling it out." I asked him why he had attended the concert. His reply: "Duty."

Babbitt's music can produce a curious reaction in some listeners. After listening to the Second Quartet and the Fifth Quartet (at a Tanglewood concert, 18 August 1983), a musician friend said she found, after a few minutes, that concentration grew difficult. Her mind flagged for a moment. And at once, the tremelos, pizzicatos, pointillistic effects, and abrupt bowings fused together in her mind into a kind of wallpaper sound, like an updated bit of Muzak.

In the late 1950s, Babbitt worked with the RCA Electronic Sound Synthesizer at the Columbia-Princeton Electronic Music Center. The medium provided him with "full satisfaction." After realizing a work, he could walk out with the tape under his arm, knowing exactly how it would sound."[33]

When Babbitt joined synthensizer sound with the human voice, he produced his most successful works. The *Vision and Prayer* (1961) for soprano accompanied by synthesized sound, and *Philomel* (1964) for soprano, recorded soprano, and synthesized sound are high points in his output. The first composition leads a dichotomous existence, one human and related to the voice's natural richness and the words of Dylan Thomas, the other dehumanized and related to electronic sounds and the angular, *Sprechstimme* manner of singing. The music's vision occurs in a transitional space, neither of the earth nor of another world, as if in an existential void.[34]

Philomel is an effective but numbing work. John Hollander's reinterpretation of a story in Ovid's *Metamorphoses* concerns a tormented woman fleeing through the woods, tongue torn out, lamenting her inability to make any sound. Then transformed into a nightingale, she regains her voice and finds she can sing. The atmosphere invoked by the music is bleak and divorced from earthly matters. The artist, in the person of Philomel, is utterly alone and destitute. The voice moves through unstable intervals and mockingly echos or fails to harmonize with itself. As if awakened from a desolating dream, one comes away aware of an eery, bodiless, and nightmarish quality to the sound, yet recalls very little of what was heard.[35]

If Babbitt composed for orchestra, he was confronted by mu-

sicians irked at his idiom, and a relentless economics that limited
rehearsal time and forbade repeated performances of the music.
When *Relata I* (1965) was performed by Gunther Schuller and the
Cleveland Orchestra, the orchestral musicians were neither persuaded about the music's value nor sufficiently rehearsed to play
it correctly. Application of serialization to all aspects of the work,
finicky timing, swift textural changes, unpredictable and ceaseless
rearrangements of instrumental combinations, and avoidance of
repetition made the players' task difficult and the audience's ability
to comprehend nil.[36]

Babbitt says the musicians of the New York Philharmonic hated
Relata II (1968), and the audience was massively uninterested. The
only people who might be curious about the work, he says, are
his "associates across the country [who] will not have any oppor-
tunity to hear it."[37] The orchestra could scarcely play it, and when
it did, the audience booed.[38] As Owen Anderson wrote in the
Music Journal, "One can only hope that it will now be quietly left
to molder on the shelf."[39]

Babbitt's music has met with almost no takers. Even the students who have taken his course in twelve-tone music refuse to
go back to Babbitt's room later in order to further experience
twelve-tone music.[40] Aaron Copland, normally sympathetic to most
new American music, has remarked on the chaotic impression made
by Babbitt's music. Whatever control there is cannot be heard.
What is heard is atomized sound, without themes or continuity.[41]

Ralph Shapey (b. 1921), never a total serialist, offers an alternative to Babbitt, according to champions of his music. He was a
student of Stefan Wolpe, and to some degree similar to Wolpe in
the style he evolved. Shapey befriended few musicians and stood
guard over his individuality. His moving from New York in order to teach at the University of Chicago in 1964 severed him
from whatever help he had. Few performances led to bitterness.
For a period, he went on strike against the musical world and
opposed anyone's playing his music.

As for his individual manner of organization tones, he states
that it reflects his radical traditionalism. He wants his music to
sound lyrical, but also powerful and intense—and thus show his
respect for Bach and Beethoven. He wants structures to be recognizable and not to exist only as theoretical constructs. By dis-

covering distinctive materials (usually in the shape of sound blocks), which are clearly exposed, placed side by side, repeated, and exchanged through one idea ending while another begins, he builds works meant to be recognizably individual.[42]

He likes neither quoting from the past nor experimenting for the sake of experimenting nor resorting to electronics. Although he insists he has some audience in mind, his musical statements make no concessions to sensuous appeal. More than a few writers have linked Shapey's style with that of New York's abstract expressionist painters, like Franz Kline and Willem de Kooning. In discussing this group of painters, Dore Ashton approvingly quotes a 1961 review of a Shapey work, written by Allen Hughes: "What Mr. Shapey has produced is a composition of abstract expressionism that seems to lay bare the most secret and elemental doubts, yearnings, torments, and despairs of the human soul trapped in the chaos of the urban jungle." This same connection has been made by Matthew Baigell. Baigell points out that Kline and Shapey have much in common, then speaks of Kline's "tumultuously fashioned nonobjective forms . . . that seemed improvised, but which in reality were carefully meditated and grew slowly . . . only after many adjustments." Rockwell also sees parallels between the violent and impassioned statements of these painters and the gestures of Shapey.[43]

When we consider a work like *Rituals* for orchestra (1959), the several observations made about the style fall into place. Shapey divides the orchestra into several sections that are carefully situated on the stage—wind soloists close to the conductor, violinists behind the violists, percussionists on the stage's sides, and the string basses in the rear. The music progresses in bold lines, at times in massive unison, or in persistently driving rhythms, or in an intricately woven polyphonic web. Contrast is provided by quiet lyricism from the woodwinds and a fascinating layering of string part onto string part. In the second of the two movements, improvising saxophonists accompanied by a pianist's heavy repeated blows on the keyboard achieve a frenzied climax.[44] The sound overpowers, as if one were a witness to an ancient primitive ceremonial.

The music is serial, based on the opening material. Repetition comes as variation, in line, motive, texture, and orchestral color. The effect is both static and discontinuous: stop-and-go sound, tense whispers followed by passionate outcries; music wandering with the blind passion of King Lear but without catharsis at the conclusion.

In *Rituals*, Shapey's music verges on the theatrically dramatic. In his *The Covenant*, for soprano, sixteen players, and two tapes, he is indeed theatrical, yet with a granitic intensity like that of Ruggles's music, writes David Moore. "The music is almost always loud; even when only one instrument is playing, it plays loudly. Dramatic it is; enjoyable it's not."[45]

Shapey scorned the listener's enjoyment as a goal for his music. He demanded that the listener "bring his brain" to concerts. "I am trying to write unforgettable music. You might hate it, but you are not going to forget it."[46]

The Sixth String Quartet (1963) and the Seventh String Quartet (1972) are separated by almost a decade. The former stresses the individuality of the players, each part independent of the others. In performance, the musicians, save the cellist, are asked to stand far apart in order to project Shapey's concept of "the graven image." In one movement of six sections, the work relies on motives (of serial provenance). The latter composition, Shapey claims, is his most "classical" work and written in response to his deep love for Beethoven's last quartets. In four movements, it starts with a series of interludes and fantasies. Next come a scherzo and trio, an arioso-like slow movement, and a passacaglis. He states the quartet, like his oratorio *Praise*, rests on tonality. As with the previous quartet, in performance, Shapey discards traditional placement of the players. They are spread across the stage, with the two violinists standing in the middle of the stage, facing each other. He wants the four music parts heard as independent lines but given an overall coherence by a controlling idea.

The *Fromm Variations* of 1973 produce a similar effect. Describing the piece's effect, Peter Davis refers to "rigorously self-disciplined and abstract" ideas, "granite-like strength," and "fierce integrity."[47]

Save for performances by his own Chicago ensemble, the Contemporary Chamber Players, Shapey's music is little heard. In part, the neglect is owing to his reclusiveness. It also is a consequence of his quarrelsome and less than magnanimous attitude when he speaks of other musicians.[48]

Gunther Schuller (b. 1925) admits to a jazz influence. However, it is often blanketed by twelve-tone effects. He has an excellent ear for instrumental combinations, and orchestrates impressively. When a work is brief, he can hold the listener's interest. His conversion to serialism came early in his career. In 1950, Schuller completed a Symphony for Brass and Percussion that introduced serialism into traditional structures. *Variants*, for jazz quartet and orchestra (1960) enlivened the symphony orchestra with jazzlike colloquialisms given to a vibraphone, piano, double bass, and piano. *Symphony* (1965) attempts a version of Babbitt's total control of all musical parameters.

Undoubtedly, one of Schuller's most effective compositions is the *Seven Studies on Themes of Paul Klee* (1959). All seven musical interpretations of the pictures are brief. Not always are serial procedures followed. Schuller's flair for varied orchestral colors and textures are everywhere apparent. The music ranges from atonal to tonal, from American jazz to Arabic orientalisms, from thirteenth-century organum to late–twentieth-century serialism, from the softest and most delicate restlings to loud tonal conglomerates, and from somberness to laughter.

The first movement, *Antike Harmonien* (Antique Harmonies), marked "Lento," conveys Klee's brownish colors and solidly compact shapes. It is expressionistic, nonrhythmic, and mostly atonal but not serial. The harmonies are thick and weighty. Strings hold very long tones. A medieval cadence occasionally appears. Above the strings, open fifths crowd on each other to produce a restrained climax (some triadic writing occurs here). Then all becomes quiet again. It strikes the ear as highly effective tone painting.

The second movement, *Abstrakte Trio* (Abstract Trio), allows only three instruments to play at any one time. Thin textures are controlled by serial techniques. All passages sound subdued. Here "abstract" means music abstracted from emotion. Schuller makes his point economically, then quickly closes the movement.

The third movement, *Kleiner Blauteufel* (Little Blue Devil), starts with a *fortissimo* bang. A *pizzicato* bass line starts up, after the style of Gil Evans and George Russell, during their cool-jazz collaboration. I am reminded especially of Russell's *Stratusphunk*, in the recording *Out of the Cool*.[49] Curiously, both this album and Schuller's composition date from the same year. Here, however, the tonal center is far less obvious. A bluesy trumpet tune is heard in nine-measure sections, not in the normal twelve-bar blues format, over a walking-bass line. Clarinets in their low *chalumeau* register add to the mood.

In *Die Twitschermaschine* (The Twittering Machine), Schuller turns to post-Webern pointillistic serialism. The brief movement squeaks, as if the composer were subjecting the style itself to light ridicule. The fifth movement, *Arabische Stadt* (Arabian Village), encourages the listener to imagine himself floating in the air. He hears a melancholic flute, throbbing drums, and an oboe playing nasal dance tunes from far below. For the first time, the composition sounds unequivocally tonal, focusing on the tone *B*. Harmony, nevertheless, is not functional, dissonance is not avoided or resolved. The scene exists in a dreamy twilight.

Ein Unheimlicher Moment (An Eerie Moment) is a successful atmosphere piece. Heard is the sort of music that movie makers and television producers dote upon for use in murder mysteries or perhaps to accompany a scene where an unsettling and shadowy figure moves through the night.

If Schuller intended to create a serene and bucolic mood, the final movement, *Pastorale*, misses its mark. The repetition of high eighth notes, a half-tone apart in the strings, later heard in a lower octave, and the unsettled phrases played by the woodwinds and French horn prevent relaxation.

The *Seven Studies* contains nothing profound but is one of the pleasanter works written in the serial and atonal styles.

A final consideration is Schuller's opera of 1966, *The Visitation*, which he wrote for the Hamburg Opera. The theme is of a young black man rejected by white and black American society. Intentional was the libretto's restatement within an American setting of Kafka's nightmarish *The Trial*. The condemnation of twentieth-century American society and culture, so popular among European intellectuals and artistic types, probably pleased the German audience attending the premiere. In 1969, the opera was televised by BBC of London.

Although Bessie Smith's recording of "Nobody Knows You When Your're Down and Out" is heard along with allusions to jazz, blues, spirituals, and gospel song, the music relies mostly on twelve-tone expressionistic procedures after the example of Berg. Voices usually declaim in the tortured nonlyrical manner of Vienna. In addition, electronic tapes are heard. After attending the Hamburg performance, Winthrop Sargeant wrote about the ovation that the opera received. Yet for him the America depicted was unbelievable, the score inexpressive and riddled with the commonplace of serial and electronic music.[50] When the Hamburg company brought the opera to New York in 1967, it was less well received. A new production in San Francisco later in the same year proved more successful.

SERIAL AND QUASI-SERIAL COMPOSITIONS: ONE OF THE YOUNGER GENERATION

Charles Wuorinen (b. 1938) at first had a Stravinskian style. Then he went over to serialism. Like Babbitt, he had no interest in jazz, folk music, or experiments in indeterminacy. Wuorinen could not tolerate other composers experimenting with styles differing from his.[51]

In 1961, with *Evolutio Transcripta*, he began to rationalize the relationships between tones and rhythms and increased his use of contrapuntal devices. The work sounds as if between two styles and shows the composer in search of an identity. The music plunges vehemently ahead from one set of thematic ideas to the next. The profusion of new departures gives the impression of undiscipline. This last may explain why, in the next year, he accepted Babbitt's methods, although he did try reconciling them with the less rigid styles of Wolpe and Carter.[52]

The Chamber Concerto for Cello and Ten Players (1963), a major work, incorporated his new ideas. The instrumentalists are divided into two groups; the players on cello, flute, oboe, clarinet, bassoon, violin, and viola in one; the two percussionists, pianist, and contrabass player in the other. Extremely difficult to play, the music is as idiomatic to the instruments as serialism would allow. The one-movement work is in five sections, each differing in structure, rhythm, texture, and so forth. A contrapuntal flow with many interruptions characterizes the music. Within sections, the music of one soloist often melts into that of the other, the stress placed on the ensemble. At the end the music of the beginning is heard in retrograde.

The next year he completed the Chamber Concerto for Flute and Ten Players. Heavy textures appear initially. Then the flute enters and the textures continuously thin out until the flute is heard almost alone. Oftentimes a musical thought is articulated in single notes handed from one to another instrument. The flute is given more legato music; the other instruments, save for the bass, produce either plucked or percussive sounds. Although the treatment guarantees clarity, it also results in a certain hardness of sound.

In 1966, a Piano Concerto backed the soloist with an orchestra that included nine percussionists. Four years later came *Time's Encomium*, a work completely realized in an electronic medium and to be listened to through a recording. Wuorinen defines twelve basic pitch classes and from these derives all musical relations. He tells us that on side one of the recording he exposes and develops the basic pitch and time relations. On side two, he varies the resultant materials within a complex fabric. The composition can be interesting to hear if the listener has an interest in unusual sound combinations. At times purely electronic sound bursts or less strident bleeps come through the speakers; at times the simulated tones of a music instrument, particularly of the vibraphone, take over. Familiarity produces the strange effect of not remembering the actual music but of being able to anticipate the general effect of specific spots in the music.

Around the mid-seventies, Wuorinen's style began to show modifications in the total serialism he had usually favored. *Arabia Felix*, for example, indicates a different direction. The severe dissonances of the earlier works are less obvious. A greater rhythmic drive, owing much to Stravinsky, appears. Some reference is made, especially near the close of the piece, to Middle Eastern music. The one-movement work calls for violin, flute, bassoon, piano, guitar, and vibraphone.

The different style is more obvious in the *Percussion Symphony*. Why percussion? Wuorinen answers in the liner notes to the Nonesuch recording: "Because it seems to me that (whatever the reason) our age has witnessed the rise of this class of sound-producers to true equality with older instruments. Even more to the point, I *like* the sound of the instruments: they have—and this is true, I think, not just of drums, gongs, and other ancient instruments, but of vibraphones and celestas, too—a marvelous combination of clarity of sound (sharpness of attack) with a very ancient, layered set of associations, reaching well back into the distant past."

At the time he wrote the composition, much in evidence was a decrease in the dissonant content of contemporary works. (Consonance and triadic harmonies occur in this piece.) At the same time, some composers were taking interest in gamelanlike percussive sounds, like those associated with Java. (They occur in this symphony.) An inclination to reclaim music from Europe's past, for use in new settings, was gaining in popularity. (Music from the early Renaissance is found in the work.)

MUSIC WITH AFFINITIES TO SERIALISM

During the thirty-five years under consideration, several composers, although not affirmed serialists, wrote music often indistinguishable from that of serialism, at least to the average listener. The best known figure in this group was Elliott Carter (b. 1908). From Walter Piston he learned neoclassic control over all elements of a composition; from Nadia Boulanger, a sensitivity to musical events as sound rather than as explications of theory. The results of Charles Ives's freewheeling experiments also shaped his formative years. Onto all of this was layered information on the highly chromatic and rhythmically complex ways of arranging sound that he had gleaned in his study of modern scores from disparate sources.[53]

The incipient contradictions of style were welded into logical disparities of one element coming to be while another ceases or tends toward an opposite. The disparities of tempo and dynamic were exploited—one instrument decelerates and softens its voice while another speeds up and grows vociferous. The disparities of instrumentation are common—harpsichord against piano, staccato winds and percussion against legato strings, delicate choir against massive tutti. The disparities of expression are frequent—one or more instruments sounding cold and aloof, proceeding in plodding fashion while another turns rhapsodic and declaims with ardor.

Confusing to listeners was Carter's aesthetic need for always making an original statement, each one unlike the music of other composers and even of his own earlier compositions.[54] Adding to listeners' difficulties was Carter's deliberate suppression of regular metrical pulsations. He made certain the accents were irregularly placed and had few correspondences between instruments or groups of instruments. In addition, different instruments or groups of instruments were likely to have distinct rhythms and speeds, however proportionally related they were one to the other. No recognizable themes sounded. Instead, short motives were introduced and instantaneously began lives of ceaseless development. In addition, a characteristic "source chord" was used to organize a work and to produce a differentiative sound for the entire composition.[55] For example, the Double Concerto for Harpsichord, Piano, and Two Chamber Orchestras (1961) is based on a twelve-tone chord that serves as an originating harmony and "tonic" anchor for the work.

According to Ned Rorem, Carter's was a grand style, icy, serious, and without charm or "carnal appeal."[56] The subtitle for this section refers to affinities with serialism. John Rockwell finds affinities in Carter to "the Columbia-Princeton club." In Carter's music serialist rationalism joins the "crabbed, indomitable spirit" of transcendental composers like Ives and Ruggles, though with less of their vitality.[57]

His earliest compositions, the *Pocahontas* ballet, the First Symphony, the *Holiday* Overture, the Piano Sonata, and *The Minotaur* ballet, all written before 1948, were concessions either to the Americanist styles of Copland and Harris or the atonal expressionism of Sessions.

One of the first compositions to indicate he had found his own voice was the Cello Sonata, completed in 1948. The distinctions of timbre and tone production between cello and piano are used to advantage. The independence of each instrument is established, especially through shifts in rhythm and tempo in one instrument, while the other continues with an already defined rhythm and pace. A six-tone row is employed in a resemblance of serial practice, and from the row is derived the intervallic conduct of line and an identifying harmonic resonance.

Carter then rethought his creative position. In the liner notes to Nonesuch H 71249, a recording of String Quartets No. 1 and 2, Carter states: "I had felt that it was my professional and social responsibility to write interesting, direct, and easily understood music. With this quartet [No. 1], however, I decided to focus on what had always been one of my own musical interests, that of 'advanced' music and to follow out, with a minimal concern for their reception, my own musical thoughts along these lines. . . . If a composer has been well taught and had had experience (as was true of me in 1950), then his private judgment of comprehensibility and quality is what he must rely on if he is to communicate importantly." Schiff, the biographer of Carter's creative life, writes: "The desert years [in isolation] liberated Carter from the tyranny of the audience," and made him decide to write work interesting to himself "and so to say, to hell with the public and with the performers, too."[58]

A cadenzalike cello part opens the First Quartet's first movement, Fantasia. It sets forth the characteristic intervals and the identifying resonance of the work. Frequent tempo changes and a complicated approach to speed and rhythm widely described as metric modulation go a step beyond the writing in the Cello Sonata. Each of the following movements (Allegro Scorrevole, Adagio, Variations) is given its own musical character and coloration. The players' virtuosic abilities are taxed. The listener is overpowered by the wealth of ways any given idea can be restated. Despite the tremendous demands on listener's understanding, the quartet conveys a sense of tension and relaxation and can prove enjoyable to some members of the general public. However differentiated the roles of the four instruments, they still seem to work together rather than each isolated from the others.

To the Carter devotee, the Second String Quartet is the most transcendentally sublime work that he composed before the 1960s. For others, it is difficult to digest. Fragmentary phrases seem to move disjointedly, producing an effect similar to those in serial compositions. Even though each instrument is allotted its own distinguishing intervals, the material undergoes constant alteration without repetition. At no point is one instrumental part subordinated to another, so that all parts demand equal attention. What is more, no instrument exchanges any material with another instrument until the last movement. Carter's is an authoritative voice. The work exemplifies his concentrated logic and the immense demands he makes on players.

The Double Concerto for Harpsichord, Piano, and Two Chamber Orchestras embodies another creative problem that the composer sets out to solve, which includes balancing the two solo instruments and their respective orchestras so that each is separate but equal. Each group develops its own set of materials. Motives and melodies are banished. The central ideas are combinations of invented sound materials, including textures, linear patterns, and figurations. Once heard, nothing returns. During a concert, the audience is often bemused by the sight of instruments busily playing music that is impossible to hear. One writer described the Double Concerto as a "landmark work by America's leading mandarin composer," but containing music that "seemed austerely imposing without being altogether quite yet comprehensible, even presenting—no mean achievement, this—a clear basis for honest dislike."[59]

The methods of composition applied to the works written between 1950 and 1965 continue in those that come after. Cut from the same cloth are the Concerto for Orchestra, the Third String Quartet, the Duo for Violin and Piano, and the Symphony of Three Orchestras.

Carter has written two compositions for voice in his mature style, *A Mirror on Which to Dwell*, six poems by Elizabeth Bishop, for soprano and nine instrumentalists, and *Syringa*, text by John Ashbery, for mezzo-soprano and eleven instrumentalists. Both are solemn compositions. A confirmed Carterite, Andrew Porter is fervid in praise of the music. Atonal and similar to serialism it may be, he writes, but in *A Mirror*, "Sandpiper" is a picturesque song built on the double imagery of the "quick, finical bird" and "the motion of the huge slow sea." The rapid, delicate piping of an oboe is heard simultaneously with low chords in the double bass, cello, and piano, thus illustrating Carter's favorite device of exploring "two kinds of musical gait, simultaneous but not synchronous." Porter continues writing about the rest of the music in a similar vein.[60] On the other hand, a veteran song composer,

Ned Rorem, calls both works failures because the music neither heightens, adds a new dimension to, or even illustrates the poems. He finds the sound fussy, continually disjunct, and undifferentiated from one poem setting to another. Paul Turok says similar things.[61]

Carter is so highly respected by the music academicians, one is brave indeed to wonder about the ultimate worth of his music. Pierre Boulez, Charles Rosen, and others have given it their blessing. Yet there have always been critics, including academic ones, who have found his reputation inflated and his music ungrateful to the ear. Paul Snook has made an important comment about Carter's inaccessibility and about his setting the standard by which influential modernists judge other composers. He writes: "I'm quite certain that if a poll were taken among a cross-section of reasonably sophisticated listeners, Carter's kind of arcane solipsism would have no chance—now or in the future—of capturing and holding a substantial audience; whereas many of the American composers he currently eclipses might just achieve that goal. For years, everybody who pretends to care has been lamenting the unhealthy status of contemporary music but few consider the possibility that the condition is partially self-induced—that the wrong aspects of 20th-century music are being emphasized and promoted as being exclusively worthy of consideration and study."[62]

Andrew Imbrie (b. 1921) believes music is not about anything, but "just *is*." What happens in music are musical things "having a concrete existence of their own."[63] The theory, unfortunately, is easier to state than to carry out.

Recognition came in the 1950s, with his Second String Quartet, Third String Quartet, and Violin Concerto. The music divides its allegiances between the austerity of the Sessions style and the hypersensitive expressionism of the early Schoenberg and Berg styles. Atonal linear movement holds the attention, not harmony. The concerto, in particular, may remind the listener of Berg's Violin Concerto and *Wozzeck*. Unlike Berg's concerto, this one frequently conceals the busy soloist in heavy orchestral textures. Woodwinds, brasses, and percussionists prevail over the strings. The concerto ends up sounding little different from many other serial and atonal works written in the 1950s and 1960s.

Arthur Bloomfield's description of *Legend*, a brief nonprogrammatic orchestral work, tallies with what was said. *Legend*, he states, "deals in spurts and sprinkles of sound," which are chromatic, fragmentary, and complex in rhythm and part writing. "The spirit of Imbrie's teacher, Roger Sessions," is heard "frowning through the music." No positive personality can be detected in the sound. "In mood the music emerged suspended in some minus area between that of effective, bittersweet lyricism, and that of rippingly tortured expressionism."[64]

The Fourth String Quartet and the opera *Angle of Repose* also underline the problem of distinguishing Imbrie's music from that of serialists.

A more interesting composer is Leslie Bassett (b. 1923). Like Imbrie, his atonality can be indistinguishable from serialism. The music alternately holds the attention through a somewhat graspable structure and an exposition of motives in somewhat recognizable shapes, or it defeats communication owing to the way sound wanders from one passage to another, without strong linear movement. Whatever the tempo mark, the music gives the impression of moving slowly and lacking energy.

His Trio for Clarinet, Viola, and Piano (1953) is cool, neoclassical, and tonal though highly chromatic; it seems to contradict what was stated above. However, the music represents a style not in evidence in later years. He comes closer to his mature style in the Variations for Orchestra (1963). Bassett states that the variations are not based on a single theme. The initial material consists of four small musical areas, each memorable as color or mood rather than as theme, and each the springboard for one or more of the variations. Although a twelve-tone series from earlier composed choral music forms part of the material, it is not used serially. Furthermore, the composer is sensitive to orchestral texture for its own sake. At the work's conclusion, Bassett reintroduces the initial materials "in climactic contest." The composition won the Pulitzer Prize.

One of Bassett's best-known compositions is the *Echoes from an Invisible World*, completed in 1975. The title comes from a remark made by Giuseppe Mazzini. An opening three-chord piano figure lines out the twelve tones that are developed throughout the composition, though not strictly in serial fashion. Unmeasured passages also occur. In three movements (fast, slow, fast), the middle movement in particular succeeds in capturing the implication of the title by encouraging quiet, subjective meditation. For the most part, the music passes as in a dream. Melody is absent. Carefully articulated and sometimes unusual orchestral colors are designed to produce the desired effects. It may not win over many listeners, owing to its unmelodious and seemingly directionless drift, but it does make an individual statement that one must honor.

With Jacob Druckman (b. 1928), we come for the first time upon a composer whose style has altered not in one direction but in several. Atonality, however, seems to be what most of his works have in common. Sonorities, whether orchestral, percussive, electronic, or vocal, fascinate him. The insertion of music from the past into his compositions occurs. I examine him in part because of the prominence given his music, especially in New York City, beginning with his "music as theater" pieces, and in part because he illustrates a type of avant-garde musician, commonly met with in postwar America, who appears to keep his fingers on the pulse of modernism and to accommodate his creativity to changing modernist trends.

Dark upon the Harp (1962), for mezzo-soprano, brass, and percussion, draws its text from six of the psalms of David and its musical inspiration from the polyphonic practices of the baroque era. Druckman describes the composition as highly personal, dramatic, and atonal. None of the tranquility he claims for portions of the work comes through.

The Second String Quartet (1966) is his last effort at writing in a rational, serial mode. Following Carter's lead, Druckman treats each instrument as a theatrical performer, whose role is summarized in a cadenza. The music's resemblance to Carter's Second String Quartet, a much talked about work in the early 1960s, is not inadvertent. The viola is rhapsodic; the violin, flamboyant; the cello, "dramatic in a stentorian" way. The second violin is asked to reproduce the last part of his cadenza with "the effect of whimpering."

While he studied at the Columbia-Princeton Electronic Music Studio in 1965, he believed electronics "was going to be a promised land of precision, control, and exactitude. No longer would I have to worry about making demands (particularly rhythmic) on the performers that were beyond their human limitations.

Whatever I could conceive, the machine would execute for me perfectly."[65] *Synapse*, a purely electronic work, came out in 1971. Around 1966–67, his thinking changed. He found boredom in sounds unconnected with human energy. Vitality and communicativeness were missing. The same reservations held true, he said, for "the rigorously logical and rational thinking of the 'post-Webern' years."[66] It was also a time when the idea of music as theater had grown popular in avant-garde circles.

Animus I through *IV* and *Valentine* (all composed between 1966 and 1977) represent his altered viewpoint. In the first *Animus* electronic sounds are set in opposition to a trombone, a symbol for humanity. In the second, a mezzo-soprano, woman as artful and adroit arouser of desire, incites two percussionists into activity against an electronic-tape background. In the third, clarinet and tape vie with one another, reveling in "mindless virtuosity," according to the composer. In the last *Animus*, the sounds of tenor voice, instruments, and tape entwine around music borrowed from Chabrier and Liszt. *Valentine* features a virtuosic double-bass player who is expected to interact with his instrument in a sexually suggestive manner. The second *Animus* is the most intriguing of the lot. In the performing notes prefacing the score, Druckman says he conceived it as a sybaritic ritual.[67] Percussion instruments are set up on five stations around the auditorium. Percussionist and singer move about "in stylized, ceremonial fashion." The singer is "slightly in advance, leading, seductive, ultrafeminine; the two percussion players . . . following, watching, potentially menacing, directing their playing at her."[68]

Druckman noticed in the 1970s that the use of theatrical elements in music seemed, in his words, "to be losing some steam. At one point, there was a great titillation as soon as anything theatrical happened on the stage. The shock value is no longer there."[69] He acted to keep his options open. *Windows* (1972), his first work for large orchestra, sounds serialistic but exhibits greater flexibility than did his earlier atonal compositions. Strikingly textured mosaiclike blocks of sound melt into each other. Here and there openings ("windows") are provided. Texture lightens and one looks out on musics from the past, intended as fleeting moments out of time, as "memories, shadows of ghosts," according to the composer. One hears vague references to waltz, to rag, to Debussy;

but for the most part, atonality dominates. The work did catch the fancy of contemporary modernists. Ten years later it sounded outmoded. Witness Nicholas Kenyon's remark that " 'Windows' now sounds clever but dated; it looks through a glass darkly at a rather trendy image."[70]

In the early 1970s, magic, sorcery, and mystery in the music was "in," and George Crumb's music of this nature, for voice and instruments, was in the limelight. Responding to this new direction, Druckman wrote *Lamia* (1974, expanded in 1975) for soprano and orchestra. Lamia is a sorceress in Greek myth. Female sorcery is depicted in a text patched from diverse sources. A variety of orchestral textures are expertly realized. The music sounds richly atonal, save for tonal quotations toward the end from Wagner's *Tristan und Isolde* and Cavalli's *Il Giasone*.

Around the mid-seventies, it was no longer reprehensible in the most advanced circles to attract a substantial audience, which Del Tredici, Corigliano, Glass, and Reich were doing. Druckman in 1976 wrote *Chiaroscuro* and at the same time said he wished to reestablish communication with the larger public.[71] Three years later, his *Auriole* was premiered. In it, he pays his respect to Bernstein by quoting from Bernstein's Third ("Kaddish") Symphony. It was, however, improbable that either work would impress a large public. Yet the orchestral effects in *Aureole* are skillfully made. On occasion long, drawn-out lyric lines stand out against the general athematic sound (as in the string parts at the beginning). More prevalent than in earlier works are persistent rhythmic patterns, which offer relief from the arhythmic portions of the work. One is reminded of the moods found in Schoenberg's *Five Pieces for Orchestra*, op. 16.

Theodore Libbey, in a review of Druckman's cantata *Vox Humana*, summarizes the criticisms of the composer's music. He heard well-written orchestrations and tight motivic and intervallic construction. But the piece was static and ended inconclusively. Craftsmanship, invigorating rhythms, and powerful scoring "failed in the long run to compensate for an absence of an overall feeling of direction and development, nor could they disguise the fact that much of the choral writing was repetitious and awkward."[72]

TOWARD A MORE BENIGN ATONALITY

Some composers have produced atonal compositions that go at least a little way toward communicating with the general public. After discussing composers of somber music, it is a pleasure to note a trifle like Peter Westergaard's chamber opera *Mr. and Mrs. Discobbolos* (1966) for soprano, tenor, and six instrumentalists. The sound is pointillistic, even dry. Now and again, the voices sing in thirds with each other. The music is witty and abets a nonsensical but surrealistic libretto about a couple who live and reproduce on a wall until the man decides he has had enough of such living and blows everybody up—himself, his wife, and twelve children. Joan Tower also injects wit into an atonal idiom. Her *Petroushskates* (first performed in 1981) buoyantly conjoins nontonal material with portions of Stravinsky's *Petroushka*.

George Rochberg (b. 1918) is a more prominent and controversial composer than the two just named. Until the early 1950s, he composed in a style influenced by Stravinsky, Hindemith, and Bartók. From the 1950s to almost the mid-sixties, he was a serialist. After that his music became an eclectic amalgam of his past styles, modified by imitations of or quotations from various tonal musics from earlier times. He serves as an example (not uncommon) of a postwar composer seeking to expand his expressive techniques beyond the limitations imposed by one modern viewpoint. In the liner notes to CRI SD 337, Rochberg states that behind all of his music is the "urge to compose the most beautiful melodies I could imagine, and an obsession with creating a sense of rightness of harmony and harmonic progression." What is more to the point, Rochberg can impress many a listener with the rightness of his melodic writing and his harmonic constructions. Furthermore, he seems to have tested his ideas aurally before setting them down on paper.

Rochberg's First Symphony, completed in 1949, contains a curious mixture of several twentieth-century styles—Stravinsky, Bartók, Schoenberg, and Berg. One moment tonal, the next chromatic, the work is by a still-ripening composer. Intense feeling, brute power, and sharp-edged rhythms are projected along with quietly subjective and delicate contrasts. When in 1952 he turned to twelve-tone writing, with his *Twelve Bagatelles* for piano, Rochberg insisted his voice was the same; only his language had changed. In the same year he completed his First String Quartet. Its expressive content is similar to that of the symphony but more unified and more his own. Flashes of tonality light up the otherwise dark atonality.

The *Chamber Symphony for Nine Instruments* is his second serial composition. His indebtedness to his teacher Luigi Dallapiccola is acknowledged in the Adagio movement, which quotes a motive from Dallapiccola's *Il Prigionero*. The other movements combine twelve-tonalism with Stravinskian neoclassicism, but with more lyrically expressive melody than Stravinsky would have countenanced. Fascinating is the basing of his *Serenata d'Estate* (for flute, harp, guitar, violin, viola, and cello), two years later, on the same row. Now the music is athematic, cool, relaxed, and dainty. He proves that he is not fixed in one expressive practice or routine.

His Second Symphony, Second String Quartet with Soprano, *La Bocca della Verità* for oboe and piano, and Piano Trio are other works from his serial period. In none is serial technique rigorous. In each, melody consists of brief, recognizable motives. Structure and rhetoric tend toward the familiar, even traditional. The dominant mood is one of intense feeling—angry or subdued and long suffering.

Creative ferment and an inner need to expand his style grew after the composition of the trio. Quotations from past musics, he hoped, would point him in the right direction. By 1965, he was moving away from serialism and toward college. *Music for the Magic Theater* shows him fashioning a more flexible and inclusive language. The title comes from Hermann Hesse's novel *Steppenwolf.* The intention is to produce a "cinematic series of shifting ideas and levels which, nevertheless, combine in an inevitable fashion, despite sharp contradictions and paradoxes, to produce a totality, a unity."[73] In the first part we hear a conflict between brief tonal and atonal passages. The listener is whipsawed with styles that are reluctant to mix. Recurring ideas are forcibly injected into the music for no logical reason. Then the movement just stops. When Rochberg reworks the Adagio from Mozart's Divertimento, K. 287 in the second movement, the ear may want to hear Mozart, not Rochberg, whose musical commentaries seem unnecessary. Mozart ceases to sound toward the end, when Rochberg reverts to aggressive secundal sounds. The contrast is upsetting to the ear and the music seems to fall apart. The third movement opens on a scurry of sound that is a *non sequitur* after the Mozart music.

A personal crisis affected the composer in the mid-sixties after his son Paul died from a brain tumor. The urgency to express his bottled feelings grew. Serialism ceased to have value and was supplanted with what he describes as a "new romanticism." Apparently the new romanticism was a continuation along the lines laid down in the *Music for the Magic Theater*.

Why did Rochberg dip into older styles? At least four reasons can be advanced. The composer appropriated music from the past in order to express what modernistic sounds could not express. Sometimes the borrowings were intended for redeployment but deprived of their original implications. Possibly, the composer hoped to achieve his expressive goals by an interplay of the old and new. Finally, the investigation of the past was a means for discovering essential metaphors in sound, which could substitute for something missing in the composer and his society.

Later, Rochberg's strong reliance on quotation waned. On the other hand, he still wanted to reenter expressive areas abandoned by modern composers, areas of serenity, exuberance, energy, and clarity, writes Gus Freedman after interviewing the composer.[74] When he composed the Third String Quartet in 1972, he wished to achieve a synthesis of his previous stylistic experiments. He abandoned notions of originality and ego fulfillment. The quartet avoids obvious quotation, although reminders of Beethoven and Mahler occur. Tonality and atonality exist beside each other. (Rochberg likens this to the major-minor, side-by-side practices of the past.) The determination of which to use is regulated by the nature of the musical gesture desired. The first movement, an Introduction and Fantasia, opens on a brief *ff* motive, meant to sound vehemently and to contrast the slower, smoother passages. Agitated and peaceful ideas are juxtaposed. At measure 87, suddenly and startlingly, a B-major triad appears—one of many bits of dramatic coloration in the movement. Still, everything holds together and interest is sustained.

The second movement is a Bartókian march; so much so, one wonders if Rochberg was indulging in a direct imitation. The third movement, a set of Beethoven-like variations, even employs some of Beethoven's part-writing idiosyncracies. For example, Rochberg makes use of Beethoven's exaggerated separation of the first violin's line high above the other three instrumentalists. Next, the march returns, although the material is entirely reworked. The finale, a grouping of scherzos and serenades, is somewhat reminiscent of parts of the first movement. At one moment, the music sounds like a driving, rhythmic, fugal section out of Stravinsky's *Le Sacre du Printemps*; at another, an eccentric but tonal serenade out of Mahler. The movement ends on a scherzo marked "vivace," then "violent," then "wild to the end!" At the close, themes from the first movement are recalled. The quartet was the most accessible work Rochberg had written up to that time. The structures are simple; the ideas easy to follow. Much of the music can appeal to the general listener.

One of Rochberg's most effective compositions is the Violin Concerto (1974). Its five movements allow the soloist plenty of virtuosic display. The rhetoric is comprehensible to the music lover whose stylistic tastes go beyond Beethoven and Tchaikovsky. Abundant melodies, many of good length, some quite pleasant, sustain the listener's attention. Structures prove easy to grasp. The music may recall Brahms, Prokofiev, Shostakovich, Hindemith, Bartók, and Berg. Yet the concerto does not sound as atavistic as several earlier works. Assuredly, the concerto was a significant attempt at bridging the gap between contemporary music and the general music public.

On 20 January 1979, the Concord Quartet premiered Rochberg's Fourth, Fifth, and Sixth String Quartets, known as the *Concord Quartets*. The music exploits almost every conceivable string-quartet technique and coloristic effect. References to past composers, especially Beethoven, Schubert, and Pachelbel, are obvious, as are the swings between tonality and atonality. Some music lovers have loved them; witness John Ditsky's comment that he had expected only parody but found profundity. Though others might object to the echoes from the past, he found the results very moving. Ditsky accepts the eclecticism, and finds nothing to be banal, not even the variations on the Pachelbel *Canon*.[75]

In a 1980 interview, Rochberg warns budding composers not

to underestimate audiences, since most music lovers are intelligent and sensitive listeners. People cannot be force fed; taste cannot be imposed. "Nor have you the right to demand of audiences that they spend a lifetime listening to or studying a handful of pieces because you say they're good. They don't have the time." He describes new-music concerts as forms of segregation and "ghettoization." Works from the present and past need to be tested against each other. One cannot erase everything that has gone before and work in isolation: "We are involved in an on-going tradition and continuity. We can't claim that the things of the past no longer have a connection. . . . If you are ready to erase everything that preceded you, then you are erasable by your own standards."[76]

However brave his advice, Rochberg has yet to reconcile the past with the present for himself in any consistent fashion. Nor is he the first postwar composer to discover the past or romanticism, as he seems to claim. Many composers who have never left the traditional mainstream have always held to this viewpoint. Nevertheless, he deserves respect for his awareness that music has to exist for some audience of more than miniscule size and for his desire to refashion his serial style in order to win over a larger public.

If amongst the atonalists any composer fits best the romantic designation, it is Leon Kirchner (b. 1919). He first was influenced by Stravinsky, Hindemith, and Bartók; then by Bloch, Sessions, Schoenberg, and Berg. Adhering to no theoretical system, his music is variously described as subjective, dramatic, rhapsodic, emotional, and disquieted. Free atonality is occasionally leavened with tonality, secundal harmony with some thirds and sixths, rhythmic drive with expansive declamatory or lyric lines.

As with other composers, the introductory measures of a work prefigure the rest of the music: "A few measures, an idea, constitute a gesture; the purpose of the work as a whole is to extend this in time. A phrase sets up the need for balance and extension, which is satisfied by what follows. This then constitutes a larger complex which sets up still more implications. The entire piece is built up and forms an entity with infinite implications," states Kirchner. When he composes, he does worry about the relationship between composer and audience. Nevertheless, he knows that

without an audience's participation, music will die and, while listening, "the audience has to remember what has happened before
to appreciate what comes next."[77]

Kirchner's First String Quartet (1948) brought him to public
attention. Its statements are big and melodic. Dense in sound and
powerful in expression, the composition offers no relief from the
relentless pressure of fiery emotion, not even in the Scherzo. At
the conclusion of the piece, slowly moving sounds convey hopelessness and despair. Similar comments can be made about his
Sonata Concertante for Violin and Piano and the First Piano Concerto.

His most ambitious composition, one he began in 1959 and
completed in 1977, is his opera *Lily*. The libretto's subject is taken
from Saul Bellow's novel *Henderson, the Rain King*. Its message, a
timely one for the America of the 1970s, bears on so-called saviors
who end up destroying those whom they wish to set free.[78] The
score abounds with novel theatrical effects, striking musical sections, and deeply felt lyricism, which now and again show kinship
to nineteenth-century romanticism. When staged, however, nothing compellingly dramatic took the audience from one stage of
conflict to another. Yet the opera contains so much listenable music, it is unfortunate that the expense of staging and rehearsing the
work precludes revival. Perhaps it stands a better chance if presented in concert form. Certainly, the music makes a more immediate and emotionally powerful impact then does that of Sessions and Carter, writes Joan Peyser.[79]

When I look back at the composers taken up in this chapter, I
must respect them for their craftsmanship and the huge amount
of time they took from their lives to devote to musical composition. Some, like Babbitt, continue to labor in isolation and suffer
mostly neglect. A fortunate one or two, like Carter, have won a
certain renown in advanced circles, though no love from members
of the general audience. Even those composers, like Rochberg,
who have tried to make their sounds more palatable, have not
won as wide a public as they had hoped. One suspects that serial
and atonal compositions may find no real acceptance in the music
world. Even when modified to include some tonality and traditional gestures, the music has not usually made a lasting impression. In part, this is owing to listeners' resistance; in part to the

workings of the American cultural marketplace, which has managed to suppress all but the most notably successful and instantaneously effective of contemporary offerings; and in part to the biases of conductors, concert managers, and boards of trustees. Suffice it to say that several compositions have been mentioned that deserve a fate better than dismissal from concert hall and opera house. What is needed is a mechanism to keep them alive before the larger public, whose usual attendance at performances by estalished and influential music groups does not include exposure to much beyond what is already well known and over a hundred years of age.

NOTES

1. Harold C. Schonberg, "Where Are They?" *New York Times*, 14 January 1962, sec. 2, 11.

2. Gregory Sandow, "Lost Generation," *Village Voice*, 24 January 1984, 79. See also John Rockwell, *All American Music* (New York: Knopf, 1983), 33–34.

3. Donal Henahan, "What Does Today's Music Owe to This Quartet?" *New York Times*, 4 December 1983, sec. 2, 1.

4. Richard Franko Goldman, "Current Chronicle, N.Y.," *Musical Quarterly* 48 (1962): 93.

5. Dore Ashton, *The New York School: A Cultural Reckoning* (New York: Penguin, 1979), 224; Cole Gagne and Tracy Caras, *Soundpieces: Interviews with American Composers*, (Metuchen, N.J.: Scarecrow, 1982), 164.

6. Gagne and Caras, *Soundpieces*, 156.

7. Leonard Meyer, *Music, the Arts, and Ideas* (Chicago: University of Chicago Press, 1967), 264.

8. Jean Duvignaud, *The Sociology of Art*, trans. Timothy Wilson (New York: Harper & Row, 1972), 23–25.

9. John Shepherd, in *Whose Music?* (London: Latimer, 1977) 42–43.

10. Gagne and Caras, *Soundpieces*, 379.

11. Milton Babbitt, "Who Cares if You Listen?" *High Fidelity* (February 1958): 39*ff*; *Contemporary Composers on Contemporary Music*, ed. Elliott Schwartz and Barney Childs (New York: Holt, Rinehart & Winston, 1967), 368.

12. Ned Rorem, *An Absolute Gift* (New York: Simon & Schuster, 1978), 60; Ned Rorem, *Setting the Tone* (New York: Coward-McCann, 1983), 155.

13. Milton Babbitt, "The Composer as Specialist," in *Esthetics Contemporary*, ed. Richard Kostelanetz (Buffalo, N.Y.: Prometheus, 1978), 281.

14. Meyer, *Music, the Arts, and Ideas*, 290–92.

15. Harold C. Schonberg, "Are We Entering a More Exciting Decade?" *New York Times*, 4 January 1970, sec. 2, 15; Dmitri Shostakovich, reprint from *Pravda*, in the *New York Times*, 11 September 1960, sec. 2, 19; Robert Claiborne, letter to the *New York Times*, 11 October 1970, sec. 2, 15; Peter J. Pirie, "A Reprieve for Romanticism," *High Fidelity* 10 (October 1960): 130.

16. Tim Page, "Concert: Atlantic Quartet and Contemporary Works," *New York Times*, 13 November 1983, 78.

17. Theodore W. Adorno, *Introduction to the Sociology of Music*, trans. E. B. Ashton (New York: Seabury, 1976), 4–8.

18. Henahan, "What Does Today's Music Owe to This Quartet?" 25.

19. Gagne and Caras, *Soundpieces*, 184.

20. Jeanne Belfy, ed., *The Louisville Orchestra New Music Project: Selected Letters* (Louisville, Ky.: University of Louisville, 1983), 28.

21. Alfred Frankenstein, in *High Fidelity* 12 (March 1962): 80.

22. David Ewen, *American Composers: A Biographical Dictionary* (New York: Putnam's, 1982), s.v. "Weber, Ben Brian."

23. Benjamin Boretz, in *Dictionary of Contemporary Music*, ed. John Vinton (New York: Dutton, 1974), s.v. "Babbitt, Milton."

24. [Roger Sessions], *Roger Sessions on Music*, ed. Edward T. Cone (Princeton, N.J.: Princeton University Press, 1979), 84.

25. John Cage, "Recent Publications of Advanced Music, Old and New," *Musical America* (February 1950): 333–34.

26. Jeffrey Hirschfeld, "Milton Babbitt: A Not-so-Sanguine Interview," *Musical America* (June 1982): 16.

27. Paul Henry Lang, ed. *Problems of Modern Music* (New York: Norton, 1962), 14; Herbert Russcol, *The Liberation of Sound* (Englewood Cliffs, N.J.: Prentice-Hall, 1972), 133.

28. Lang, ed. *Problems of Modern Music*, 13.

29. Virgil Thomson, *American Music Since 1910* (New York: Holt, Rinehart & Winston, 1971), 120.

30. John Rockwell, *All American Music*, (New York: Knopf, 1983), 32.

31. [John Cage], *John Cage*, ed. Richard Kostelanetz (London: Allen Lane, Penguin, 1971), 14.

32. Andrew Porter, "Musical Events," *New Yorker* (12 December 1983): 163.

33. Russcol, *The Liberation of Sound*, 130.

34. For commentaries on *Vision and Prayer*, see Richard Franko Goldman, "Current Chronicle, N.Y.," *Musical Quarterly* 48, (1962): 94–95;

Eric Salzman, "Music from the Electronic Universe," *High Fidelity* 14 (August 1964): 56.

35. For commentaries, see Paul Rappoport, review of New World Records NW 307, *Fanfare* (January/February 1981): 59; Rockwell, *All American Music*, 29; David Moore, review of New World Records NW 307, *American Record Guide* (January/February 1982): 8–9; Salzman, "Music from the Electronic Universe," 56.

36. Milton Babbitt, in *The Orchestral Composer's Point of View*, ed. Robert Stephen Hines (Norman: University of Oklahoma Press, 1970), 35–36; Elaine Barkin, in *The New Grove Dictionary of Music and Musicians*, s.v. "Babbitt, Milton (Byron)," (New York: Grove Press Inc., 1980). I have also obtained information directly from two members of the orchestra, as well as two members of the audience.

37. Peyser, "The Affair Proved Traumatic," *New York Times*, 12 January 1969, sec. 2, 17.

38. Harold C. Schonberg, "Music: Bernstein and Stern Team Up," *New York Times*, 17 January 1969, 33.

39. Owen Anderson, review of Milton Babbitt's *Relata II*, played at the 16 January 1969 concert by Leonard Bernstein and the New York Philharmonic, in *Music Journal* 27 (March 1969): 77.

40. Hirschfeld, "Milton Babbitt," 18.

41. Aaron Copland, *The New Music, 1900–1960*, rev. ed. (New York: Norton, 1968), 175.

42. Clifford Jay Safane, "An Interview with Ralph Shapey," *Music Journal* 37 (May/June 1979): 23–24; Rockwell, *All American Music*, 61–62.

43. Ashton, *The New York School*, 200–1; Matthew Baigell, *Dictionary of American Art* (New York: Harper & Row, 1979), s.v. "Kline, Franz"; John Rockwell, "Ralph Shapey at 60—He Defied Neglect," *New York Times*, 10 May 1981, sec. 2, 17; Rockwell, *All American Music*, 62.

44. Gagne and Caras, *Soundpieces*, 372.

45. David W. Moore, review of CRI S 435, *American Record Guide* (February 1983): 46.

46. Ewen, *American Composers*, s.v. "Shapey, Ralph."

47. Peter G. Davis, "Pianos Still Stir Composers' Souls," *New York Times*, 7 June 1981, sec. 2, 23.

48. Rockwell, "Ralph Shapey at 60," 17.

49. See the album *Out of the Cool*, MCA 29033.

50. Winthrop Sergeant, "Musical Events," *New Yorker* (15 July 1967): 106.

51. For more on Wuorinen's attitudes toward native American music, critics, audiences, and composers, see Kenneth Terry, "Charles Wuorinen, Atonal Tonalities," *Downbeat* (February 1981): 16; Gagne and Caras,

Soundpieces 396; Harvey Sollberger, in *Dictionary of Contemporary Music*, s.v. "Wuorinen, Charles."

52. Sollberger, op. cit.

53. David Schiff, *The Music of Elliott Carter* (London: Eulenberg, 1983), 14.

54. Ibid., 21.

55. Ibid., 63–66.

56. Rorem, *An Absolute Gift*, 111–12; *Setting the Tone*, 146–47.

57. Rockwell, *All American Music*, 39.

58. Schiff, *The Music of Elliott Carter*, 132, 152.

59. Richard Buell, "American Composers," *Boston Globe*, 10 March 1984, 9.

60. Andrew Porter, *Music of Three Seasons: 1974–1977* (New York: Farrar Straus Giroux, 1978), 306.

61. Rorem, *Setting the Tone*, 245–46; Paul Turok, review of CBS M 35171, *Fanfare* (January/February 1981): 98.

62. Paul Snook, review of CRI SD 475, *Fanfare*, (January/February 1983): 132; reply to a letter from a reader, *Fanfare* (May/June 1983): 22.

63. Ewen, *American Composers*, s.v. "Imbrie, Andrew Welsh," 349.

64. Arthur Bloomfield, "New Imbrie Work Premiered by San Francisco Symphony," *Musical America* (January 1960): 5.

65. See Druckman's remarks in the liner notes of CRI 167 and VOX SVBX, which contain recordings of *Dark Upon the Harp* and *String Quartet #2*, respectively.

66. Jacob Druckman, "Stating the Case for the 'New Romanticism,' " *Ovation* 4 (June 1983): 6.

67. Jacob Druckman, *Animus 2* for soprano (mezzo), two percussion players, and tape (New York: MCA Music, 1973).

68. Gagne and Caras, *Soundpieces*, 158.

69. Jacob Druckman, "Performing Notes," *Animus 2* (New York: MCA Music, 1973), n.p.

70. Nicholas Kenyon, "Musical Events," *New Yorker* (4 May 1981): 142.

71. Harold C. Schonberg, "Can Composers Regain Their Audiences?" *New York Times*, 4 December 1977, sec. 2, 1.

72. Theodore W. Libbey, Jr., "Live Appearances," *Ovation* 4 (February 1983): 26.

73. Rochberg, in the liner notes to Desto DC 6444 (Music for the Magic Theater).

74. Gus Freedman, "Metamorphosis of a 20th-Century Composer," *Music Journal* 34 (March 1976): 13.

75. John Ditsky, review of RCA ARL 2-4198, *Fanfare* (May/June 1982):

193–94; Daniel Webster, review of the concert by the Concord Quartet, *Musical America* (May 1979): 29–30.

76. Gagne and Caras, *Soundpieces*, 341–45.

77. Eric Salzman, "No 'System' for Him," *New York Times*, 21 February 1960, sec. 2, 9.

78. Joan Peyser, "For Him, Music Is Its Own Compensation," *New York Times*, 1 January 1984, sec. 2, 13.

79. Ibid.

4
Musical Countercurrents

During the 1950s, serialism and atonalism predominated. Even as this music achieved its zenith, avant-garde music based on an opposite postulate grew in influence and, in the 1960s, achieved equal strength. Its composers repudiated the rational systems, mathematically derived constructs, and discipline that had characterized the modernism of the fifties. They preferred unscientific schemes, ad hoc use of available sound materials, and less predictable ways of creating musical compositions. The resultant compositions were in accord with the libertarian principles of the time.

The 1960s, according to the newly installed President Kennedy, were to usher in the Great Society; they also saw an increase in America's involvement with the Vietnam War. The decade was to remake America and unify it through prosperity, concern for its members even to the lowliest, and an enlightenment to come with the availability of higher education and high culture. It also saw the American society afflicted by inflation, war casualties, and the military's appetite for men, goods, weapons, and money. Unrest grew and, with it, the aggressive assertion of the political, economic, and social rights of blacks, women, and the poor. Public demonstrations, arrests, general lawlessness, political terrorism, increased crime and use of drugs, race riots, and assassinations threatened whatever consensus had given a sense of community.

The number of Americans under the age of thirty burgeoned.

Many youths began defining their elders as failed humans and set out to alter established ideas, practices, and institutions. A young "beat" generation spurned the safety of their parents' middle- and upper-class homes, and chose to live outlandishly and precariously. Personal freedom sometimes amounting to license was a primary objective. The writers who spoke for the "beat" generation were apolitical, anti-intellectual, and nihilistic: Allen Ginsberg, Jack Kerouac, Gregory Corso, Lawrence Ferlinghetti. Paul Goodman and Norman Mailer sponsored this group, writes Wolfgang Bernhard Fleischmann, which had as common denominator the "exaltation of ecstatic, visionary states of emotion and apperception. For that reason, its more religious votaries" tended to "subscribe to forms of mystical adoration." This included Roman Catholic, Jewish, and Buddhistic modes of thought. On the other hand, the more secularly minded placed "explicit faith in the visionary powers of drugs."[1]

David Harris, who married Joan Baez, has spoken about his life at Stanford in 1966 as follows: "I went through a big Nietzsche thing . . . the idea that a man could build himself into anything he could see, talking about the base of power being the self, consciousness. I remember going through a very heavy existential thing. . . . We were all into a motorcycle thing. It's the most existential position possible. . . . We were riding life like a motorcycle, on top of it, opening it up as far as it would go."[2]

The movement represented by David Harris had roots in California. It first came to national attention through the student revolts of 1964 at the University of California at Berkeley. Soon, campuses throughout America were radicalized.

What is most important to keep in mind is that the musical counterparts of the "beat" writers had a share in this radicalization and created works that were extreme departures from what had been accepted as music, whether traditional or modern. Though their styles were divergent, these composers were united in their opposition to completely rational and controlled processes of creative expression.

THE REPUDIATION OF AUTHORITY

The creative people who typified this reshaped avant-garde criticized the lack of connection between the modernity of the 1950s and the environment, the psyche, and people's need to be allowed to be themselves, uncontrolled by others. According to Marshall Berman: "One of the crucial tasks for modernists in the 1960s was to confront the expressway world; another was to show that this was not the only possible modern world, that there were other, better directions in which the spirit could move." They required "affirmative visions of alternate modern lives." They found life sources, energy and affirmation to oppose Moloch, and the expressway world of Robert Moses by looking at the everyday life of the street, as Jane Jacobs did in *The Death and Life of Great American Cities* (1961).[3]

Modern dance, for example, hoped to assimilate the life of the street. Merce Cunningham, Twyla Tharp, and members of the Grand Union tried for nondance ("antidance") movements and patterns, often incorporating randomness and chance, with dancers not knowing at the start of a dance how it would end. At times they eliminated music and opted for silence, street sounds, or radio static. To get away from the formality of theater performance, they danced on bridges, roofs, and the streets, seeking to interact with whoever and whatever was around. Simultaneously, artists in New York's Lower East Side, among them Allan Kaprow, Jim Dine, Robert Whitman, Red Grooms, George Segal, and Claes Oldenburg, created art that took space and everyday objects into account. They experimented with nonart materials like junk and debris in order to evoke "real" life. They staged "happenings"— nonverbal, frequently spontaneous, theatrical presentations—as forms of interaction with life. Oldenburg wrote in 1961: "I am for art that is political-erotic-mystical, that does something other than sit on its ass in a museum. I am for an art that embroils itself with everyday crap and comes out on top. I am for an art that tells you the time of day, or where such and such a street is. I am for an art that helps old ladies cross the street."[4]

The connection between creative works and the street was obvious in the popular music of the 1960s. One recalls Bob Dylan ("Talkin' World War Three Blues" and "Desolation Row"), Paul Simon, Leonard Cohen ("Stories of the Street"), Peter Townshend, Jim Morrison, and various Motown writers. Berman points out that hordes of performing artists appeared in the streets. They played and sang music of every kind; danced, performed or improvised plays; created happenings, environments, and murals; filled the streets with "political-erotical-mystical" images and sounds; involved themselves with "the everyday crap." At times they came out on top. At times they "mystified themselves and everyone else as to which way was up."[5]

As for the avant-garde composers not connected with the popular musical world, without question the most significant mentor to the radical generation was John Cage (b. 1912). His collaboration with the dancer Merce Cunningham and the painter Robert Rauschenberg and his influence upon younger creative people in all artistic fields have been often remarked upon. Indeterminate music, meditative and mystical music, music as theater, electronic and acoustical experimentation, recorded montages of natural sound, text-sound concepts, new-wave and jazz-fusion attempts were all touched by his ideas. Until the 1960s, he had had problems with getting the attention of others and making a living. Not until 1960 was he able "to live as a musician, so to speak—lecturing and concerts and so on."[6]

The composer David Diamond had been abroad for many years and had thought that serialism and atonality were ascendant in the American art-music world. When he returned in 1965, he saw "the other side of the nightmare world." To him, "the sixties were the most anarchistic period in the history of art, the product of society's natural tendency to vomit back hostility and protest in a tasteless, valueless, speculative culture." All that was once known as avant-garde "had gone out of business," even Schoenberg and his followers.[7]

Interest in aleatory (chance) experimentation, guided at times by throws of the dice, the Chinese oracular book of *I Ching*, cuts of playing cards, or the like had commenced. Later came graphically notated music (Earle Brown), works prolonging their tones and silences out to an eternity (Morton Feldman), environmental music (Max Neuhaus), total music theater (Robert Ashley), musical satire and social commentary (Salvatore Martirano), music structured on marvelously novel sonorities (George Crumb), chaotically computerized sounds (Lejaren Hiller), and synthesized collage and improvisation (Lukas Foss). Assertions were made that composers should no longer attend concerts, write scores, or study subjects like theory and orchestration. No wonder that to Diamond, a composer who still valued older practices, it seemed a nightmare world.

John Cage preached the necessity for drastic change. He dismissed neoclassicism and serialism. Carter, he said, had merely "put a new wing on the academy" and opened "no doors to the world outside the school."[8]

The posttriadic modernists of the 1950s did mount counterattacks against what they claimed was musical charlatanry and anarchy, but failed to beat back the New Left. As the polemics shot back and forth, caught in the middle were those contemporary mainstream composers who still were beholden to tradition and believed in evolution, not revolution. The demolition of traditional musical values that characterized the 1950s increased in the 1960s. The composers occupying the musical center found themselves set upon forcefully from both sides of the modernist dispute. Meanwhile, the general public was alternately amused and annoyed by the antics of the New Left, indifferent to the modernists' infighting, and unreceptive to most of the contestants' compositions.

THE NEW LEFT

Several composers belonging to the New Left were either born, brought up, educated, or employed in California. Many commentators have pointed out that these California-connected musicians, whatever the final decision about the value of their music, represented a native movement. Thus, they were unlike New York's serialists, whose modernism came from Europe. Here, an observation made by Godfrey Hodgson has relevance: "Americans believe . . . that America's destiny is to supersede what they alone still call the 'Old World.' California is America raised to the nth power." Naturally, Californians "assume that they stand to the East Coast as America stands to Europe. They take it for granted that the way they live is a preview of the new society that must come to birth."[9]

Rober Irwin, the painter, has described his growing up in Los Angeles. What he says about himself may possibly apply to Cage, born in the same city. Irwin was allowed to live freely, even irresponsibly, and developed a freewheeling attitude toward the world. In addition, he learned never to give a straight answer and to play games all the time. When he became an artist, he was exposed to the work of New York's Abstract Expressionists, but soon discovered that New York's ways were not necessarily his. He recalls: "In those days you just got yourself in a good Zen mood and emoted."[10] Anybody who has conversed with Cage or heard him during question-and-answer sessions will recognize how closely these words fit him.

Richard Felciano, a Californian and a musical New Leftist, states that a Californian had not only a sense of Europe but also of the Orient, which made him "another kind of American."[11] This parallels Roger Dettmer's remark about Cage being, like Cowell and Harrison, a far-west composer, "who broke with the traditions of New England Transcendentalism to embrace oriental philosophies as alternative inspirations for a good deal in his music."[12]

The California viewpoint soon cropped up in New York and was incorporated into the views of the musicians known as New York's "Downtown" composers. Many of them were from, or had been taught by teachers of, the Pacific Coast, not the least being Cage himself. Others were followers of one or another of the Western musicians. Joan La Barbara, for example, attended a concert given by Downtown musicians in 1982 and heard Carl Stone's *Sukothai*; he was a Californian composer inspired by non-Western influences. She also heard music by Arnold Dreyblatt and Rhys Chatham, both of whom had studied with La Monte Young, a composer who grew up and studied in California. The remainder of the program that night was by people who had connections with the California scene and with Cage in particular.[13]

Cage was a prime mover for much of the artistic innovation in all fields that began in the 1950s and extended through the 1960s. Dore Ashton explains how painters took Cage seriously and were among the first to comprehend his emphasis on the separateness of musical "events," applying the term to aspects of their paintings. They admired his tearing down of the barriers between art and life and his unorthodox treatment of his materials. As might be expected, Cage's Zen Buddhist rhetoric soon got into the vocabulary of artists. Feldman describes the fascination with Cage, saying that Cage was asked to speak or demonstrate his music at many New York gatherings of artists. "It was like a vote of confidence. A lot of artists turned up: Kiesler, Kline, Ferren, Pollock, and of course de Kooning, and a lot of literary people were interested in him, too."[14]

Meanwhile, the academic rationalists were angered by the Cageian assaults on their positions. Schuller, seeing the principles he
believed in repudiated, said that nobody should be offended by
the academic's insistence on control: "The *really* serious, dedicated, thoughtful composer of today [written in 1967]" accepts
"intellectuality as a necessary counterbalance" to emotion or feeling, and does not prize anti-intellectualism. Yet a "large segment
of the so-called avant-garde" is anti-intellectual and tempted "to
go the easy route of psychedelic art and the musical happenings,
of the whole gray area of choiceless, decisionless music." As a
result, "a genre of music has . . . arisen which represents the real
subversion of our time."[15]

The New Left challenged intellectual standards. It declared artistic works requiring close attention and specialized knowledge
to be elitist. They were lies, representing an age of oppression of
minorities, of social inequality, and of catering to the rich and
well born. Obviously they should be banished. And the banishment included Beethoven, Rembrandt, and Shakespeare. Drop-
outs from college and tradition began describing Frederic Chopin,
George Elliot, and Auguste Rodin as just so much "bullshit." Once,
when Cage heard a recorded Brahms symphony during a social
evening, the sound bothered him. In the midst of the work, a
telephone rang and a door slammed and Cage said to a neighbor,
"Isn't that beautiful?"[16]

The "masterpiece" concept was denounced, writes Barney Childs.
The Cage coterie held that nothing possessed permanent aesthetic
value. The art product was of less importance than the process for
realizing it. Any hierarchical, systematized, and nonrandom ordering of music was tyrannical and stultifying. No such thing as
artistic responsibility existed.[17] Exemplifying a polarization akin
to that of the Italian futurists at the beginning of the century, Cage
explained his notion of "art" as "criminal action, because it con-
forms to no rules." Claims Richard Kostelanetz, this opposition
to conventional thinking made possible an unlimited range of in-
termediate syntheses.[18]

Cage thought art had meant a separation of music from life, "a
compendium of masterpieces." True contemporary music does not
make that separation and "is not so much art as it is life." The
contents of any work had to be so arranged that they sounded

different in different performances; that is to say, every performance of work had to be a premiere in order to be regarded as
contemporary.[19] To him, high culture merely passed along the
values of the ruling establishment. The notion of "masterpieces"
was elitist in origin. The world contained an infinite assortment
of sounds, which were constantly changing and producing con-
fused impressions. To attempt to transcend this disarray and give
it order was a falsification of experience.

As Christopher Lasch has indicated, two undesirable after effects of such advice were a new illiteracy and an uninformed insistence on relevancy to replace the store of knowledge and cultural traditions.[20] Virgil Thomson, looking more directly at Cage's
ideas, warned that trying to destroy the past was "a losing game."
The past might wear out, but it could not be destroyed. Real change
came only slowly, he said, and without our knowing it was happening. He says: "I cannot see today's mass-conscious celebrities
as anything but a danger to art. . . . Music has its fashion indus-
try and its novelty trade." Cage "seems today's leader in novelty-
fashions."[21]

THE AESTHETIC OF DISINTEGRATION

Cage's attitudes had their roots in the early twentieth century,
in Futurism's art of noises, Dadaism's cultivation of the absurd
and repudiation of revered art objects, and Surrealism's fantastic,
distorted, and discontinuous representation of dream states. Dada
was the principal antecedent to Cageian practices. The word itself
was chosen to represent absolute freedom, even to make non-
sense, and described a movement launched in 1916 by Tristan Tzara,
Hans Arp, Hugo Bell, and Richard Huelsenbeck. Three years later,
Dada arrived in Paris and was immediately espoused by rebellious
French youths disillusioned with the idealism, morality, and reason of their parents. In exhibitions, performances, and demonstrations, they juxtaposed unrelated words, sounds, and objects randomly chosen to represent a unit that defied logic.

Tzara, in *Memoirs of Dadaism*, says he made his Paris debut in a
performance where he read aloud from a newspaper while a bell
kept ringing so loudly nobody could hear what he said, thus con-
veying the idea that his mere presence on the stage should have

satisfied any onlooker and that what he said had no importance. The artist Marcel Duchamp came to New York City in 1920 and brought Dadaism to America by exhibiting his "Readymades," which were found objects from nature or man's manufactures, presented as art without modification or artistic interference. On his arrival, he presented the collector Walter Arenberg with his *Paris Air*, a glass globe whose space had been sealed off in Paris. Other Readymades were *Bicycle Wheel*, a wheel mounted on a stool, and the widely talked about *Fountain*, a urinal. These exhibits illustrated his contention that nothing lay outside the artist's scope, nobody should abide by established rules, and antiart was as important as rationalized art.

According to Carla Gottlieb, what Duchamp actually achieved was of a questionable nature—a further disorientation of a public "already badly in need of orientation. Instead of training our sensitivity to art, and thus helping us enjoy art properly, Duchamp obliterated the line between art, craft, and nature, between masterpiece, ornament, and curiosity." Yet crucial critics and artists "declared the Readymades to be masterpieces of art, and believed "that the spirit of Duchamp has breathed art into a bottle rack or a urinal."[22]

In the 1950s, Duchamp's ideas attracted John Cage, Robert Rauschenberg, and Jasper Johns. Cage also was attracted by the whimsical eccentricity of Erik Satie (1866–1925), whose music ridiculed the claims of modernists and traditionalists alike. Cage was, in part, provoked into a stance like that of Satie and Dadaism by his disenchantment with rationalistic and academically oriented colleagues, inflexible audiences, and the hostility to his early works. He attacked them through nihilistic provocation. Morris Dickstein writes that destruction and chaos, "a form of aesthetic terrorism," were the outcomes of his experiments. "Where this polemical side is dominant, we often find publicists rather than artists, dada rather than symbolism."[23]

After adding his own interpretation of Oriental philosophy to Dada, Cage tried to remove what he called "inherited aesthetic claptrap" through compositions stressing unplanned events, purposelessness, and dissociation of every moment of a work from every other moment, all pushed to an extreme of irrationality. His message to younger composers, says Rockwell, was to "do any damn fool thing they wanted to."[24] The performers of his works might also exhibit odd behavior. Charlotte Moorman, a cellist, once decided to put on Cage's *26' 1.1499"*, which called for a loud, sharp sound. Moorman thought breaking glass might be appropriate, therefore tried smashing an electric light bulb in a wastebasket. Still unsatisfied, she experimented with bricks. Next, she turned to David Tudor for advice. He recommended shattering a Pepsi-Cola bottle, "because it was abrasive." It worked for her. She then turned her attention to finding a second sound and eventually settled on the striking of a garbage-can cover with a hammer while she plucked a cello string.[25]

Exhibiting an eccentricity stemming from Dada and Cage, the composer Nam June Paik's *Hommage á John Cage* called for the simultaneous playing of three tapes while the composer hurled eggs at a mirror, threw a rosary at the audience, and attacked a piano with oversized scissors. Then there was Kirk Nurok's *Sonata for Piano and Dog*, with a dog featured as vocal soloist.[26]

The absurdities embodied a playfulness meant to amuse, but also to criticize contemporary society. Harold Schonberg stated that the outrageous behavior could be "much more fun than, say, a concert of post-Webern serialism by grim young composers." The trouble was, he adds, that some admirers of the New Left took such antics much too seriously and missed the entire point.[27]

Admirers of Cageian Dada increased in the 1960s, most of them under the age of thirty and "turned off by the Establishment." A lesser number were middle-aged, among them former devotees of the serial and atonal compositions of the 1950s. Their earlier enthusiasm had been skin deep. By the beginning of the 1960s they were looking for something different to approve. The need to remain modish, however, prevented a return to traditional styles. Therefore, after the New Left's extremisms came to their attention, they made them the new fashion.[28]

When members of the New Left like Cage spoke, their logic was often impossible to fathom. On nonmusical matters, for instance, Cage on occasion spoke in terms seemingly detached from conventional human feeling, whether in reference to a young man who contemplated suicide,[29] the evils in Iran under the Shah,[30] or the destructive acts of China's Red Guard.[31] According to Cage, suicide might be a good; the staging of modern spectacles amidst tyranny was acceptable; and the mayhem in China might improve the world and revolutionize thinking.

A similar reversal of conventional logic invests Cage's comments about music. To give historical sanction to the chance procedures he favored, Cage announced that Bach, too, believed in indeterminacy since "timbre and amplitude characteristics of the material" is not given. Undiscussed were understood performance practices of Bach's time and the definite configurations of melody, harmony, and rhythm given in the score. Cage strongly endorsed originality in music, criticizing audiences for not seeing its importance. But what was the nature of his criticism? He began: "Why are people opposed to originality? Some fear the loss of the *status quo*. Others realize, I suppose, the fact that they will not make it. Make what? Make history. That one sees that the human race is one person . . . enables him to see that originality is necessary."[32] What he did not mention was that audiences may not value originality as much as other attributes of a composition.

A final example of Cage's reasoning concerns his advocacy of painfully loud sounds. He first erroneously states that only some people still object to loud sounds. What objection exists arises not because people dislike the experience but because they are afraid of hurting their ears. He then stated that at one time he sat down for an hour with his ear close to a resonating loudspeaker. Afterward his ears continued to ring through the next night. When the ringing subsided he was examined by an ear specialist who told him his hearing was normal. Ergo, listening to loud sound was not at all harmful. Basing his proof on this one experience, Cage advised listeners not to be fearful for their hearing.[33]

The potential for harm from such assumptions is obvious. Cage tells the story about once reading that skunk cabbage was edible. He entertained the idea without questioning it. One day, he cooked a mess of the stuff and fed it to himself and six other people. All became quite ill. He says he almost died because of it.[34]

After looking over the statements of Cage and other New Leftists, many people learned to be wary of accepting what they said. When they claimed that their music led to self-awareness, self-fulfillment, the transformation of consciousness, the eternal verities of Zen, the reform of society, the profound understanding of the ways of the universe, and a coming to terms with all of life itself, the burden they made music bear was too much for it. Note what Cage had to say about his *Etudes Australes* for piano and *Freedman Etudes* for violin when performed in Boston in 1983: "We are surrounded by impossibility. Very frequently . . . the situation is hopeless. I tried to put both the pianist and the violinist in a hopeless situation. If we as an audience can see that they are able to come through that, if it turns out that the impossible is not so difficult after all, then maybe we could change our government and everything else we need to change."[35]

Of all the curious ideas advanced by the musical New Left, one of the most peculiar was the elevation of boredom to a positive value. Cage stated: "In Zen, they say: If something is boring after two minutes, try if for four. If still boring, try it for eight, sixteen, thirty-two, and so on. Eventually, one discovers that it's not boring at all but very interesting."[36] Radicals dedicated to the principles of the New Left accepted words like these on faith.

Reviewing a concert of music by Morton Feldman, a Cage follower, Andrew DeRhen spoke of minimal contrasts and little perceptible movement. At any other time in musical history, "someone of Feldman's nontalents could have never attracted notice." DeRhen continues: "But during an age when nihilism has thrived in music—particularly the avant-garde—there is obviously a place for a composer who has plumbed new depths of boredom, uneventfulness, and navel contemplation."[37]

A Winthrop Sargeant article printed in the *New Yorker* in 1963 contains a report on the views of Leonard Meyer, a respected writer on music, concerning the two different musical modernisms evident in America at that time. Meyer, says Sargeant, distinguishes between two opposed aesthetics, the teleological, art as goal oriented and structured (and characteristic of the modernism of the 1950s); and the antiteleological or radical empirical, art as accident, without preconceived traditions, and resting on ever-fresh experience (and characteristic of the New Left's modernism of the 1950s). Furthermore, Meyer relates this latter modernism to Zen and Existentialism and states that it cannot be a form of communication ("since communication depends on an understood vocabulary and a set of logical expectations on the part of the audience), and also that it cannot be subjected to criticism (since it involves no anticipations and no meanings). Antiteleological art has no purpose, it just *is.*" It exists to challenge our beliefs and values.[38]

Cage himself has said an audience's value judgments are invalid; that its attempt to find only a limited number of musical relationships is mistaken and beside the point since each sound is only meant to be authentically itself. He and his colleagues are engaged in an errorless art, because error presupposes an idea of what should have occurred.[39]

At times vulgarity and bad taste were seen as values. This is the way Kenneth Gaburo meant his *Lingua II: Maledetto,* "for 7 Virtuoso Speakers," to be understood. It begins as a learned discourse on the word "screw," but soon turns unambiguously obscene. For three-quarters of an hour verbal excrement at the lowest sophomoric level, unrelieved by any musical sound, assails the ear. In liner notes to the work's recording, Gaburo tries to make a case for the coarseness, implying a profundity not readily perceptible to the listener. He discourses on paralangauge—vocal effects that are supposed to communicate meaning beyond that of the words themselves. Regrettably, the reader-listener remains mystified.

Some criticisms of the New Left's position and of its music are not easily put aside. If a concept fails to come across and if a performance proves unsatisfactory who is to blame? Is the counterculture's position meant to protect its practitioners against failure, since without standards, failure is impossible? Was the resultant anarchy, called freedom, in truth, a way to shun responsibility for one's actions?[40]

THE "UNSELFING" OF SOUND

Speaking for the New Left of the early 1960s, Cage rejected emotional expression in music as a form of selfishness linked to ego. This ego erected a wall between the individual and experience. Music should be just sound, expressing nothing at all in itself. The laudable composer attempted to control neither performer nor listener through his music.[41]

The representation of the composer as making profoundly expressive statements in response to the dictates of personal feelings was anathematized. Preferred was the image of the composer as an inventor of novel sounds. Interestingly, Cage's father, whom Cage held in high regard, had been an inventor and possibly passed the inclination for novelty on to the son. Virgil Thomson states that the inventor's view of novelty had been Cage's view since Thomson first knew him, in 1943. Cage, Thomson says, "prizes innovation above all other qualities—a weighting of the values which gives to all of his judgments an authoritarian, almost a commercial aspect, as of a one-way tunnel leading only to the gadget-fair."[42] Donal Henahan commented: "At some point, John Cage must have decided he was not going to be one of the world's great composers so he invented a fallback career for himself." Schoenberg told him "he was 'not a composer, but an inventor— of genius,' " so Cage became one of the leading wits in music, "a man whose influence went on expanding even while his compos- ing pretensions seemed to shrink."[43]

Other New Left composers imaged themselves as inventors. For example, Lejaren Hiller said: "I get wrapped up in each successive compositional (or research) project and its necessities seem (to me) to override other considerations."[44]

To single out one work, *Night Music* is a tape composition with all sounds invented by Richard Maxfield. If the piece is heard be- fore reading the composer's liner notes, its electronic noises sound like the jangle of slot-machines being actively manipulated in an arcade. Maxfield says in the liner notes that birds, insects, and summer nights at Riverside and Central Parks were the ideas mo- tivating the work. He then describes how he went about invent- ing his sound material aided by an oscilloscope and tape recorder.

After "hearing" a New-Left composition, critics often complain that invention comprises attention-getting gimmickry, the more ingenious and quirky, the better. They single out works like Cage's *Imaginary Landscape*, which calls for an ensemble of radios, and *4' 33"*, where a pianist sits before a keyboard for three movements of silence. The gimmickry might include the title of a composi- tion. For example, when David Tudor performed *66 West Twelfth Street* at the School for Social Research, the title represented the school's address. Why? Because Cage wanted the name of the mu- sic always to be the address of the place in which it was being performed at the time.[45]

Visual gimmickry was *de rigueur*. Witness Arthur Paxton's *Blood Lines*, which Jack Hiemenz says "is predicated on the notion of locating a horn amidst a woodwind quintet at the front of the stage, then having it gradually relocate to the back of the stage where it takes its place amidst a grouping of brass instruments— its 'blood' kindred. It was an intriguing idea, but one that ultimately came across as a mere gimmick, given the dreariness of Paxton's music."[46] One gimmicked composition that never got to be heard was by Philip Corner, who in 1968 invented a work with the following instruction for performance: "One anti-personnel type CBU bomb will be thrown into the audience."

The ultimate Cageian statement is to inscribe a concept meant to be realized in sound onto paper, then not have the music performed at all, instead merely exhibiting the concept. Hilton Kramer in 1972 attended just this sort of exhibition, titled "Concept and Content." Kramer writes: "In the basement (an apt location) we find the work of John Cage, the composer. He shows pages of music manuscript, framed as if they were pictures (which they are not. . . . As a visual artist Mr. Cage is an amateur dealing in stylish clichés. His work in the graphic media shows a keener appreciation of the current art market than of anything serious in the realm of artistic expression."[47]

Another approach is to leave music out altogether, and put down a concept using the most general terms, as in "prose music." For example, La Monte Young in 1960 issued several compositions as brief prose writings and left it to the performer to realize the "music." Or, if preferred, one could read the piece and, it is assumed, find his senses stimulated without the interference of actual sound. An example is Young's *Composition 1960 #10 to Bob Morris*. It consists of a single sentence: "Draw a straight line and follow it."[48]

Anything that could be interpreted conceptually became a matter for music, whether one read the concept, saw it as a picture, or freely realized it through silence, noise, text-sound or pitched tones.

RESIDUAL EFFECTS

Some radicals in music left a residue that remained effective for some time. When they introduced revolutionary concepts into their musical compositions, they could not help but influence the course of music education. In the era where youth questioned most aspects of Western tradition, those who were music students wondered about the need for a thorough study of traditional theory, techniques, and literature. One or two composer-teachers advocated music schools with no set curriculum, no classes, and no required areas of study. They gave it as their opinion that students themselves should decide how to spend their time and should use libraries and music faculty only in ways they themselves desired.[49]

It follows that the accusation of charlatanism would arise against leaders of the New Left. Cage's *Etudes Australes* was based on patterns suggested by a map of the stars in the southern hemisphere. The composer also took direction from the map's colors and a vague numerology based on the number 64. Henahan writes: "This is the sort of shamanistic approach that sets conservative critics to grinding their teeth and has led many to dismiss Mr. Cage as a charlatan." Henahan then speaks of Cage's *Empty Words*, which consisted of words and syllables from Thoreau's journals, arrived at through chance operations, and of slide projections from Thoreau's drawings. He says it raises the issue of charlatanism.[50]

Certain members of the New Left, however much some of them might not condone it, set up a climate where incompetence and fraud could grow. Anyone could "compose music," though he or she lacked training and talent; somewhere admirers could be found to support his or her pretensions. If a composition struck a sufficiently radical pose, it had to "be given the breaks on the probability that there is more there than meets the eye," while another, more traditional work "must be regarded with suspicion on the probability" that it is less good than it sounds. We have reached "the point where it is amusing to dismiss" old music "with a quip, but dangerous to one's critical reputation not to discover in any second-rate . . . [radical] exercise some cosmic implication."[51] The fear to criticize, the forcing of one's self to believe in the "emperor's new clothes," already a residue of the 1950s, was reinforced in the 1960s and persisted into the 1970s.

The principal supporters of music's New Left, it is true, were young people. However, as Morton Feldman astutely realized, these "kids" bought his, Cage's, and Brown's gestures but not the music. "The kids make an anti-hero stance, wear a cape, and say 'I'm not a composer,' the dramatic gesture. To them, John Cage, the person, has become a hero, not his music."[52]

Older attendants of a New Left concert frequently "left in droves during the performance," writes Anitra Earle, who watched an audience of 550 shrink to 40 at a San Francisco concert in 1970. Boredom seemed to be the motivating reason for leaving.[53] At a performance of Cage's *Variations II* and *III*, the biggest sensation was Cage's drinking down a glass of water while a microphone placed at his throat transmitted his gulps over loudspeakers. The amplification was so loud, it hurt eardrums and caused most people to flee. The committed ones "remained for that last mammoth gurgle" and gave Cage "a standing ovation."[54]

So long as some men and women remained radicalized, the music of the sort described above was supported. Meanwhile, the general concert-going public found its conclusions about the modernism of the 1950s reinforced by that of the 1960s. It increasingly turned away from all contemporary music.

INDETERMINACY

I have already had occasion to refer to chance or indeterminate music—that is to say, sound heard in a performance that is of unforeseeable outcome, and unrepeatable—each performance being unique. Therefore, any recording of an indeterminate composition can only inform you of something that has already happened. Indeterminateness could apply to a musical work in several different ways. The procedure for creating a work could be based on chance actions, like the fortuitous instructions derived from dice throwing or I Ching, which eventually produce a notated score of some sort. Or deliberately vague drawings, graphs, or other schemes might indicate approaches to any aspect of a composition—tones, durations, loudness or softness, and so on—with a more precise implementation left to the performers. Or a composition might exist only in a number of brief interchangeable passages, with the performer allowed to combine these passages in any fashion for any given performance. Thus, indeterminacy means unpredictability either in the way a piece is put together or in the way it is performed or both.

Why resort to indeterminacy? First, it objectified music and, thus, feeling. By obliterating past and future, the composer could devote himself to "Thisness" and "Nowness." This iconoclastic cleansing action was a means to an end—to effect change in aesthetic concepts of what constituted the ultimate nature of music.[55] "Those who envisage art as a bulwark against the irrationality of man's nature, and as a monument to his constructive powers," said Aaron Copland, "will have no part of the Cagean aesthetic. But those who enjoy teetering on the edge of chaos will clearly be attracted."[56]

John Cage had studied with Henry Cowell, Arnold Schoenberg, and Adolph Weiss. He also knew Varése's experiments with percussive sounds. An early work, *Metamorphosis* (1938), showed passing interest in the twelve-tonalism of Schoenberg. About that time, he also wrote *Bacchanal*, a tentative attempt at writing for prepared piano. The next year, *First Construction (in Metal)*, for several percussionists, found him leaning toward Cowell (his *Pulse* of 1939) and Varèse (his *Ionization* of 1933). A variety of metallic objects were struck to produce sounds somewhat related to the delicate emanations from Asian gamelan ensembles. A *Second* and *Third Construction* soon followed.

In *Imaginary Landscape No. 1* (1939), he experimented with metal cans, buzzers, a wastebasket, water gong, and amplified wire coils. In *Imaginary Landscape No. 2* (1942), he tried out audio frequency oscillators and the possibilities of sound-frequency changes available in a variable-speed record turntable. His works based on chance would begin in the 1950s.

The Seasons (1947), first performed in New York City in conjunction with a dance presentation by Merce Cunningham's company, calls for a chamber orchestra to perform notated music meant to depict the seasonal divisions of the year. In the liner notes to the recording, Cage refers to the "Indian view of the seasons as quiescence (winter), creation (spring), preservation (summer), and destruction (fall)." A rythmic structure with fixed time lengths in proportional relationship between the smallest units and the largest sections gives order to the work. For the most part, gentle plucked and staccato like sounds or soft, longer held tones predominate. Except for occasional loudnesses, a sameness of procedure predominates. The overall effect is one of quiet beauty, enhanced by subtle shifts in tone color, and telling use of instrumental timbres. *The Seasons* is composed music, not chance or noise.

Similar comments can be made about the *String Quartet in Four Parts* (1950), a composed piece also about the seasons of the year, only now it is French-summer and American-fall music, a canon for winter, and a quodlibet for spring. Indian philosophy, nevertheless, with its seasonal division of preservation, destruction, quiescence, and creation influences the sound. Vibratoless tones, very slight bow pressure, and a restricted number of pitches flatten the expressive content. Also composed music is the *Sonatas and Interludes* for prepared piano, written between 1946 and 1948. Screws, nuts, bolts, and rubbery items added to the piano's strings alter the pianist's tones, resulting in an approximation of a Javanese gamelan ensemble. Sixteen sonatas and four interludes focus on tiny percussive tones, which are pleasant, capricious, unaggressive, repetitive, and mesmerizing.

Then in 1951 came Cage's renunciation of individual taste and memory and his search for expressive freedom through chance procedures. An early example of this new departure is the *Music of Changes*, for piano solo. Charts with sixty-four elements in each were suggested to Cage by the Chinese oracle book *I Ching*, according to the toss of yarrow stalks or coins. Cage made up a chart for each aspect of sound—pitch, duration, dynamic, tempo, and so forth. Coin tosses decided combinations of these aspects. Regular pulse was eliminated. Instead, durations of sound and silence determined by chance were notated graphically and formed no rational pattern.

Other compositions of similar kind came out. *Landscape No. 4* (1951) is scored for twelve radios, the indeterminate element being the content of the programs. In *Water Music* (1952) a pianist combines a whistle's squeal, a radio's static, the shuffling of cards, and the tinkling of poured water. *Williams Mix* (1952) amounts to a fanciful but chance mingling of city and wind noises. In the same year, Cage conceived *4' 33"* for a silent performer, the indeterminacy residing in the surrounding noises of the room itself and the audience waiting for something to happen. In *Variations I* and *Variations II*, any number of performers on any number of instruments or objects were invited to produce any sounds they desired, perhaps by abrasively stroking a piano's strings with a microphone, or by the amplified scratching of pen on paper—the possibilities were limitless.

Writing about Cage's activities in the 1950s, Eric Salzman states: "Under his influence a whole 'junk music' school of tape and electronics has sprung up . . . an aural equivalent of junk sculpture."[57] What occasioned this remark was Cage's *Fontana Mix* (1958) and the use of four tapes in a random sound collage, combinable in any number of ways. Indeed, the work could be realized in limitless ways, the so-called score being merely an outline of possible actions. One realization, on a Turnabout recording, is for magnetic tape alone. Emitted is a jumble of everyday sounds. Another recording, by David Tudor, is for amplified piano; still another, by Max Neuhaus, is for percussion. A version by Cornelius Cardew is for guitar.

Cage was indifferent to criticism. Once a work left his desk, it was outside of him. He explains: "If someone kicked me—not my music, but me—then I might complain. But if they kicked my music, or cut it out, or don't play it enough, or too much, or something like that, then who am I to complain?"[58]

Yet once he did complain vociferously, when both he and his music were being "kicked." The occasion was the performance of *Atlas Eclipticales* (1961) by the New York Philharmonic. It combined the orchestra with electronics manipulated by an assistant to the conductor (Bernstein). Star tracings guided the score, which was realizable, as usual, in a number of different ways. Each instrument had been given its own electronic amplification. The players hated the piece. As Cage later described it: "The New York Philharmonic is a bad orchestra. They're a group of gangsters. . . . In the case of *Atlas*, they would tear the microphones off the instruments and stamp on them and the next day I would then have to buy new ones to replace them for the next performance."[59] Some time after that event, I met a Philharmonic player at a dinner given by a Boston Symphony member. I asked if the talk about the performance and the sabotage of Cage's equipment were true. Without the hint of a smile on his face, he replied that the players' actions had been in the spirit of Dada, so why was Cage complaining?

Cage's contributions to nihilism continued with *Variations IV*, which throws together street noises, sounds taped at an art gallery exhibit in Los Angeles, and snippets of older music—all of it electronically distorted and indiscriminately mingled. A determined modernist, Alfred Frankenstein likened the piece to Robert Rauschenberg's "combine paintings," into which Cage's friend collaged anything he could find—cast-off clothing and bedding, stuffed birds, posters, metal signs, and reproductions of older paintings. He adds that Cage loves garbage.[60]

On 17 November 1967, came an exercise in complete anarchism, *MUSICIRCUS*, mounted in the University of Illinois, at Urbana's Stock Pavilion, built as a livestock-exhibition center. No score was offered; anybody who would care to perform something, anything, was invited to come and do so. About five thousand people, most of them young, were a party to the mayhem that ensued. The "performance" lasted four hours.

A similar gigantic intermedia piece centered on random environmental sound was tried in 1969, *HPSCHD*, which Cage conceived with the assistance of Lejaren Hiller. Seven harpsichordists, a fifty-two–tape "orchestra," visuals of all sorts, and the noise of thousands of young spectators—yelling, dancing, throwing objects around—guaranteed chaos.[61]

In all probability, hardly any of Cage's compositions will outlive his own lifetime. Those that are candidates for future life are most likely to be found among the composed pieces written before the 1950s.

Morton Feldman (b. 1926) composes for the psychrophilic listener, one who thrives on music of low temperature. His works sound one-dimensional, as if fixed in one place. Quiet dynamics and cool tones are resorted to. Scores or graphs introduce elements of indeterminacy (usually in pitch, rhythm, and/or time values) and allow performers much freedom of choice.

Feldman's teachers had been the atonalists Wallingford Riegger and Stefan Wolpe. Then, in the winter of 1949–50, he met Cage, David Tudor, and Earle Brown. As Feldman describes it in the liner notes to Time Records 58007, he showed Cage a string quartet. Cage asked "How did you make this?" The reply: "I don't know how I made it." This admission excited and pleased Cage, who jumped up and down and screamed: "Isn't that marvelous. Isn't that wonderful. It's so beautiful, and he doesn't know how he made it." Thus, states Feldman, did Cage give him "those early permissions to have confidence in my instincts." Feldman adds: "There was very little talk about music with John. Things were moving too fast to even talk about. But there was an incredible amount of talk about painting. . . . The new painting made me desirous of a sound world more direct, more immediate, more physical than anything that had existed heretofore."

Early results of Feldman's acquaintanceship with Cage and his circle were a group of works called *Projections* (1950–53), intended for various chamber combinations, notated graphically, and structured indeterminately. The high, middle, and low of sound gamuts were indicated, but no specific pitches were given. Duration was to be decided by relative lengths of rectangles located above dotted vertical lines meant to indicate pulse. The resultant sound lacks harmonic depth and rhythmic impulse. Tones do not link up but are heard as separate entities.

In 1951 Feldman extended his experiment to the orchestra, with *Intersection I* and *Marginal Intersection*. Graphs with a high, middle, and low register loosely designated within a time length are given as guides. The performers choose when to enter, what pitches to play, and where to modify their dynamics. An impression of constant improvisation permeates the performance. The effectiveness of any presentation relies on the ideas of the players, an incipient weakness.

Aware of this weakness, Feldman wrote *Structures* for String Quartet with a different approach. He first sketched out and graphed a series of musical events, then himself realized these events in a correctly notated score. The opening is pointillistic and sparse; next come several quasi-ostinato passages; another pointillistic section sounds; then two more quasi-ostinato passages; and the concluding section refers back to the opening.

In *Pieces for Four Pianos* (1957), Feldman desired indeterminacy between the performers and asked that they not listen to each other during playing: "It works better if you don't listen."[62]

Durations (1960–61) comprises four pieces for various chamber combinations. Again, each player is asked to conduct his performance as if he were alone. The actual sounds are given; the general tempo indicated; all performers begin together, but from then on freely choose their own durations.

The composer had always kept modern painterly procedures in mind when he composed. In some works he makes specific reference to painters, as in *For Franz Kline* and *De Kooning*. One of his most interesting compositions, written as a memorial to the painter Mark Rothko, is *Rothko Chapel* (1972), for chorus, two solo voices, viola, celesta, and percussion. The quiet, sad, and meditative music does make some connection with Rothko's mysterious and reflective paintings.

His opera *Neither* (1976), for soprano and orchestra, is not nearly as communicative. The one dominant feeling the observer comes away with is of isolation and aloneness. The singer, in a long white robe that stretches downward and then covers the stage, remains motionless. Soft murmurs and light rushes of sound introduce the singer on one tone, enunciating individual syllables without vibrato or other expressive shading, icy and detached. Nothing ever happens. Repeated chords, some long tones, and occasional dynamic distinctions are heard. The performers go through their motions as if without wills of their own. Then at last it is over and the listener rejoins reality. As here, much of Feldman's music has, at the close, the effect of a return to waking life.

Writing around 1961, Earle Brown (b. 1926) remarks on the influences of Alexander Calder and Jackson Pollock. "The integral but unpredictable 'floating' variations of a mobile, and the contextual rightness and Pollock's spontaneity and the directness in relation to the materials and his particular image of the work show an awareness of the 'found object' tradition as well as establishing unique and personal conditions of control of the totality." Then Cage provided him with a means for dealing with "given" material and for liberation "from the inherited, functional concepts of control."[63]

Noncontrol, spontaneity, and unpredictable "floating" variations are operative terms in Brown's creative vocabulary. He wanted to conjure up a musical environment that was always in motion and whose meaning was constantly being altered. Yet, he did not believe in unguided "randomness." He developed the concept of "open forms," where performers choose in what order to play pages of music. He provided pitches, durations, and dynamics, which performers modify according to their own sense of time.

He tried a graphic notation that to some extent imaged the connection of the music to the actions requested of the performers. As Brown explains, in the liner notes to CRI S-330, an open-form composition is one where "all of the sound materials in the work are notated and controlled in the score but . . . their sequence, juxtaposition, tempi and repetitions are left to the spontaneous decisions of the conductor [or in chamber pieces, the performers themselves], during the performance, as the performing process develops and unfolds between himself, the written sound materials and the musicians. . . . The form of the work is therefore unique in each performance, but it is always [the same composition] . . . because only those composed sound events may be used."

In *December 1952*, specific pitches are missing; a scheme of lines differing in length and position prompts any number of players to improvise for whatever length of performance time they desire. *Available Forms I*, written in 1961, is an exercise in "conceptual mobility," for eighteen instruments. Six pages contain five musical events each. A conductor determines the order in which events are played by moving an arrow on a numbered board in front of the podium, and by holding fingers up to indicate what particular event is then to be played. *Available Forms II* (1962), is for two orchestras, each led by an individual conductor. Each conductor is totally independent of the other and has his own pages and events to choose from. The two streams of music, however, are heard simultaneously.

Lukas Foss, born in Berlin, in 1922, came to the United States with his parents in 1937. Categorizing his music is difficult since his considerable talents have been expended on one stylistic fashion after another. He has been, in turn, a musical Americanist, a serialist, an experimentalist, and a "new romantic." Because he is best known for his works calling for some form of improvisation, he is discussed here. Early works, like the Capriccio for Cello and Piano and the *Song of Songs* (1946), a cantata for soprano and orchestra, are tonal, triadic, and lyric, pleasant to hear and skillfully crafted. Both were written in 1946. *The Prairie* (1943), for soloists, chorus, and orchestra, and the string quartet of 1947 exhibit Americanisms from jazz to Copland-folk.

In 1957, he founded the Improvisation Chamber Ensemble (piano, clarinet, percussion, cello, and at times a French horn) and began to experiment with improvisation based on guide sheets. Three years later came *Time Cycle*, for soprano and orchestra (1960), with four selections as its text, two in English, from Auden and Housman, and two in German, from Kafka and Nietzsche. Most of *Time Cycle* sounds atonal. Between movements, the Improvisation Chamber Ensemble takes over with sounds having no relation to the composed material.

The Concerto for Cello, Orchestra, and Tape (1966) electrically amplifies the soloist and permits him to select one from three given orchestral accompaniments. The two not selected are then combined to become the accompaniment to the next movement. Graph composition is tried out in *Elytres* and *Fragments of Archilochos*. His *Phorion*, meaning "stolen goods," is for orchestra and electric organ, harpsichord or piano, and guitar. A part of Bach's Partita in E for solo violin is first heard intact before it is completely demolished. In 1967, *Baroque Variations* for orchestra was completed. Foss again uses the Bach partita heard in *Phorion*, plus a Handel concerto grosso and a Scarlatti sonata. The original music is taken apart and distorted in order to achieve a dreamlike quality. Some eight years later, interviewed by Gagne and Caras for *Soundpieces*, Foss said he was fishing for new ideas and meanings in *Baroque Variations* and that it was written at a time when he was obsessed with the idea of destroying his love for Bach.

His Third String Quartet (1976) has irritated several people whom I know. It is minimalistic, unmelodic in the extreme, a busy skirl of strings on a couple of notes at a time, in unison or slightly out of synchronization. Also minimalistic is *Music for Six*, playable by any six instruments. By the mid-seventies, Foss was discovering good things in the work of La Monte Young and Terry Riley. *Music for Six* shows him appropriating their style.

Foss changed style again in 1978, with *Thirteen Ways of Looking at a Blackbird* for mezzo-soprano, flute, percussion, and piano. The text is a poem by Wallace Stevens. All kinds of novel ways of producing sound à la George Crumb, are tried out. The singer sometimes speaks and sometimes really sings in tonal fashion. The accompaniment resembles sound-effect music.

ENVIRONMENTAL MUSIC

Environment refers to conditions surrounding or within a person that can or do impact on human life. Already mentioned are

works by John Cage, such as *HPSCHD*, which center on environment. Mentioned earlier, though briefly, was the experimentation
of Alvin Lucier, a strong advocate of environmental music. Lucier
said: "I follow my instincts and continue making pieces with brain
waves, echoes, room resonances, vibrating wires, and other natural phenomena."[64]

In the early 1960s, still less noticed as a composer than he liked,
Lucier discovered the brain-wave equipment of Edmond Dewan,
which inspired him to try a new direction. The result was *Music
for Solo Performer*. Electrodes attached to Lucier's scalp detected
the ten-cycle rhythms of alpha waves, which were then heard over
loudspeakers. The emitted sounds then triggered off several percussion instruments and also started up tapes of prerecorded brain
waves. At its premiere, the audience endured the sound for almost
a half an hour, then booed until it ceased.

Later in the 1960s, he invented *Shelter*, a work based on the
filtered sounds of vibrations detected in the walls, floors, and ceil-
ings of a building. That same year, Pauline Oliveros invited him
to California. During a visit to the ocean shore, he was fascinated
by the resonances coming from sea shells and from a canyon near
the shore. The result was *Chambers*, for several performers blow-
ing into conch shells. Interested in sounds from the solar system,
he produced *Solar Sound Systems*. Solar panels of different sizes,
shapes, and capacities were placed at various on-site locations, facing all points of the compass but aligned to the sun's pathway
from morn until dusk. When sunlight fell upon the panels in these
various locations, with unpredictable intensities at different times
of the year, electric voltage was created and drove electronic music modules, amplifiers, and loudspeakers, thus producing sound
continuously in flux.

Sferics, performed January 1983, was a record of natural radio-
frequency emissions from the ionosphere. These electric distur-
bances were supposed to make listeners realize that "art needs no
shape," and "music is where you find it." Edward Rothstein, who
attended the performance, said he had no such thoughts. Instead,
the sounds "provoked speculation about how such 'avant-garde'
activities can still be taken seriously; Mr. Lucier has been exploring similar regions for nearly two decades."[65]

A special kind of environment, that of constantly changing sound, was explored by Elliott Schwartz in his *Elevator Music*. A twelve-story building was converted into a performing environment. Performers were stationed on each floor, near the elevator doors, while the audience rode up and down the elevator listening to the different musics fading in and out.

A well-known environmental composer, Max Neuhaus, began around 1966 to investigate music making that was free of the concert hall. He is perhaps best known for *Water Whistle*, an installation using a swimming pool as a concert area. Water pumped through cheap whistles piped sound underwater. Members of the audience had to at least put an ear to the water's surface, or duck their heads under, or better still don swimsuits and dive below the surface, in order to take in the sounds. One person who did so in the swimming pool of New York University said he heard a dissonant, high-pitched drone, similar to a power tool's hum.

Another environmentalist, John Hassell, has put together a *Landmusic Series*, beginning in 1979. One of this series, *Elemental Warnings*, installed in Connecticut in 1969, had twenty oscillators buried in the ground, where they beeped at passersby. Two months later the oscillators were attached to balloons and released to beep into the stratosphere, with the expectation that eventually they would come down in different parts of the earth and continue to beep away.[66]

Liz Phillips is another environmentalist, one who concentrates on sensors that respond to wind, sunlight, or body heat. She had started as a visual artist, went into light sculpture, then found her way to sound. Her *City Sounds* was an outdoor installation in a pedestrian area of a New York college campus. Nothing was visible. As people walked through, they entered microwave fields and set off electronic sounds. Some walkers responded with surprise or confusion. Others rushed through, as if the spot were haunted. All reactions were acceptable, and under the circumstances represented a new form of "applause" to the "composer."[67]

MUSIC AS THEATER

Several works previously described can be categorized by the phrase "music as theater." These include Druckman's *Animus* compositions, and several of Cage's, Hiller's, and Lucier's productions where the visual elements are of equal, if not more, importance than the aural elements. In fact, one of the important origins for music as theater, in the sense referred to here, was the happening (combinations of action, sounds, and images heard sequentially or simultaneously) that was fostered by Cage and his artistic friends, including Allan Kaprow, at Black Mountain College in the 1950s.

Depending on the composer, the neodramatic music described here has been classified as mixed media, multimedia, or performance art, as well as the older term "happening." It is nothing new. At the beginning of the century, Scriabin, the dadaists, the constructivists, and Bauhaus-connected artists had tried something similar. Moreover, the mixed events of circuses and the way motion pictures wed sound to sight are related to it. Although the various terms for neodramatic music are used with inexact meanings, certain characteristics hold true. Usually they give off an aura of impermanence. They require the participation (or at least the supervision) of the originator in order to bring off the performance with the intended effects. In many instances little musical skill is necessary to the artifactor—indeed, the "musical" content of some compositions reveals little or no music, as the term is commonly understood.

Why did several well-known American composers veer strongly toward music as theater in the 1960s and 1970s? One obvious explanation centers on the youth culture of the time and the surfacing of tastes toward which the composers were sympathetic. A goal of this culture was the altering of states of consciousness. Often this was achieved through drugs. The psychodelic painter attempted to make connections with others through comparable visual means, through what Timothy Leary called "retinal orgasm." Light shows combined sound, slide projections, tinted smoke, and stroboscopic lights in an endless variety of patterns. Multimedia groups, like USCO and Mark Boyle's Sensual Laboratory induced vivid subjective sensations "by bombarding several senses simultaneously. By amplifying the sound of the music to ear-deafening levels, and by tuning the oscillations of the strobe light to the frequency of brain rhythms, they succeeded in disorientating normal consciousness and provided, in effect, a synthetic trip."[68]

Some composers wanted to reintroduce music's time-honored connection with drama, but (they said) with the artificiality and untruthfulness of traditional musical theater eliminated. Unlike traditional theater, their neodramatic music (like the theater of the absurd of Beckett, Ionesco, and Genet) downplayed narrative, ignored established time and place, and presented characters who did not necessarily play roles. Meaning was to be intuited by the audience. On its simplest level, neodramatic music was meant to have visual impact, as in William Penn's *Fantasy* for harpsichord, where the composer has the audience watch the performer thrash about on and around his instrument, projecting unrestrained and unconventional humor, as the music changes from the completely organized to the completely disorganized.

An important function of some neodramatic music was the making of a political statement, as in the notorious *L's G.A.* (1968), by Salvatore Martirano, which called for a gas-masked politico, "helium bomb," two-channel tape, and movie projector. It bitterly denounced the Vietnam War and domestic social evils by means of painfully loud electronic sound, and a gas-masked narrator frenetically shouting out Lincoln's Gettysburg Address. That music of this sort sometimes failed in its purpose is made clear by one viewer, Robert Hall, who writes: "One stumbles to the exits after such music of pain more enraged at the composer's heavy-handedness than indignant over the willful perversion of the American dream."[69]

Frequently the meaning was elusive. Elias Tanenbaum's *Rituals and Reactions* requires a chorus on stage, another in the audience, a soprano singer, five brass players, three percussionists, and electronic tape—plus mimes or dancers, if available. The "Rituals" are fully composed sections; the "Reactions" are free responses of the performers to the tape and to each other. The conductor comes on stage to the applause of the audience (ritual), which is picked up by the chorus on stage. A shout of "Hey!" starts up the instrumental playing and the tape. Then the soloist appears in the back of the hall, dressed in robe and mask, and walks slowly to the stage like a high priestess, all the while singing, "She is the 'Em-press of Ice Cream.' " (The composer says the words mean nothing at all.) Now words from books on the occult are sung. When the section ends, everyone shouts: "It's on sale!" This begins the second ritual, that of shopping. Finally is heard the poem "East of Atami" by Jack Shoemaker, which depicts the ritual of Japanese prostitutes going home after a night's work. Words can be used in any order. Various sound effects are heard, including calls and whines from individual voices and choral interpolations.

Robert Ashley, born in Ann Arbor, Michigan, has continuously been identified with experimental neodramatic music. From 1958 to 1966, he and Gordon Mumma operated the Cooperative Studio for Electronic Music, located at Ann Arbor. In 1963 he helped commence the ONCE festivals—an important Midwest showcase for neodramatic music that was, at once, visionary and preposterous. Ashley left for California in 1969 and there became the director of the comtemporary music center at Mills College. In California, he met Terry Riley, Steve Reich, Morton Subotnick, and Pauline Oliveros. Eventually he would move to New York City. His early music education was worthless, Ashley claims, because he was set to studying an "exotic tradition, something that had nothing to do with my reality." He saw no reason to imitate a European-derived music, and so turned to a study of psychoacoustics and to speech research.[70] To him, anything outrageous was interesting, anything shocking was good. He was once asked about a letter he had sent to Larry Austin, in which Ashley wrote: "They'll probably invite you to play there [in Los Angeles] eventually. When they do, do something outrageous." Ashley replied with: "Oh, I always say that. Oh, God—I mean, it's only interesting to do something outrageous. I only hope I haven't lost touch! . . . There's a long tradition for shocking audiences, and I don't think that's necessarily bad."[71]

Outrageous and shocking was his 1964 composition *The Wolfman*. One critic heard it done at New York's Kitchen in 1979 and said it consisted of Ashley yelling and screaming "with maximum amplification against a deafening electronic roar." Possibly it was meant to express "primal rage," but it also "seemed designed to enrage the audience."[72]

Another of Ashley's shockers, written in the 1960s, was *Purposeful Lady Slow Afternoon*, in which a female narrator gives a dramatic and erotic recitation about forced oral sex, accompanied by chimelike electronic effects and a Tibetan horn. Viewers found it embarrassing.

A lengthy ongoing composition, the product of several years of work, is *Perfect Lives (Private Parts)*, which Ashley describes as a "video opera," a compendium of what he has aimed at in all previous works with the addition of minimalistic, rock-derived music. It was first heard more or less complete in New York in 1981. Fragmentary narration, more an unconnected interior monologue, is monotonous and often adolescent in its profundities. It is backed with music originating as much from Ashley's assisting musicians (Blue Gene Tyranny, pianist; David Van Tieghem, percussionist; Jill Kroesen, singer; and Peter Gordon, rock-band leader) as from Ashley himself. Purporting to be about somebody named Isolde and her brother and making reference to a bank robbery, the narrative is so cut up into bits and pieces it ceases to hold an audience's interest. The ever-the-same rock beat and brief, incessantly repeated music passages executed on saxophone, percussion, electric guitar, and electronic keyboard vary from Hollywood soundtrack love-story sound to aggressive street-wise pulsation.

Other composers of music as theater are Larry Austin, Eric Salzman, Gordon Mumma, and Pauline Oliveros. Of these, the most individual and the most difficult to classify is Oliveros. She was a performer on the accordion, a student of karate, and a lover of outrageous music. Her other areas of interest were dreams, telepathy, Zen philosophy, ritualism, and mythology. As a composer, she has busied herself with theatrical music, improvisation, electronics, conceptual realizations, musical mediation, and politico-art works. Her raw material has come from the natural environment, the inner biological world, the technological area, and her own fertile imagination. Her biographer Heidi Von Gunden writes: "Some of her music requires that performers sit out-of-doors and respond vocally to the sounds of automobiles and airplane noises. She has written a two-hour–long piece in which runners circumnavigate a circle while musicians sound exotic instruments, perform sonic meditations, and move with colored sheets while a nude couple stands within a black-and-white circular tent." Oliveros prefers her music be performed anywhere but on a formal stage.[73]

The going phrase amongst aficionados of modernism in the 1980s has been performing art. It embraces the performance activities of Diamanda Galas, who sings, screams, groans, shouts, and whines her way through a performance, to the accompaniment of electronic noises, all at a numbingly high volume of amplification. Another woman involved in performance art is the dancer become composer Meredith Monk. She has been called "a kind of vocalists' John Cage," because she experiments "with the limits of vocalism." Whatever music there is tends to be simplistic and repetitious. A little goes a long way, writes John Ditsky, after hearing her *Songs from the Hill*.[74] A more recent *Turtle Dreams* and other pieces show her going the direction of minimalism, but without the attractive rhythms and tones of Philip Glass and Steve Reich.

When performance art became a trendy pursuit, the performance artist who gained widest recognition was Laurie Anderson. She cared a great deal about contemporary musical innovations like electronic amplification and alteration of instrumental sounds, manipulation of recording tape (including backing herself with herself on tape), and examining topics of the day within a rock-music format. Although she had taken lessons in violin playing, she also devoted years of study to painting and sculpture and did write some art criticism. Beginning in the 1970s, she devoted her activities to performances combining speech with song and violin playing. Her earliest works were brief, cunningly set forth, and patterned after the happenings made familiar by Ashley and post-Cageians. *It's Not the Bullet That Kills You, It's the Hole* asks the singer to fire a bullet into an arm. *Time to Go* is a constantly repeated museum guard's prodding of visitors to leave at closing time.

One of her most ambitious pieces, writes John Rockwell, was *United States I-IV*, in four one-hour–long sections, which Anderson premiered at The Kitchen in New York. It was a sort of solo opera, plus a "highly attenuated art-rock concert," plus a lecture, poetry, and aural and visual imagery. "The subject is herself on one level, but more generally, in the tradition of all autobiographical artists, her observations on whatever it is that is the subject of a given piece." Her singing "is not so much song as wildly varied and inflected narration."[75] Anderson does have a cult following. Beyond her performance art, she is limited as a musician; witness her *It's Cold Outside*, for orchestra (orchestrated by Bill Obrecht), which sounded embarrassing when premiered in 1981.

In this chapter, we have examined those postwar experimenters who have moved the farthest away from what the world has known as music. Whether their experiments have succeeded or not, whether what they have produced is genuinely music or something else altogether will eventually be decided by the public. None of it has caught the fancy of the general art-music public. The older the piece and the farther away American society travels from the conditions that called it forth, the more the special audience for it shrinks.

NOTES

1. Wolfgang Bernhard Fleischmann, in the *Princeton Encyclopedia of Poetry and Poetics* ed. Alex Preminger (Princeton, N.J.: Princeton University Press, 1965) s.v. "Beat Poets."

2. Godfrey Hodgson, *America in Our Time* (New York: Random House, 1976), 309.

3. Marshall Berman, *All That Is Solid Melts into Air: The Experience of Modernity* (New York: Simon & Schuster, 1982), 313–14.

4. Ibid., 318–20.

5. Ibid., 320–21.

6. [John Cage] *John Cage*, ed. Richard Kostelanetz (London: Allen Lane Penguin, 1971), 15.

7. Francis Crociata, "Our 'Youngest' Symphonic Composer Turns 60," *New York Times*, 6 July 1975, sec. 2, 11.

8. John Cage, *Silence* (Cambridge: M.I.T. Press, 1966), 72.

9. Hodgson, *America in Our Time*, 288.

10. Lawrence Weschler, "Profiles (Robert Irwin. Part I)," *New Yorker* (8 May 1982): 69–70.

11. David Ewen, *American Composers: A Biographical Dictionary* (New York: Putnam's, 1982), s.v. "Feliciano, Richard."

12. Roger Dettmer, "Cage: Sonatas and Interludes for Prepared Piano," *Fanfare* 6 (January/February 1983): 130.

13. Joan La Barbara, " 'Concerts by Composers' Illuminates Downtown School," *Musical America* (May 1982): 13–14.

14. Dore Ashton, *The New York School: A Cultural Reckoning* (New York: Penguin, 1979), 3, 224–25.

15. Gunther Schuller, "Can Composer Divorce Public?" *New York Times*, 18 June 1967, sec. 2, 17.

16. Herbert Russcol, *The Liberation of Sound* (Englewood Cliffs, N.J.: Prentice-Hall, 1972), 142. See also Morris Dickstein, *Gates of Eden: American Culture in the Sixties* (New York: Basic Books, 1977), ix; Robert Brustein, in *The Culture Watch: Essays on Theatre and Society, 1969–1974* (New York: Knopf, 1975), 20–21.

17. Barney Childs, in *Breaking the Sound Barrier: A Critical Anthology of the New Music*, ed. Gregory Battcock (New York: Dutton, 1981), 106.

18. See Richard Kostelanetz, ed., *Esthetics Contemporary* (Buffalo, N.Y.: Prometheus, 1978), 27.

19. Cage, *Silence*, 44.

20. Christopher Lasch, *The Culture of Narcissism* (New York: Warner, 1979), 259.

21. Virgil Thomson, *American Music Since 1910* (New York: Holt, Rinehart & Winston, 1971), 80.

22. Carla Gottlieb, *Beyond Modern Art* (New York: Dutton, 1976), 349.

23. Dickstein, *Gates of Eden*, 235.

24. John Rockwell, *All American Music* (New York: Knopf, 1983), 57.

25. Marjorie Rubin, "Musicians Using Bizarre Sounds," *New York Times*, 17 August 1963, 21.

26. Elie Siegmeister, "Humanism and Modernism," *Keynote* (January 1984): 9.

27. Harold C. Schonberg, "Dada, Dada," *New York Times*, 25 August 1963, sec. 2, 9.

28. For more on this change of allegiance by the fashionable set, see John Canady, *Embattled Critic* (New York: Farrar, Straus & Cudahy, 1962), 78–79.

29. Cage, *Silence*, 63, 267, 272.

30. Ibid., 63; Berman, *All That Is Solid Melts into Air*, 31–32.

31. John Cage, *M* (Middletown, Conn.: Wesleyan University Press, 1973), "Foreword."

32. Cage, *Silence* 35, 75.

33. Cage is quoted in *Esthetics Contemporary*, ed. Richard Kostelanetz, 288–89.

34. Cage, *Silence*, 261–62.

35. See the *Dictionary of Contemporary Music*, ed. John Vinton (New York: Dutton, 1974), s.v. "Dlugoszewski, Luisa"; Jean Duvignaud, *The Sociology of Art*, trans. Timothy Wilson (New York: Harper & Row, 1972), 28; Rockwell, *All American Music*, 54; Daniel Yankelovich, *New Rules: Searching for Self-Fulfillment in a World Turned Upside Down* (New York: Bantam, 1982), 5, 9, 20, 30, 34; Lasch, *The Culture of Narcissism*, 285–91. The Cage quotation was printed in the *Boston Globe*, 3 April 1983, sec. A, 9.

36. Cage, *Silence*, 93.

37. Andrew DeRhen, in *Musical America* (June 1971): 23.

38. Winthrop Sergeant, "Musical Events," *New Yorker* (14 September 1963): 120–21. Leonard Meyer's views had appeared in an article in the *Hudson Review*.

39. Cage is quoted in Leonard Meyer, *Music, the Arts and Ideas* (Chicago: University of Chicago Press, 1967), 80–81.

40. Michael Steinberg, "Tradition and Responsibility," *Perspectives of New Music* 1 (Fall 1962): 157; Jesse Pitts, in *The Seventies*, ed. Irving Howe and Michael Harrington (New York: Harper & Row, 1972), 144; William Mayer, "Live Composers, Dead Audiences," *New York Times Magazine*, 2 February 1975, sec. 6, 35.

41. John Cage, *For the Birds* (Boston: Boyars, 1981), 56; Cage, *Silence*, 15, 17; [Cage] *John Cage*, ed. Richard Kostelanetz, 29.

42. Thomson, *American Music Since 1910*, 74.

43. Donal Henahan, "The Riddle of John Cage," *New York Times*, 23 August 1981, sec. 2, 17.

44. Ewen, *American Composers*, s.v. "Hiller, Lejaren Arthur, Jr."

45. See "Contemporary Piano Music," in *Musical America* (May 1952): 26.

46. Jack Hiemenz, in *Musical America* (May 1983): 28.

47. Hilton Kramer, *New York Times*, 8 January 1972, 25.

48. Frederic Rzewski, in *Dictionary of Contemporary Music*, s.v. "Prose Music."

49. [John Cage] *John Cage*, ed. Richard Kostelanetz, 13–14, 25, 33.

50. Donal Henahan, "John Cage, Elfin Enigma, at 64," *New York Times*, 22 October 1976, sec. C, 1.

51. The words enclosed in quotations are from Canady, *Embattled Critic*, 31–32.

52. Feldman is quoted by Harold C. Schonberg, in an article in the *New York Times*, 24 September 1967, sec. 2, 19.

53. Anitra Earle, in *Musical America* (September 1970): 25.

54. Ross Parmenter, "Music: Avant-Garde Sound Mosaic," *New York Times*, 22 August 1963, 20.

55. Christian Wolff, in *Dictionary of Contemporary Music*, s.v. "Cage John"; Cage, *M*, "Foreword"; Charles Hamm, *Music in the New World* (New York: Norton, 1963), 609; Henahan, "John Cage, Elfin Enigma, at 64," 7; Battock, ed., *Breaking the Sound Barrier*, 101; David Kingman, *American Music* (New York: Schirmer, 1979), 520.

56. Aaron Copland, *The New Music, 1900–1960*, rev. ed. (New York: Norton, 1968), 178.

57. Eric Salzman, "Music from the Electronic Universe," *High Fidelity* (August 1964): 56–57.

58. Quoted in the liner notes to Turnabout TV 34046S.

59. Cole Gagne and Tracy Caras, *Soundpieces: Interviews with American Composers* (Metuchen, N.J.: Scarecrow, 1982), 75.

60. Alfred Frankenstein, review of Everest 3230, *High Fidelity* 19 (February 1969): 84.

61. The description of the performance and the quoted comments may be found in Stephen Husarik, "John Cage and LeJaren Hiller: HPSCHD, 1969," *American Music* 1 (1983): 4–6.

62. Gagne and Caras, *Soundpieces*, 165–66.

63. Liner notes to Time Records 58007.

64. Ewen, *American Composers*, s.v. "Lucier, Alvin."

65. Edward Rothstein, *New York Times*, 16 January 1983, 51.

66. Tom Johnson, in *Musical America* (November 1974), 14.

67. Joan La Barbara, in *Musical America* (May 1979), 12–13.

68. John A. Walker, *Art Since Pop* (Woodbury, N.Y.: Barron's 1978), 40–41.

69. Robert Hall, "England's American Music Society, *Music Journal* 29 (January 1971): 38.

70. Gagne and Caras, *Soundpieces*, 17.

71. Ibid., 22–23.

72. Rockwell, *All American Music*, 105.

73. Heidi Von Gunden, *The Music of Pauline Oliveros* (Metuchen, N.J.: Scarecrow, 1983), viii.

74. John Ditsky, review of Wergo SM 1022, *Fanfare* (September/October 1980): 164.

75. Rockwell, *All American Music*, 125–27.

5

Modern Music, Visionary Connections

On 8 April 1983, the Musica Viva ensemble of Boston performed *Rotae Passionis*, for piano, violin, viola, cello, flute, clarinet, and percussion, by Christopher Rouse. Divided into three sections, the first was concerned with Christ's agony in the garden of Gethsemane; the second, with the stations of the cross; and the last, with Christ's entombment. Speaking to the audience about the work, the composer made reference to mysticism, mystery, ritual, and Eastern viewpoints. Rouse's sensitive ear for special effects was everywhere in evidence. For example, at one point, the clarinetist played with his bell resting on a timpani's head, while the percussionist altered the skin's tautness by means of the pedal, producing unique fluctuations in the clarinet's sound. In the second section, each of the fourteen stations of the cross began with a ritualistic loud whack of a mallet on a wooden box. The work's close had a strangely withdrawn, dreamlike atmosphere. The composer's subject, the music's extraordinary instrumental colorings, and the listener's feeling of being transported to another world and time dimension, all serve to introduce the music discussed in this chapter.

Like a ritual observance, a work may advance in a manner designed for a solemn ceremony—incantatory, magical, or religious. Another work may invoke images of enchantment and mystery, with or without a ritualistic component. Neither work is necessarily atavistic or an exercise in nostalgia or escape. Both are artistic responses to the materialistic characteristics of American society, and to the spiritual sterility these imply. Both reject the chaotic, one damn thing after another, anything is art music milieu of indeterminacy, environmental noise, and a great deal of performance art.

Without doubt, myth and mysticism are on the minds of several of the composers about to be examined—Hovhaness and Crumb, for example. They wish to throw light on the meaning of existence, joy and suffering, and life and death, and to suggest a cohesiveness and connectedness (albeit, entirely subjective) to the apparent contradictions of living. Kathleen Agena, in "The Return of Enchantment" (1983), offers Goethe's view of historical-cultural cycles as an insight into our present-day dilemmas. He writes of four stages in these cycles—the first involves striking visions and potent symbols; the second and third stages increasingly resort to reasoning and the dissecting of experience; and the last stage "is marked by banality and vulgar sensuality. There is an attempt to return to the past to restore the vitality of the initial impetus, but the effort only creates chaos." Goethe himself wrote of this final stage as follows: "Human need, aggravated by the course of history, leaps backward over intelligent leadership, confuses priestly, folk and primitive beliefs, grabs now here, now there, at traditions, submerges itself in mysteries, sets fairy tales in the place of poetry, and elevates these to articles of belief."[1]

In music, this final stage became more and more manifest beginning in the 1960s. Writing in 1983, Jacob Druckman mentioned the rationality of the 1950s. He then said that during the mid-sixties the tide changed. In the new works and ideas "we can sense a gradual change of focus, of spirituality and of goals . . . [and] can discern a steady re-emergence of those Dionysian qualities: sensuality, mystery, nostalgia, ecstasy, transcendency."[2]

Druckman, of course, was thinking of his own changed direction, commencing with his *Animus* music of 1966. He may also have had in mind the change in composers like Rochberg. The composers taken up in this chapter, however, have been more committed to the refocusing of musical expression, not so much toward a Dionysian view as toward the visionary, ritualistic, and symbolic. To be kept in mind, nevertheless, is Agena's warning that "the emergence of archaic, mystical motifs in the culture today represents" but a "groping effort to find a replacement for the world view we have lost." This view "cannot be manufactured." She then quotes Daniel Bell, who wrote that it must "grow out of the deepest needs of individuals, sharing a common wakening." This, she claims, has yet to happen and will come in very slowly: "We will have to live with confusion and uncertainty for some time. . . . For now . . . there are more questions than answers." However, the mist is thinning, she believes, and light has begun to shine through.[3]

Whatever else may be said about the compositions discussed in this chapter, most of them (though not all) employ musical tones in more or less controlled situations. Many of them place no impediments between their music and the general audience and do delight the ear. As a result, some of them have won a sizable following for the sake of their music, not their ideology.

THE ASSERTION OF THE FANCIFUL

In a letter to Ben Johnston, Harry Partch (1901–74) listed his influences as "Yaqui Indians, Chinese lullabies, Hebrew chants for the dead, Christian hymns, Congo puberty rites, Chinese music halls (San Francisco), lumber yards, and junk shops."[4] Born in California, he grew up in Arizona and New Mexico. For a long while, he held menial jobs, wandered throughout America, and got to know the underside of society. For the most part, Partch taught himself music. Because human expression was important to him, he downgraded electronic sound. He wanted logic and system; therefore he disliked chance. Feeling that discipline was essential, he spurned the anything-can-happen mixed-media events espoused by Cage. The typical Partch work is fully conceived beforehand and usually unites music to action and dance and sometimes to chanted speech or singsong vocalizing. The ritualistic, magical, incantational, and ceremonial are often bundled into a single work.

Partch would have agreed with his friend and fellow composer Ben Johnston when Johnston stated that fundamental to art are "myths, beyond ready conscious and verbal expression. This is especially true of music. Art has some of the same functions and values as dreams: it puts us into contact with less superficial aspects of ourselves." Furthermore, "the power of art lies precisely in its ability to transcend natural thoughts and put us in a mode of symbolism which interconnects all of us in an exploration of the unknown in ourselves."[5]

Partch invented a forty-three–tone scale system for his music, based on just intonation—that is to say, based on the natural or pure fifth and third. He also invented a whole series of instruments, most of them plucked or struck (among them, pitched "cloud-chamber bowls," bamboo "boos," seventy-two–string "kitharas," elongated "violas," and forty-four–string "canons"). Much of his harmony strikes the ear as nonrevolutionary and resting on some combination of pure intervals. His rhythm has muscle, plus the complexity of different metrical patterns sounding simultaneously. Dissonance is never obtrusive. Shimmering waves of brief, reiterated sound configurations rather than songlike melody are heard. The resultant music has managed to appeal to mixed audiences.

Adrian Corleonis writes that in Partch's dramas are "bardic utterances with surreal humor and bedded deeply in compassion which touches us—literally—where we live and opens the archaic springs of joy and terror." Compositions like *The Delusion of Fury*, and "its comic pendant" *The Dreamer That Remains*, leap "the stale boundaries of 'serious,' 'classical,' pop, and rock into which the music of today is partitioned."[6] To peform Partch's works, musicians must learn to understand his notation, master special playing techniques, and distinguish between non-equally tempered intervals. Several months of rehearsal usually must precede a performance. Since his death, performances have become rare. It is therefore fortunate that, before he died, several composer-supervised recordings of his works were made.

Barstow (1941) is a setting of eight hitchhikers' roadside inscriptions for chanting voice and instrumental accompaniment. Partch takes seriously these existential gestures expressing estrangement and disillusionment. His music provides a unity and exuberance that universalize the specifics of the words. A similar treatment is accorded *U.S. Highball*, "a musical account of a transcontinental hobo trip." *The Letter*'s text is a communication from a hobo acquaintance. An intoning voice, kithara, adapted guitar, and two marimbas perform. The words, satirical and funny, are about jail, a wife the writer wishes dead, and the cold outside world. The music sounds warmly ingratiating, in despite of the text's pessimism. Especially attractive are the rhythmic flow and the instrumental punctuations given the letter writer's message.

In the 1950s, Partch united music with theater, one of the first attempts a setting of Sophocle's *Oedipus*, premiered in 1952. Reviews were mixed. One of two critics thought Partch had enhanced the tragic conflict; others found the music silly and grating. In the same year came *Castor and Pollux*, "a dance for the twin rhythms of Gemini." The story is told through paired instruments and Chinese-like music. Repetitious rhythms, timbres, and phrase patterns foreshadow the minimalist styles of the 1970s. Three years later, he wrote *The Bewitched*, modeling it on the Japanese Kabuki Theater's *Noh* play. Combined are wit, whimsy, satire, and bawdiness. The work is also "primitive," in that it accepts "magic as real," says Partch, and expresses "tribal unity." In two scenes, he uses a chant of the Cahuilla Indians of California. Each episode is a surrealistic vision—incantations, screams, chanting, and talking are heard. Strong rhythmic propulsions keep the music moving. Fantastic juxtapositions characterize the sound.

Throughout his lifetime, Partch was a loner. Not until the late 1960s did he come to general notice. His was a unique voice. Because the music was so dependent on Partch's personal coaching to make it sound authentic, every year that has gone by since Partch's death has increased the problems of performance. Recordings are only an inadequate historical documentation of what he created.

John Canady once made an observation applicable to Partch, as well as to George Crumb, although Crumb's style is dissimilar. Canady said that he found some artists practicing magic, like the caveman artists. As necromancers, they took heed of the ancient function of art as the creation of magic symbols through which man relates himself to his environment. Symbols did help in examining a contemporary problem—how to stay sane in an environment where science explained everything to the intellect yet left the spirit baffled. Regrettably, no vocabulary of magic symbols existed any longer, Canady said, so artists' symbols often remained private and unintelligible to the public. He was uncertain if creative people interested in magic were merely capitalizing on a new set of textures, curious forms, and novelties in order to win "the kind of cocktail-success that endures only as long as it titillates." Were these artists really hoping, he wondered, "to meet at least half way a public that so far has been asked to make all the concessions ?"[7]

Crumb had something to say about his belief in magic and nothing to say about meeting anyone halfway. Music to him was endowed with magical properties. Substantially real and mechanistically analyzable, it yet eluded a description of its true nature, which touched on the spiritual, the psychological, and the metaphysical. He was convinced intuitively that music "must have been the prime cell from which language, science, and religion originated."[8] Crumb knew about Cowell's and Cage's innovations. The delicate atmospheric colorations of Debussy, the speech-song of Schoenberg, the twittering night sounds of Bartók, the wistful use that Mahler made of popular tunes, the transparent chromaticism of Webern, and the unusually strange effects available through electronics were also influences on his music. He liked simple designs like variation and song form.[9]

An unusual sort of virtuosity was required of both instrumentalists and singers. For example, Jan De Gaetani has said that Crumb's music represents its own kind of difficulties. "There's one piece where you have to sing into the piano, and still keep your sense of pitch despite all those billowing, bewildering harmonics; and you get a similar problem when he has you singing along with a mandolin that is not properly tuned. There are all sorts of contemporary singing devices in his music—clicking the tongue, rolling r's and what all—but for the most part it's just pure singing. . . ."[10]

Crumb built musical scenes by summoning up a wealth of subjective and sensuous sensations. The results were sufficiently attractive to win over listeners from the musical left and right throughout the late 1960s and into the 1970s. At the beginning of the 1960s he discovered the poetry of Federico Garcia Lorca and wanted to translate Lorca's powerful images of death, loss, and mystery into music. Composing *Night Music I* in 1963, first as an instrumental piece, he found that its parts refused to make a whole until he added verses by Lorca. The result was a work for soprano, piano–celesta, and percussion. The voice employs speech-song in the poems *La Luna Asoma* ("The Moon Rises") and *Gacela de la Terrible Presencia* ("Gacela of the Terrible Presence"). Highly chromatic music is heard through unusual resonances, rhythms, and melodic ranges. Ornamented motivic passages are set against loosely ordered free-fantasy passages. Hard-felt mallets strike the piano's strings; or a resonating gong is slowly dipped in and out of a tub of water. The sounds take on an eery quality.

Eleven Echoes of Autumn is for flute, clarinet, violin, and piano. Each "echo" explores a single resonance. For example, the second echo combines violin harmonics with seventh-partial tones of the piano, produced by rubbing a small block of hard rubber on the strings. The fourth echo is based on sympathetic vibrations—the alto flute and clarinet playing onto the piano's strings. The final echo features a violin played with a slack bow to produce a melancholic effect. Epigrammatic passages follow one upon the other, building in intensity to the eighth echo, before gradually fading away to silence.

Crumb's own comments are a helpful introduction to *Echoes of Time and the River* (1967): "I think that for every composer there's a natural acoustic which he inherits. If you come from Kansas, you have a certain acoustic in your ear. If you come from Charleston, West Virginia [Crumb's birthplace], located in a river valley with sizable hills around—that's an altogether different acoustic. This must influence a person in very subtle ways, but I think it's in my music. An echoing quality, or an interest in very long sounds, haunting sounds, sounds that don't want to die; this is all part of an inherited acoustic, I think." He then goes on to say that also in his ear were the hymns, revival songs, and popular music he heard while he grew up.[11]

This orchestral suite consists of four "processionals," which are meant to have aural and visual impact. They are linked neither to Thomas Wolfe's writings nor to a program. Each processional is a metaphor expressing "qualities of metaphysical and psychological time." The river of time, an ancient metaphor, stands for the continuous passage of time, with neither beginning or end. Crumb asks for the ritualistic marching of percussionists and wind players, who perform as they move. Three mottos, whispered or shouted by the players, add an enigmatic dimension to the music: "*montani semper liberi*" ("mountaineers are always free"), the motto

of West Virginia; "*los arcos rotos donde sufre el tiempo*" ("the broken
arches where time suffers"), from a Lorca poem; and "*krek-tu-
dai*," a phonetic invention of Crumb. Writing about the work's
reception in Chicago, Donal Henahan heard boos amidst an enthusiastic ovation. Although many enjoyed the delicate sonorities,
the musically trained audience was split down the middle about
the composition. Some rejected it completely as gimmickry that
could topple the already shaky structure of tradition.[12]

   Black Angels (Thirteen Images from the Dark Land), finished "*in
tempore belli*" (1970), expresses fright and fury over the murder of
innocence and longs for faith and connection with the past. Sym-
bolically, these are represented by the fundamental opposition of
the Devil and God, and by the soul's fall from grace, spiritual
annihilation, and redemption. Written for an electrified string
quartet, the effects are nightmarish. Schubert's *Death and the Maiden*
melody floats in and out; also, the plainchant "Dies Irae." Bowing
takes place on the underside of the strings. Trills are executed with
thimbles on the fingers. At times, the players perform on mara-
cas, tam-tams, and water-tuned glasses. Weird is the whirring,
ghostly fluttering of wings in "Night of the Electric Insects." The
listener remains in the grip of a bleak and terrifying vision from
which he struggles to free himself. The Devil and the damned,
not redemption and the saved, dominate the work.

   In the summer of the same year he composed an impressive
work, *Ancient Voices of Children*, a cycle of songs to Lorca's poetry, for mezzo-soprano, boy-soprano, oboe, mandolin, harp,
electric piano, and percussion. In the introduction to the C. F.
Peters score, Crumb says he was taken over by the powerful,
haunting imagery of life, death, love, the smell of earth, and the
sounds of wind and sea, stated in primitive and stark language.
Flamenco, Arabic music, Bach's "*Bist du bei mir*" and Mahler's
despairing "Der Abscheid," from *Das Lied von der Erde*, are heard.
Drama, passion, and subtle emotional inflections prevail. A woman
trembling and alone searches for a lost child, her search stated in
song and solemn dances. Her final words beg Christ the Lord to
give back one's ancient soul of a child. The child, heard offstage,
joins the mature singer at the end, to symbolize the giving back.
The composition is indeed moving.

   Later pieces continued to mine the vein uncovered in *Echoes,*

Black Angels, and *Ancient Voices*. Of the many compositions Crumb has written, two stand out as his finest efforts—*Echoes of Time and the River* and *Ancient Voices of Children*. The remainder can seem too mannered to listeners. The death-preoccupied moods and the similar way every work reveals itself do produce a sensation of *déjà vù* and a desire for expressive variety.

Born in Los Angeles, Morton Subotnick started off as a serialist, then, after 1960, turned to multimedia and electronics. As with Crumb, a fanciful imagination directs his creativity. *Play! 4* (1966) was a multimedia composition using chance, theater, films, and games. The next year, he put together two tape compositions for Nonesuch Records, titled *The Wild Bull* and *Silver Apples of the Moon*, whose recondite sounds addressed a limited audience. Indeed, according to Subotnick's admirer, Richard Norton, the composer chose to ignore the general audience, his experience being a private one to be shared with a few appreciators.[13] The traditional listener is apt to hear pops, tweets, clucks, and other noises follow each other as if in response to an interior monologue. Every now and again, in the latter work, a vaguely Eastern melodic phrase breaks in.

In the 1970s he wrote compositions for live performers. Sound was fed into an electronic synthesizer. There, a "ghost score" (a digital control system), which is never heard, altered the sound. After Subotnick's "ghost score" reshapes the music, it comes over the loudspeakers in novel configurations. Some "ghost" compositions are *Before the Butterfly, Liquid Strata, The Wild Beasts, A Sky of Cloudless Sulphur, Parallel Lines, The First Dream of Light, Axolotl*, and a series of works, first appearing in 1981, titled *The Double Life of Amphibians*. Some auditors, like Alfred Frankenstein and Richard Norton, sense profound realizations of the stated program; others, like Donal Henahan, find recognizable structures. The problem is to get more than a few listeners to agree with Frankenstein and Henahan.

THE EAST

Borrowing the music of exotic cultures has a history going back to Mozart and his Turkishisms, and proceeding from one romantic composer to another to the twentieth century. These borrowings added piquancy to an already established style. On the other hand, several composers in the postwar years immersed themselves so totally in one or more exotic cultures that their pieces greatly modify the characteristics of Western music.[14]

The move to identify with other, especially Eastern, cultures received a strong impetus in 1889, when an Indonesian gamelan (an instrumental ensemble made up mostly of chimes, gongs, other hammer-struck metal objects, and drums) was brought to the West to play at the Paris International Exhibition. Debussy, for one, was fascinated by the sound. Soon the Far East influenced the subject or the music of compositions by quite a few composers—Puccini, Stravinsky, and Bartók, among them. By the 1950s, some Netherlands musicians were performing on Indonesian gamelans. In the United States, Henry Cowell and Colin McPhee showed this fascination with the East. In fact, from 1934 to 1939, McPhee lived in Bali, studied its music, and wrote his seminal *Tabuh-Tabuhan* for orchestra in 1936 and his *Balinese Ceremonial Music* for flute and two pianos in 1942. Also, Mantle Hood and faculty at the University of California at Los Angeles began reproducing the music of the East in performance. The stage was set for certain of the postwar composers to start where McPhee had left off and Hood was pointing. As with so many other aspects of postwar music, Cage in his early work for percussion ensembles and for prepared piano had begun to explore the Eastern musical ambiance. Moreover, his writings and talks extolling Zen Buddhism had an influence on younger composers.

Eastern music tended to be purely melodic, limited in range, and based on modes, which were not simply scalar structures but traditional ways of grouping notes. Each mode had certain melodic phrases associated with it that distinguished it musically and expressively from other modes. Performers played either compositions or improvisations based on these characteristic phrases. Far Eastern musical cultures preferred some form of pentatonic spacing of intervals, with microtonal ornamentation. In Japan, a melody might have similarities to the Western Lydian or Dorian modes, though whole-tone intervals were the most commonly heard. From India to the Mediterranean, however, highly ornamented, microtonally inflected equivalencies to the ancient Western church modes could be heard. Instead of harmonizing with each other, most

Eastern musicians engaged in a free heterophony—that is to say, two or more players simultaneously played variations on the same melody, the higher pitched instruments moving faster than the lower ones. A persistent low-toned drone was frequent. Sometimes parallel fourths or fifths sounded. Rhythm might be free, percussive sounds used to punctuate the end of melodic phrases; or steady, especially in dance, with a constant pulse and several superimposed rhythmic patterns heard at the same time. Throughout Asia, plucked string instruments and a variety of tuned and untuned percussive instruments were favored. In addition, an instrument from the flute or double-reed family was often added. When a string instrument was bowed, the bow's hairs were usually slack, producing softer, less brilliant tones than those of the violin. Indeed, dynamics were normally quiet. The one distinction between soft and loud was that between indoor and outdoor performance—the latter often resorting to the more assertive instruments. When the American composers turned to the East, they wished to share in the openness and sensitivity to aesthetic beauty that seemed a part of Asian musical culture.[15]

In most cases, although an American composer consorted with Asians and visited the East, he chose to live and work in the West. He remained, in short, an American. This was true for Alan Hovhaness, who was born to an Armenian father and Scottish mother in 1911. It was his Armenian cultural heritage that he first concentrated on understanding and absorbing. From Armenian musical practices he derived his own style, one owing little to any contemporary fashion. At nineteen years of age, he was asked if he would like a scholarship to travel to Paris and study with Nadia Boulanger. "I said no. I felt I didn't want to be a part of contemporary music. I didn't want to be a part of this very intellectual approach. A very cold approach, I felt." Soon he won the admiration of a considerable international following, attracted by what it perceived as his music's profound and simple beauty. Hovhaness himself said: "The greater the emotional intensity, the greater the simplicity. This is not intellectual music, but music of pure feeling."[16]

He wished to picture the universal and the melodic. He rejected serialism and atonality as unnatural and coreless: "The reason I liked Oriental music is that everything has a firm center. All music with a center is tonal." He preferred just intonation, "the scale of nature," to the tempered chromatic scale, because humans unconsciously used it when left to their own devices. He knew true simplicity, though the key to beautiful sound, was hard to achieve. Nevertheless, a work of excellence had to remove all adornments, the essence alone remaining.[17]

In 1959, he traveled to Asia and studied Indian, Chinese, Korean, and Japanese music. Returning to the United States, he described the music that gave him pleasure as: "Seventh Century Armenian religious music, classic music of South India, Chinese orchestra music of the Tang dynasty, Ah-ak music of Korea, gagaku of Japan, and the opera-oratorios of Handel."[18]

Four attractive songs, composed in the 1940s and recorded on Poseidon 1008, demonstrate his fondness for Armenian-like, but nevertheless original, melody of limited range. Melody is an entity in itself, the accompaniment not essential to its existence. Simplicity, repetition of a limited number of phrases, the creation of mood with spare brushstrokes of sound, and an unobtrusive exoticism characterize the music. Hovhaness, in the liner notes, describes the first song, "Gurge Dikran," as "an inconsequential tale about a horse and carriage ride to an unimportant place." For almost the entire song, the music remains in a "white-key" diatonic Dorian mode. Heard are infinitely varied statements and restatements of brief, narrow-ranged melodic patterns. The vocalist's tune is delightful; the setting graceful and airy; and the sentiment refreshingly unburdened with weighty meaning.

The second song, "Gantznin Orern," describes how the "days pass in pain and love for my beloved," a common subject in Mideastern songs. The piano imitates an oriental lute. The sensuous cantillation describing the ruinous passage of time and the separation of lovers sounds fresh and affecting. The third is a dance song, "Dulhey, Dulhey," on the words: "There is singing under the willow tree; but I shall pick apples. Come, take!" Entirely in the diatonic Aeolian mode, the music is sprightly, strophic, and rhythmic. Flutelike melody in the pianist's right hand sings with the voice. The last song, "Ararat," sets the words: "Old dome of Ararat, centuries have come like seconds and passed." Unmeasured, contemplative melody, and organumlike accompaniment create a sense of timelessness.

A culminating work of this early, mostly Armenian-centered period is the Symphony No. 9 (*"Saint Vartan"*), composed 1949–50. It contains twenty-four movements, each under two minutes long, some dignified in tone, others energetic, dancing, and canonic. Included are solemn chants intoned usually by a solo trombone or trumpet, processionals featuring the brass section, lyric "arias" for the strings, and dances (sometimes titled "estampies") whose sound varies from the Oriental to the medieval. The admirable instrumental writing gives the impression of a rich, colorful sonic tapestry, sometimes gay, sad, impassioned, ritualistic, or mystical.

In 1955, Stokowski and the Houston Symphony gave the premiere performance of one of his most well received compositions, *Mysterious Mountain*. The music sounds unlabored, serene, and warmly human. A resonant chorale opens the first movement; a faster middle section features woodwind solos with harp and celeste in the background; then the movement closes on the chorale. The second movement starts softly with a fugue in the strings; next comes a sudden change to a fast tempo, where quicksilver strings play unusual cascades of notes; brasses then intone a chorale accompanied by the swiftly moving strings; and the close brings in the full orchestra on the chorale. The last movement is to be played slowly and expressively. Cast in ternary form, it returns to the earnest and serene hymning heard in the first movement.

Hovhaness was also repeating himself. Though compositions like *And God Created Whales* (with its gimmicky whale "songs"), are superficially attractive, they can prove tiresome when heard several times. The same must be said of some of the works incorporating non-Armenian Easternisms—the *Fantasy on Japanese Woodprints, Fuji, The Rubaiyat of Omar Khayyam,* and *To Vishnu.*

The several symphonies written in the 1970s are usually less interesting than his music from the 1940s and 1950s. The songs of these years are pleasant enough, but the mannerisms are obtrusive, the simplicities overdone. Hovhaness has been an overly prolific composer. Nevertheless, at its best, his music is individual, effective, and communicative. More than a few music lovers have been enthusiastic about the sounds he makes.

Lou Harrison, born in Oregon, grew up in California. Early in his career, he felt the contradictory influences of Cowell's and Cage's experiments with percussive sounds and of Schoenberg's serialism. He also grew familiar with Partch's music and his ideas about just intonation. The *Symphony on G*, written between 1947 and 1954, with a new finale added in 1966, was a work constructed on serial principles but centered on the tone G. The piece was more colorful, perceptibly connected, and recognizably more lyric than most serial works. The adventurous listener may well be attracted by its romantic character.

From 1961 to 1962, Harrison journeyed to Japan, Korea, and Taiwan in order to study the music of these countries. *Novo Odo*, for chorus, Oriental instruments, and orchestra soon followed as a protest against nuclear war. He also completed *Pacifika Rondo*, for Oriental instruments and orchestra, a protest against the atomic bomb and its destructive effect on the Pacific.

Lou Harrison's leaning toward the music of Indonesia was already evident in the gamelanlike sounds and rhythms of the Suite for Violin, Piano and Small Orchestra of 1951 and in the *Concerto in Slendro* for violin, celesta, and percussion of 1961. In the 1970s, he wrote several compositions that were more obviously the result of his research into Indonesian music. Among them, *La Koro Sutro*, for chorus and gamelan, and the Suite for violin and gamelan, come to mind.

Three of the four compositions written in 1978 and 1979 require an Indonesian gamelan ensemble for their performance. *Main Bersama-Sama* was composed for the Gamelan Sekar Kembar (a matched bronze gamelan imported from western Java and to be played on by eleven musicians), a French horn whose valves are set in a special pattern in order to reproduce the gamelan's tuning, and a *suling* (flute). The piece begins on the percussive gamelan sounds. Shortly the flute enters, then the horn. Each soloist repeatedly plays a limited number of melodic phrases, either exactly or in slight variation, to the rhythmic-melodic accompaniment of the gamelan. The *Threnody for Carlos Chavez* is written for the same gamelan and a viola. Harrison says he had in mind music expressed in an eight-layered European medieval rhythmic mode over a single maxima, entirely in triple (perfectum) divisions. He claims that the approach has its counterpart in Javanese music. Slow, dignified gamelan sounds accompany the lyric lines of the viola, whose tune is similar to that of the previous work. (Both compositions, of course, are limited to the tones available to the Gamelan Sekar Kembar).

The *Serenade* for Betty Freeman and Franco Assetto, for the Gamelan Sekar Kembar and *suling*, is cast in a lyric style "normal to the Gamelan Degung of West Java." As with his other pieces, the tones, melodies, limited instrumental colorations, and repetitions produce a static and somewhat plain effect, monotonous yet pleasant and easily graspable.

Like Hovhaness, Lou Harrison tried to bridge the space separating East from West. Both composers synthesized exotic and Western styles in compositions that without apology or self-consciousness feature gratifying melody. If at times their music seems one-dimensional and lacking in variety, it can also bewitch the ear when heard buffered by other composers' compositions written in contrasting styles. They are not the only composers inspired by the East. But they are among the few who thus inspired also give pleasure to the general listener.

MINIMAL MUSIC

Minimalism in art had been practiced in the early part of the century by artists like Marcel Duchamp and Piet Mondrian and the composer Erik Satie. The term "minimal art," however, waited for Richard Wollheim to invent it in 1965, applying it to works of negligible artistic substance, as in the Readymades of Duchamp. In music, minimalism meant essentially a work thought of as an object, whose surface melodic-rhythmic patterns and the relation of these patterns to the beginning, continuation, and end of a composition are of the greatest importance. Meaning derives from the connection of these patterns to the composition as a whole. Normally, a minimal piece makes do with a limited number of ideas endlessly repeated and imperceptibly altered. Absent is a sense of progression and rhetorical contrast.[19]

During the postwar years, practitioners of minimal art in painting and sculpture included Frank Stella, Donald Judd, and Ellsworth Kelly. Amongst musicians, four loomed importantly—La Monte Young, Terry Riley, Steve Reich, and Philip Glass. Precedents for these composers had been established during the 1940s and 1950s by Cage, Partch, and Hovhaness, both in the music they wrote and in their East-facing perspective.

La Monte Young, though born in Idaho, grew up and received much of his musical training in California. In 1963 he married the artist–illustrator Marian Zazeela and with her performed a number of "Sound/Light Environments." By the beginning of the 1970s, he had become a follower of Pandit Pran Nath, an Indian musician. He visited India for a while in order to school himself in Indian philosophical and musical ways.

Creative eccentricity was revealed in *Composition 1960 #2*, which directs that a fire be started in front of the audience; in *Composition 1960 #7*, where the performance requires that the tones *B* and *F*-sharp "be held for a long time"; and *Composition 1960 #13*, whose score consists of the words "play anything you like." His composition of 1962, *The Second Dream of the High-Tension Line Stepdown Transformer* centers on a continuously sounding chord: *G, C, C*-sharp, *D*. Two years later, Young conceived *The Tortoise, His Dreams and Journeys*, a very long work, sections of which were to be performed on successive days. Sustained tones and harmonies chosen from frequencies related to a common fundamental were sounded by motors, musical instruments, and voices. The sounds were amplified to painful levels. At the same time, the room was lit up by projections of Marian Zazeela's calligraphic light art. Young's intention was to have stationary sounds represent themselves alone and not to become shapes determined by human will.[20]

La Monte Young's *Dream House* was presented at New York's The Kitchen in 1974. It avoids dissonance, climax, variety in mood, and any sense of direction in order to express motionless, static, meditative, and mystical existence. Sine-wave generators, voices, and musical instruments sustained drone tones, while Young's and his wife's voices improvised after the Indian-style singing of Pandit Pran Nath, sliding between three or four notes without articulating words. The expected light show, conceived by Marian Zazeela, helped achieve the effect that Young desired. Why the prolonged tones? To provide an experience that seems endless, said Young. His assumption, of course, was that whoever came would have a liking for meditation and a willingness to absorb India-induced influences. Although he did have an impact on other avant-garde composers and on listeners, usually youthful, who had a countercultural mind set, the sameness of his music found few enthusiasts in the general audience.

Terry Riley, born in California, was also a disciple of Pandit Pran Nath, introduced to him by La Monte Young, and also a temporary resident in India. In 1964 he made a tremendous splash in avant-garde waters with his *In C*, often described as the first truly minimalist composition. The score is performable by any number of musicians on any instruments of their choosing. A basic piano part provides a pulse beat of steadily repeated eighth notes playing octave *C*'s for as long as the performance lasts. Every instrumentalist is asked to play the fifty-three figures given in the score in agreement with the pulse, proceeding in sequence from the first to the fifty-third figure. How long a figure is repeated, where the accents are placed, and when silences are introduced is decided independently by each player. The performance is completed when the last player finishes playing the last figure. The slow change from one figure to another, the constant overlapping of several figures heard simultaneously, and the persistent diatonicism focusing on one tone have proved hypnotic to some, abhorrent to others.

Predictably, the California writer on music Alfred Frankenstein proclaimed it a definitive masterpiece of the twentieth century: "It is probably the most important piece of music since Boulez's *Marteau sans maitre*; conceivably it is the most important since the *Sacre*. For it defines a new aesthetic and a most important one." He admits the repetitions numb the senses but claims the subtlest changes take on monumental meaning. "The hearer is thrown into a kind of trance and at the same time is made infinitely more alert than ever before to what sound is all about."[21] Similar virtues would be discovered in the music of Steve Reich and Philip Glass.

Harold Schonberg reports that once he attended a Lukas Foss–directed concert at Carnegie Recital Hall, where he sat through a sixty-seven minute work by La Monte Young and was grateful when it was over. Then came Terry Riley's *Kundalini Dervish*— "A Primeval Dance in which the Participants Try to Shake the Snakes," according to the program notes. This piece lasted ninety-eight minutes. Young's composition was one loud amplified note with occasional interjections by dimly seen performers. Riley's piece was also one loud note, stated as a drone bass to which some doodles from the woodwinds were added. The shadowy hall reverberated at ear-spliting levels with the sound even as an accomplice saturated the air with burning incense. "People walked in, blanched, stood it for a while, and walked out. . . . Lukas Foss, the impressario of the concerts, was in and out. He said that he could not take too much of it, either."[22]

Shri Camel premiered in 1976. The composer describes it as his "most concentrated work yet" and "some of the finest and most inspired moments I have ever felt in a studio." A modern electronic organ (a Yamaha YC-45D), tuned in just intonation and modified by a computerized digital-delay system, is played on by Riley. This permits him to play two and three parts against the solo line. The music, in which very little seems to happen, stems from North Indian raga singing. Riley's devotees praise the trancelike states it induces in them.[23]

The composers most strongly impressed on the minds of audiences, both in the United States and abroad, as minimalists are Steve Reich and Philip Glass. Both men take for granted an awareness of, and a responsiveness toward, music in their listeners that is entirely different from the reactions found in the usual art-music audience. To at least some degree, they demonstrate a susceptibility to the philosophy and sounds of the East. Thus, music however simple is to be meditated upon and appreciated through a recognition of the intricacies and the shadings in meaning found within the most abbreviated of musical ideas. This viewpoint rejects the reasoned intellectualism of serialism and the disintegrative structures of indeterminacy.

Robert Jones, a former *Times* critic, after making a study of the two composers, wrote: "Glass's cultural influences are Indian and North African, Reich's are Jewish and Balinese (also, he's crazy about canons). Both men use static harmonies, repetition, modular construction, and phase shifting, and neither writes music with the narrative quality of 'normal' Western music. Reich's music is generally delicate in texture and sensuous in sound, while Glass's is more dramatic and sometimes downright scary in its violently driven quality. Glass aims his music at the stage [this was written in 1983, after Glass had devoted his energies to the writing of several operas], Reich thinks solely of concert performance. Both composers share an enormous audience."[24] Repetition, of course, is basic to their styles, as is the use of no more than a handful of readily absorbed motives in any given composition. During the late 1960s and early 1970s, their followers related the sound of Reich and Glass to their own reactions to it by describing it as "trance music," thus connecting the two to Young and Riley.

The music of both composers first was heard in New York around 1967, in Village performances. Two years later, it was presented at the Whitney Museum, during an Anti-illusion Show, which was focused on emerging artists, among them Serra, Le Witt, and Naumann. Indeed, at the beginning of their careers, Reich and Glass won the support of contemporary artists before being taken seriously by performers and other composers. For example, Richard Serra stated: "Sculptors got involved with the manipulation of space in relation to a process. Phil and Steve do the same things with time. You start with structures, which at least avoids arbitrariness, but you end up with something new and unexpected, which is the art of it. The extraordinary thing for me is that the music is built on structures that create something other than the raw elements that are being organized. The result is an experience, a potential for joy, unlike anything else, and we happen to call it music."[25]

Eastern input and artistic approbation alone would not have won the large, mostly youthful, following that soon clustered around minimalism. Young people were attracted by minimal music's kinship to rock music—its vigor, its forceful physical activity, its strong and steady pulse, its brightness of sound, its concentration on brief, assimilable units of material, and its presentation of this material free of artistic pretense.

There continued to be adverse criticism. Asked about Reich's and Glass's minimalism, Aaron Copland replied in 1981: "It basically seems dull to me. I can't imagine staying interested in repeated long stretches of time unless you're looking for some kind of mesmerization that will work on you without really paying attention to what it is that's putting you to sleep, or whatever it's supposed to be doing to you."[26] Donal Henahan felt that minimalism sounded like "the old complex music turned upside down. One tiresome extreme had bred another." He refused to choose sides "between dreary academic clichés and the new waves' glassy-eyed simplicities."[27]

One of the more thoughtful criticisms has come from David Owens. Writing in the *Christian Science Monitor*, in 1983, he said that, yes, the young were attracted to Reich and Glass, whose ensembles seemed to close the rift between art and popular music. But Owens wondered if minimal music wasn't really popular culture. No matter how much these composers maintained they were mainly Western, their minimal music had more to do with Eastern views. "The syntactical, the connotive, and the individually redemptive belong to the Western ideal; the hypnotic, the non-confrontational, and the cancelling of a Western sense of musical cognition, belong to the Eastern." Minimalism is "about consciousness, about getting in touch with basic feelings, about transcending to more refined levels of experience. At some point, though, art music in this milieu is going to have to try . . . to be *about itself*, and not anything else. To have its own, intact, memorable, aurally engaging reasons for existing—and for being returned to." Works popular for being "about other things" will not win the permanent affection of audiences.[28]

In Steve Reich's minimal music can be heard traces of twelfth-century organum, baroque motor rhythms, propulsive block-chordal movement after Stravinsky, Bartókian figuration, and a jazzlike complex of several simultaneously sounding phrase patterns. In addition, Hebraic chant, West African drumming and Balinese gamelan practices affect his music, although he himself has claimed no interest in improvisation or in imitating exotic sounds. Reich asserts: "One can create a music with one's own sound that is constructed in the light of one's knowledge of non-Western structures. . . . Instead of imitation, the influence of non-Western musical structures on the thinking of a Western composer" like himself "can produce something genuinely new."[29]

When compositional process and sounding music unite, Reich has further stated, the listener senses the impersonality of the process and the unanticipated psychoacoustic by-products that result. These by-products may include submelodies heard when melodic patterns are repeated, stereophonic effects depending on where the listener sits, and small differences resulting from different performances, or the sounding of different harmonics and tones. "While performing and listening to gradual musical processes," Reich states, "one can participate in a particular liberating and impersonal kind of ritual. Focusing in on the musical process makes possible that shift of attention away from *he* and *she* and *you* and *me* outwards towards *it*."[30]

The music of his friend La Monte Young is stationary. In contrast, Reich's music changes gradually from within (sometimes so gradually the listener does not perceive the changes taking place). A work contains a small amount of material played repeatedly by several musicians. They begin together, then go slightly out of phase with one another, thus producing constantly new configurations and producing new melodic and rhythmic patterns. In 1964 while working with Terry Riley, he wrote one of his first minimalist pieces, *It's Gonna Rain*, a speech-tape composition consisting of only the three words of the title heard on tape loops that go in and out of phase. Two years later, he wrote *Come Out*, another speech-tape composition on the words "come out to show them," taken from a description of a beating received by the speaker in Harlem's twenty-eighth precinct. The recorded phrase is first heard in unison on all channels. Then the second channel slowly moves ahead and goes out of phase with the first. Later the two statements of the one voice becomes four, then eight, simultaneously sounding but noncoinciding statements. The composition begins as if a needle has stuck in the groove of a recording. Little by little, however, as the voices multiply and go out of phase with each other, the listener loses all awareness that it is a voice being heard and is aware only of unintelligible sounds. After ten minutes, the piece chugs like a Rube Goldberg engine that is roughly humming along. In 1967 Reich applied his in-and-out phase technique to music from a musical instrument, *Violin Phase*.

He formed an ensemble in 1966 whose sole function was to perform his own compositions. By 1971, this ensemble had grown to include twelve musicians, and his activities had shifted to the New York area. In three works written during the early 1970s—*Drumming*, *Six Pianos*, and *Music for Mallet Instruments, Voices, and Organ*, stylistic procedures are similar to the ones described. By 1976 and *Music for 18 Musicians*, he was writing more colorful and varied works—albeit loud, bright, percussive, rhythmic, and repetitive overall. The phase shifts in the musical materials were combined with timbral shifts from one instrumental group, with or without voices, to another group. Major changes in coloration marked off sections. Recognizable triadic chord sequences were also involved in the repetitions and the sectional demarcations. All instruments were acoustical ones. The use of electronics was limited to the placement of microphones before the musicians and the sending of the sound over loudspeakers. The work attracted a growing audience, most of it crossing over from rock.

Music for a Large Ensemble was commissioned by the Holland Festival and premiered in June 1979. (Both he and Glass are among the very few American composers to receive European commissions for new works.) The piece called for the largest forces he had ever used up until that time, including all of the orchestral families, plus women's voices, whose sounds were amplified by means of microphones.

The *Octet* (1979), commissioned by Radio Frankfurt, calls for string quartet, two pianos, and two clarinets doubling on bass clarinet, flute, and piccolo. The first and third of its five sections resemble each other, as do the second and fourth sections. The last section combines all of the material previously heard. Reich's interest in "melodic lines, composed of shorter patterns strung together" had roots in *Music for a Large Ensemble* and in the chanting of the Hebrew scriptures. The piece holds the interest more than do his earlier compositions. Contrasts are stronger; sounds are more varied; some richness relieves the normally spare and wiry lines. It was performed to sold-out houses in New York.

Reich's ability to appeal to an ever-growing number of listeners, not all of them necessarily youthful, is exemplified in the reception given his *Tehillim* in 1982. The title is the Hebrew word for psalms. Passages from the psalms are scored for four female voices, accompanied by four tambourines without jingles, string quintet, two electric organs, six woodwinds, and percussion. A later arrangement for voices and orchestra is not nearly as effective. The music is joyous and exalted.

Philip Glass was even more a painter's composer than Reich, having befriended Sol Le Witt, Donald Judd, and Richard Serra, who were exploring their own minimalist pathways. He was also a composer of harder, more rock-related music than Reich was. In fact, Glass was connected with the New Wave and Art Rock movements in popular music. Among his teachers were La Monte Young and Terry Riley. Later, under the Indian sitar player Ravi

Shankar and another Indian, Alla Rakha, he studied Indian ideas and music, finding attractive the Indian propensity for repetition of brief melodic-rhythmic cells (the tones in his own music would normally be based on triadic relationships) and the building of total structures based on these cells.

Glass, like Reich, formed his own ensemble in order to do justice to his music. The performing group of 1967 numbered seven people: three saxophone/flute players, three electric organ players, and one electronics-sound person. Three important works from this period are *Music in Fifths*, *Music in Contrary Motion*, and *Music in Similar Motion*. Harmony and counterpoint are absent from these works. *Music in Fifths* demonstrates Glass's style of around 1970— a simple line, consisting of two phrases a fifth apart, is played rhythmically and in unison by the entire ensemble and then repeated several times. When Glass felt ready to proceed to something else, he cued the players to take up the next section. Here, a few extra notes were added to the first line. Again there was repetition, until Glass signaled the change to the next section. Until the end, each ensuing section involved the expansion or contraction of the initial line played in unison.

The territory marked off by these early pieces was further explored during the 1970s, in *Music with Changing Parts*, *Music for Voices*, and *Music in Twelve Parts*. In the last work are rock rhythms, negligible melodies, static harmonies, and repetitions of certain designated sonorities. Usually loud, energetic, and featuring a strong pulse, the work can go on for six hours. On the whole, we find that where Reich concentrated on a phase music that involved the unison statement of a line, then each player repeating the line but slowly going out of and into synchronization with the other players, Glass concentrated on an additive approach that involved the unison statement of a line, then all the players continuing in unison but adding to or subtracting notes from the original line.

With *Einstein on the Beach* in 1976, Glass turned to musical theater. This opera had next to no plot. In fact, Glass spurned the attitude that an opera had to have musical themes, which were then to be developed, or that it had to be a play with connected narrative. As for plot, he said, his experience in theater was in the recent tradition of nonliterary theater, "the kind of work with which Robert Wilson, the Mabou Mimes, Richard Foreman and Meredith Monk are involved; and, of course, the godfather of it all was the Living Theater, which I remember seeing back in 1957." These people draw their inspiration not from texts but from ideas, drawings, poems, or images. "It would never occur to them to hire an author or work from a script."[31]

Einstein on the Beach, written in collaboration with Robert Wilson, is a four-act opera that goes on for almost five hours. Most of the sung and spoken text consists of numerals and sol-fa syllables. Certain visual images, each given its own characteristic music and presented surrealistically, dominate the stage—especially the images of a train, a trial, and a spaceship. No story integrates these images. Splinters of melody, brief chord sequences, and loud and decisive rhythmic patterns recur without end. When the music changes, as it sometimes does and without warning, the listener is startled out of the catatonic state brought on by the repetitions.

After the opera toured Europe, it came to New York and played to sold-out houses. Present were painters, dancers, photographers, filmmakers, and young people—especially the fans of new wave, art-rock, and performance art. Though most regular concertgoers and opera attenders were absent, a cult following was much in evidence. "Its like being stoned on music," said one youth. Replied Glass, "If people think my music is druggy, that's *their* problem. To me, it's just a matter of harmony and rhythm and cycles."[32]

Other operas followed in the 1980s: *Satyagraha*, commissioned by the Netherlands Opera; *The Photographer; Akhnaton*, commissioned by the Stuttgart Opera; and *The Civil Wars*, commissioned by the Rome Opera. All of them were "needle in the groove" compositions. All were greeted with enthusiasm by Glass's large following and with impatience by most of the other people who witnessed them. Several writers on music of excellent reputation have said that they liked Glass's operas. Assuredly, for the first couple of minutes of listening time, the music is viscerally attractive. One notes, however, that a good number of the young people who enjoy Glass's instrumental music are often disappointed by the operas, and those who enjoy the operas are often less enamored of the instrumental compositions. The former came mostly from the rock and disco world; the latter include a large contingent of countercultural ideologues.

A serious question arises, not easy to answer. Since the audience is mostly affianced to rock—and this includes also the artists, dancers, and filmmakers—and not to other forms of art music, when we discuss Glass's music, are we really talking about popular or art music? Does his minimalism really bridge the gap between the two or only seem to do so? His audience, at bottom, is inclined to be an exclusive one, liking what it likes and avoiding everything else. This is the impression I sometimes have when reading a criticism by Sandow in the *Village Voice* or Rockwell in the *New York Times*. Both men praise minimalists, performance artists, and Eastward-yearning composers. What they like they seem to elevate into universals. It leads to an impasse in the reconciliation of different artistic styles just as unfortunate as the impasses produced by the serialists, and the advocates of indeterminacy.

One should add, nevertheless, that along with Hovhaness and Harrison, Steve Reich and Philip Glass have supplied Americans with music far more attractive to a general audience than that of any of the other composers discussed thus far.

NOTES

1. Kathleen Agena, "The Return of Enchantment," *New York Times Magazine*, 27 November 1983, 79–80.

2. Jacob Druckman, "Stating the Case for the 'New Romanticism,' " *Ovation* 3 (June 1983): 44.

3. Agena, "The Return of Enchantment," 80.

4. Ben Johnston, in *Dictionary of Contemporary Composers* (New York: Dutton, 1974) s.v. "Partch, Harry."

5. David Ewen, *American Composers: A Biographical Dictionary* (New York: Putnam's, 1982) s.v. "Johnston, Ben (Benjamin) Burwell."

6. Adrian Corleonis, "Ferruccio Busoni," *Fanfare* 7 (January/February 1984): 109.

7. John Canady, *Embattled Critic* (New York: Farrar, Straus & Cudahy, 1962), 58.

8. Ewen, *American Composers*, s.v. "Crumb, George Henry."

9. Donal Henahan, "Crumb, the Tone Poet," *New York Times Magazine*, 11 May 1975, 17, 56; see also Shirley Fleming, in *Musical America* (September 1968): 5.

10. Jack Hiemenz, "Jan De Gaetani," *Musical America*, (April 1974): 7.

11. Cole Gagne and Tracy Caras, *Soundpieces: Interviews with American Composers* (Metuchen, N.J.: Scarecrow, 1982), 120–21.

12. Donal Henahan, "Current Chronicle: United States, Chicago," *Musical Quarterly* 54 (1968): 84, 87.

13. Richard Norton, "The Vision of Morton Subotnick," *Music Journal* (January 1970): 38, 48.

14. For further discussion of this point, see Gregory Sandow, "A Profound Influence," *Village Voice*, 14 February 1984, 86.

15. See, for example, the comments of Lucia Dlugoszewski in Ewen, *American Composers*, s.v. "Dlugoszewski, Lucia."

16. Peter Westbrook, "Alan Hovhaness, Angelic Cycles," *Downbeat* (March 1982): 27.

17. Gregory Battcock, ed., *Breaking the Sound Barrier: A Critical Anthology of the New Music* (New York: Dutton, 1981), 286.

18. Ibid., 289.

19. Matthew Baigell, *Dictionary of American Art* (New York: Harper & Row, 1979), s.v. "Minimal Art."

20. Christopher Small, *Music, Society, Education* (London: Calder, 1977), 151; John Vinton, ed., *Dictionary of Contemporary Music* (New York: Dutton, 1974), s.v. "Young, La Monte."

21. Alfred Frankenstein, review of Columbia MS 7178, *High Fidelity* 20 (February 1969): 104.

22. Harold C. Schonberg, "Music: Last Loud Word," *New York Times*, 7 May 1969, 37.

23. Hugh Garner, liner notes to CBS M 35164; Edward Strickland, review of CBS M 35164, *Fanfare* (September/October 1980): 185–86.

24. Robert T. Jones, "An Outburst of Minimalism," *Musical America* (February 1983): 26.

25. John Rockwell, "Sound of New Music Is Likened to Art," *New York Times*, 3 January 1973, 48.

26. Alan Hershowitz, "Aaron Copland," *Music Journal* (April 1981): 11.

27. Donal Henahan, "One Tiresome Extreme May Breed Another," *New York Times*, 22 January 1984, sec. 2, 19.

28. David Owens, "Minimal Music: Aptly Named," *Christian Science Monitor*, 20 June 1983, 21.

29. Battcock, ed., *Breaking the Sound Barrier*, 163.

30. Richard Kostelanetz, ed., *Esthetics Contemporary*, (Buffalo, N.Y.: Prometheus, 1978), 301.

31. Allan Kozinn, "Philip Glass," *Ovation* 5 (February 1984): 16.

32. Robert T. Jones, "Philip Glass," *Musical America* (April 1979): 4–5.

6

The Traditional Mainstream

The traditional mainstream comprehends the stylistic characteristics of the great majority of Western artworks that stem from earlier practices. Many of these characteristics can also be found in folk and popular music. It also indicates the ultimate tendencies of some avant-garde composers after they have spent years in divergent experimentation. We are talking about art music that, because of its strong links with the past, has a potential for acceptance by unspecialized listeners. Thus far this music has been tonal, with structures intelligible to the ear of the generality of music lovers. It utilizes some variety of functional harmony and of readily recognizable rhythm and melody. The traditional mainstream represents the preferences of large constituencies of the art-music world, not the specialists but the preponderant American musical society, including most musicians, music lovers, and even composers. It includes the music of past European composers—from Bach to early Stravinsky and late Bartók. It includes a number of past American composers—Gottschalk, Paine, Chadwick, MacDowell, Griffes, and Ives (in works like the Second Symphony). Some recent composers in the traditional mainstream are Moore, Hanson, Barber, Thompson, Gershwin, Creston, Thomson, and Copland in his Americanist period.

Hundreds of American composers of the post–World War II period have continued to write solid compositions that respect and build upon the past and thus facilitate communication with the general audience. Yet they have received far less attention than they have deserved. For one thing, as explained in the first two chapters of this book, the modernists have dominated the publicity about new music. To add to the problem, the general music public, after being damned as philistine and force fed works it finds incomprehensible, has become hostile to anything new. Still another problem is the dominant position within the mainstream musical society of European born and trained conductors, instrumental soloists, and opera singers whose sympathies do not lie with American music, and of managers and board members whose orientation is anything but American.

Many mainstream composers insist that they were denied most of the performance and support sources theoretically available to all contemporary composers. As Elie Siegmeister writes, the new-music leaders have "persuaded private and governmental sources to grant extensive subsidies for the future of *their* art," not of anybody else's art.[1]

As a case in point, both in 1983 and in 1984, though not a member of the traditional mainstream, Jacob Druckman was put in charge of the *Horizons* festivals in New York City, sponsored by the New York Philharmonic. He announced the new birth of romanticism in contemporary American music, then proceeded to mount the works of nonmainstreamers, composers who had been heard from and rejected by the public over the last thirty-five years. If he had only looked he would have discovered that the neoromanticism he thought was novel had been around all the time.[2] As Gregory Sandow observed in 1983: "Conservatives aren't part of the Philharmonic's festival. They *do* have an audience, though (more people have heard Menotti's *Amahl and the Night Visitors* than all Wuorinen's works combined)—as do radicals like Steve Reich and Philip Glass, who aren't in the festival either, though for a better reason: Druckman says their own ensembles play their music better than the Philharmonic."[3]

One gets the impression that it took integrity for these mainstream composers to keep faith with their own convictions in a climate hostile to everything they believed in. A bitter Siegmeister wrote in 1983 that, although he is a New Yorker, hardly anybody in New York performs his music.[4] Other composers have made similar comments. For example, the composer Jack Gottlieb, who favors tonality and an idiom deriving from American musical theater, has uttered a typical complaint: "The music establishment made me feel I was on the outside since I did not flow with the tide. In fact, some of my music was accused of being too 'Broadway.' But I never understood why this necessarily had to be a critique of opprobrium."[5]

Walter Simmons has written about the proceedings of the contemporary composers' conference sponsored by the YM-YWHA and held in New York City in 1981. He is worth quoting at length about the pressures brought to bear on contemporary thinking by the modernists: "An important corollary that emerged during the course of the proceedings was a revelation of the coerciveness with which the 'traditional' wing of 20th-century music has been suppressed by the academic musical establishment, and the degree to which dissent has been silenced through subtle forms of intimidation. For example, Gregory Sandow, composer and critic for the *Village Voice*, confessed to being unable to admit to himself an admiration for the music of Benjamin Britten until respected academics like Rochberg openly accepted it. And after Samuel Lipman . . . [extolled] the wealth of musical treasures to be discovered among American composers of the generation that produced Hanson, Cowell, Barber, Schuman, and others, Peter G. Davis of the *New York Times* admitted a long-held admiration for these composers that he had been afraid to confess publicly. The intensity of this *de facto* censorship was evident in an incident related by conductor Gerard Schwarz, in which he described being severely ostracized by the contemporary-music ensemble Speculum Musicae, of which he had been a member, when they learned that he had chosen Samuel Barber as recipient of a major commission. Even Arthur Weisberg, conductor of the Contemporary Chamber Ensemble, reportedly claims that he disliked most of the modern works he performed, but was responding to socio-political pressure. With such cowardly submission to a party line rampant, it is no wonder that audiences have become conditioned to an automatic skepticism concerning contemporary music. As Schwarz emphasized, it is foolish to expect audiences to appreciate music presented and performed with feigned conviction. Performers must exercise freedom in selecting contemporary music that they can present with honest pride, and Schwarz knows that there is plenty awaiting discovery and exposure."[6]

THE ATTITUDES AND VALUES OF THE
TRADITIONAL MAINSTREAM COMPOSER

Different artistic expressions reflect different attitudes and values and rest on different premises concerning worth. Therefore, the value systems and premises of one or another body of the avant-garde may be invalid when applied to works of the mainstream composers in order to appraise them and determine their significance. Yet such evaluation has taken place.[7] Because composers with a more traditional Western orientation have often been ill represented in publications concerned with musical matters, I have made a special effort to talk with and write to several of them. What follow are conclusions based on what they have said.

What are the attitudes of most of these composers? First, I note that they do not decry older approaches but follow them, although almost always with changes, sometimes extensive ones. Tradition is not a matter of the past but something living in the present, not frozen but always modified by new circumstances. Therefore, working within a tradition means continuation, adaptation, and renewal. In short, this contemporary music can and, in its better examples, does belong to the present. It is twentieth-century music, even while it honors the past.

These composers have no interest merely in solving problems or seeking innovation for its own sake. They ascribe to intuition a major role in their creative processes and a lesser role to intellectualization and to the realization of philosophical concepts. To start with tradition is the means for exciting the composer, priming his imagination, and making secure his touch. His departures from inherited tradition result from the exigencies of a heightened vision, which the composer lives through, tries to capture in sound, and hopes to communicate to others as his interpretation of a shared inner reality.[8]

The traditional mainstream, by definition, signifies neither right or left veering, but keeping to the wide center of moderation. To veer too much in one direction brings on the danger of second-hand mimicry of the past; to veer in the second direction brings on the danger of self-defeating and possibly sterile practices.[9] Compared to the avant-garde, composers in this mainstream are less eager to explain their theories and analyze their music. The music is meant to speak for itself. Masterliness is not just an intrinsic property of a musical work. It also is a consequence of the empathic reaction of the audience. Whether a conservative musician like Nicolas Flagello or a middle of the roader like Leonard Bernstein or an adventurer like Elie Siegmeister, the mainstream composer regards himself as a humanist whose music is concerned with most men's and women's feelings, their need for life affirmation, their tragic vision, and their yearning for dignity. Flagello, Siegmeister, and Schwantner have tried to capture much of this concern in compositions whose subject is Martin Luther King, Jr. Bernstein writes symphonies that wrestle with questions of evil and the responsibilities of divinity. Colgrass writes one composition affirming primal innocence and another confronting human anomie and offering hope.

Mainstream composers are usually modern romantics but in the wider sense of the term, for they are not only likely to be creators of warm, emotion-inducing sound, but also revolters against the doctrine of originality above everything else, the formality and restrictions imposed by the followers of Babbitt and Carter, and the nihilism of the post-Cageians. It does not matter if the scientific explorer can form no definite connection between specific feelings and specific musical sounds, the mainstream composer premises the existence of such a connection, his listener assumes that it exists, and therefore one writes to elicit and the other listens to be introduced to important human feelings, ranging from extreme sadness to extreme joy. Instruments sing in strains comprehensible to the public. Tones combine in enjoyable resonances. Harmony is to some purpose and makes sense to the ear. The listener can anticipate and perceive the return of primary musical ideas. A grammar and symbolism with antecedents in the past and couched in a tonal language common to composer and general public aids understanding, if not on first hearing, then after only a few hearings. Whatever atonality or indeterminacy is employed, it is, in most instances, introduced judiciously and in a configuration that will not lead to the listener's defeat.

Many composers taken up in this chapter have written compositions that were well received. Nevertheless, they are infrequently heard. Why? Already mentioned was the lack of conviction on the part of foreign conductors and "star" soloists; also the intimidation of new-music performers by the avant-gardists, who have managed to get more than a few mainstream works scrubbed off performance lists. Add another reason, the American enthusiasm for the new and sensational in artistic matters, which affects most judgments of worth. Furthermore, there is the premiere syndrome, where a composition is heard once, for its publicity value, then never repeated. And last, one confronts the reluctance of one conductor or performing group to do a composition already done by another conductor or performing group—thus ensuring that most composers who are performed will remain only locally known.

Whenever a contemporary American composition has won genuine approval from audiences, it has usually been a mainstream work. Exceptions to this observation are many of the compositions by composers like Rochberg, Hovhaness, Reich, and Glass. Yet these works, too, exhibit virtues ascribed to mainstream pieces—tonal centers, understandable harmony, enjoyable melodic progressions, meter of some definiteness, and unambiguous structures. And with a different arrangement of this study, the four composers cited above might easily have been placed in this or the next chapter.

The avant-garde is a recent creation in the West's history. For centuries, vital cultural statements have been made without need of provocation from an avant-garde. Today, American mainstream composers write in a variety of styles. Some compositions are dull. Others afford only passing amusement. But several are among the finest written by postwar composers, whether American or European.

THE MUSICAL CONSERVATORS

Conservators are those composers who have least departed from the practices of the past. They are usually dismissed out of hand as mere imitators and inconsequential artists. For the most part their works are strongly tonal, employ triadic harmony, and introduce dissonance circumspectly. With some, the styles of the Middle Ages and Renaissance are guides. Others find Baroque or Classical styles congenial. A greater number value the practices of the Romantic period. Immediate American predecessors who also valued these practices, like Howard Hanson and Samuel Barber, have an impact as well. We also come upon composers favoring native American musical languages—that of folk, popular, and jazz. Few composers adhere completely to one style. They may honor two or more models. Moreover, few remain untouched by the innovations introduced by the posttriadic composers. However, these innovations are used only for compelling expressive reasons.

Arnold Rosner (b. 1945) has written works with affinities to the music from around the year 1600. *A Gentle Musicke* for flute and strings, to give an instance, has a kinship to the dances and viol music of Elizabethan England. Rosner invokes a ceremonial ambiance, as if the music was intended for a formal performance before the royal court. Similar things could be said about his String Quartet No. 4, Symphony No. 5, *Canzona Secundi Toni* for brass ensemble, and French Horn Sonata, all works from the 1970s. For listeners who relish serenity and understatement, Rosner's music has much to offer. A second composer, Robert Baksa (b. 1938), admires the usages of Mozart and Beethoven. A Quintet for Oboe and Strings is patterned after Mozart's works for woodwinds and strings, though with suggestions of American song. Lucid melody and uncluttered textures reinforce its projection of pastoral peace and contentment. His *Bagatelles* for piano, which look toward Beethoven in his lighter moments, are diverting kickshaws.

A large group of composers have their antecedents in the Romantic era. Vittorio Giannini (1903–66), to name one, has composed at least two outstanding works: an opera, *The Taming of the Shrew* (1950), and a monodrama for soprano and orchestra, *The Medead* (1960). His roots are Italian (Rossini and Puccini); his leanings, unabashedly emotional and dramatic; his focus of interest, inner human conflict. The opera is satisfying theater to see and boasts strong, appealing melody. When it was mounted at the Boston Arts Festival in 1960, around 9,000 people attended its performance and at the end roared their approval. *The Medead* is a somber and dissonant work. Giannini's text makes room for highly contrasted moods and emotions. Medea in the text and

through the music becomes not an abstraction but a human sur-
charged with suffering.

Another conservator is John La Montaine (b. 1920). His Concerto for Piano of 1958 continues the romanticism of Samuel Barber. Like Giannini's *Taming of the Shrew*, this composition met
with major success but was abandoned by performers within a
few years. In three movements, the first opens dramatically with
a rhetorical assertiveness typical of the previous century's concer-
tos. It goes on to an engagingly lyric second thematic group, then
a real development and recapitulation of the exposed ideas. The
second movement, a slow and introspective elegy in memory of
the composer's sister, rises to an overwhelming climax before
subsiding again into the quieter mood of the opening. The finale
opens brilliantly and proceeds like a Prokofiev march. Twice it is
interrupted by an extended songful passage.

Later works, like *Wilderness Journal*, for bass-baritone, organ,
and orchestra, to texts of Thoreau and *Come into My Garden, Maud*
and *Conversations*, both for flute and piano, display more enriched
harmonies than those in the concerto. Colorful and convincing
portrayals of moods and pictures from nature (*Wilderness Journal*)
and of native American sentiments (*Conversations*) abound. *Come
into My Garden* is a bucolic instrumental song tinged with sounds
of the Middle East.

The tribulations of the tonal composer in a postwar world are
eloquently described by Lee Hoiby. In 1971 he stated: "I write
melody—for me, music has got to sing and dance. I studied with
Menotti for four years at Curtis, and I'm of the Barber school, if
there is such a thing. My music is lyrical, it's traditional, it's real.
It may be hopelessly out of fashion."[10] He began his career when
atonalism was dominant and revolted against it: "With what
opprobrium has the tonal composer struggled in our time! Time
will sort this out, but I have sometimes felt like a man on a dying
limb; also, sometimes, when writing down a signature, like a
freedom fighter."[11]

Hoiby's first love has been opera. Early success came with a
one-act musical drama, *The Scarf* (1955), based on a story by Anton Chekhov. Malignant sorcery, carnality, and murder are treated
naturalistically. Eloquent music invests the powerful melodrama.
In 1983 it was performed both in New York and Boston. Bernard

Holland, reviewing the New York production, wrote: "The music takes more intense a part in the drama on stage, flowing through it rather than just providing support from underneath." Although Hoiby employs familiar twentieth-century tonal techniques, his music is "imaginative and fresh," and has "sustained dramatic power." [12] In Boston, I witnessed an enthusiastic audience react with a standing ovation, proving the opera's effectiveness even after the passage of almost thirty years. Yet the modernistically oriented reviewer for the *Boston Globe*, Richard Dyer, never reported on the excitement the opera caused or the pleasure it gave. Instead, he sniffed at the "lurid little opera," whose "music doesn't aim very high." [13] The words exemplify the opprobrium Hoiby referred to earlier.

Hoiby's Piano Concerto No. 1 (1958) is an intrepidly romantic composition. Heard is rhetorical back-and-forth dialogue between piano and orchestra. Every now and again, soaring strings and piano, working together, achieve vividly expressive climaxes. In addition, light, staccato counterpointal passages in the piano are introduced to highlight a woodwind solo. A second piano concerto, completed twenty-one years later, is bolder in harmony and more percussively assertive in its rhythms.

Hoiby's first full length opera, *Beatrice*, dates from 1959; and a second, *Natalia Petrovna*, from 1964. Both have weaknesses, but also impressive moments. Walter Cavalieri writes that the latter work made a stunning effect at its premier in New York's City Center. Despite the favorable audience response, the work disappeared from sight. Fortunately the famous playwright Tennessee Williams saw *Natalia Petrovna*, liked it, and offered Hoiby the pick of his plays from which to fashion a libretto for a new opera. [14] The result was *Summer and Smoke*, premiered in 1971. Hoiby's expert score contains music that is usually restrained and often beautiful. Miss Alma, the heroine, is a Southern singing teacher. Hoiby's music centers on her inner conflicts. He frequently resorts to chords based on intervals of the second, fourth, and seventh to express her turmoil. Neither the opera nor the audience deserve the condemnation given them by a sneering Martin Mayer, when he states: "Though the tunes are not very expressive of either dramatic situation or character, they *are* tunes, offering an unsophisticated audience a real modern opera that nobody—at least, no-

body unsophisticated—could possibly dislike. Being sophisticated,
I disliked it."[15]

Adverse criticism from reviewers who feel composers must repudiate the past has also pursued Nicolas Flagello (b. 1928), that
is to say, in those few instances when he has been considered an
important enough composer to warrant criticism at all.[16] In actuality Flagello's music is made of strong stuff. His teachers were
Vittorio Giannini and Ildebrando Pizzetti, but his style stems more
from the former than the latter. He arrived at his mature voice in
1959, with two compositions, the Concerto for String Orchestra
and *The Judgment of St. Francis.* The concerto, unabashedly lyrical,
does make an impression on ears receptive to traditional sounds.
Not the least of its virtues is the balancing of romantic warmth
with classical logic. The ingratiating first movement utilizes a
strongly etched but melodious motive against simple rhythmic
backgrounds. Counterpoint relieves the usual homophonic texture; rich sonority, the othewise spare sounds. The emotional core
of the concerto is in the second movement, an attractive elegy.
The finale dispels the sadness with tangy rhythms and brief fugatos.

The Judgment of St. Francis is an opera in seven flashback scenes.
Flagello portrays episodes in the saint's life, integrated through a
recurring palace scene in which the saint's father expresses discon-
tent over his conduct. The weaving together of the scenes is skillfully done, but the opera contains little real dramatic action. A
singers' opera, it comes across as strong in melody, finished in
orchestration, and apt in its depiction of religious rapture.

His Piano Sonata, an idiomatic work, uses triadic harmonies,
with free admixtures of chromatics, unexpected dissonance, and
chords based on the interval of the fourth and second. Especially
captivating is the slow movement, an extended operatic *scena*, as
if the piano were a character experiencing emotional conflict. From
the same year comes the *Capriccio for Cello and Orchestra.* Again
are found two Flagello trademarks, the treatment of the soloist as
an actor in a drama and the restraint of rhapsodic expression by
tightly controlled form.

In 1964 appeared the *Contemplazioni di Michelangelo,* for soprano
and orchestra. Four of Michelangelo's poems are set gratifyingly
for the voice, which is allotted music in the sumptuous and pas-

sionate style that typified the compositions of late–nineteenth-century Italian composers. The music brings out the self-questioning about love, the bitter outcry over unrequited feeling and separation, the praise of a swift and happy bird able to reach the sun through ways concealed from humans, and the grief over a misery-filled and sinful existence. Heroic rhetoric combines with seductive sound to make an effective concert piece. A similar statement can be made about *The Passion of Martin Luther King*, for bass-baritone, chorus, and orchestra (1968, rev. 1973). When the work was performed in Quebec, Marc Samson wrote in *Le Soleil* (12 April 1979), of how filled with action and drama he found the composition, calling it an outstandingly "public" work, proved by the standing ovation it received. Samson then writes about its understandable and simple language speaking directly to the listener, the skillful handling of the orchestra, the easily accessible melodic substance, and the singularly striking impact it had on listeners.[17]

A Second Symphony (*Symphony of the Winds*)[18] and *Odyssey*, for symphonic band, are economical in length and give an impression of strength and tragic grandeur. I have personally observed how their persuasive expressiveness has proven attractive to both young and old listeners. The last is a one-movement piece progressing like a fantasy. At first the mood is dark and meditative; later it grows fervidly impassioned. In a work like this, Walter Simmons writes, Flagello "bridges the gap between audience tastes and the need for a living body of significant contemporary music free of gimmicks and meretricious pretensions. Whenever his works are heard, they seem to meet with both astonished enthusiasm and bewilderment that such obviously fine music is not played more often."[19]

Another romantic is Thomas Pasatieri. Like his teacher Vittorio Giannini, his roots are Italian; like several of the other traditionally oriented composers already mentioned, his more immediate influence is Samuel Barber's music. He has composed several operas that pleased audiences and reviewers in the American West and South. The Northeast has heard little of his music. Sometimes his writing shows carelessness and haste. But offsetting this is his effective sense of theater, gift for dramatic scoring, and ability to gratify the ear.[20] Pasatieri says he is interested in people, "other-

wise why write an opera?" His music is tailored to the demands
of the stage. Nevertheless, "it has to be good music, and always
music that is beautiful to sing." He writes in order "to bring joy"
with his music: "I would rather please a real audience than please
five other composers sitting in the room."[21]

A representative opera is *Washington Square* (1976), whose libretto by Kenwood Elmslie draws upon Henry James's *Portrait of
a Lady*. The score calls for fifteen instruments and eight singers.
The harmony sounds at times triadic and mellifluous, at times polytonal and strident, but always designed to support the voices
and to provide information about the workings of the characters'
minds. Melody, precisely shaped and preferably cantabile in nature, can be choppy, poignant, or seamlessly flowing depending
on a character's emotions. Reviewing the opera's initial performance by the Michigan Opera Theater, John Harvey writes that
when Catherine, a principal character, fell in love and declared her
independence of her father, her "cantabile ceased to become halt-
ing and, indeed, flowered into continuous melismatic song fla-
vored with neo-romantic, poignant dissonances." In addition,
Catherine's "meddling Aunt Lavinia was plagued with mischie-
vous trills, wide melodic skips, and mocking percussion and wind
commentary." Catherine's music is mostly in *E*-major; that of her
New York environment, *A*-flat. "Details such as these," concludes Harvey, "attest to Pasatieri's skill in musico-dramatic construction, and his ability to reveal the essential attributes of his
characters." The reviewer goes on to admit that the opera proved
quite effective despite the fact that the music often struck him as
facile and derivative.[22]

The Pasatieri songs I have seen burst with a lyricism directly
connected with Barber's vocal works, as in "These Are the Days,"
"Instead of Words," and "Discovery."

A substantial composer is Robert Ward (b. 1917). Folk and jazz
are points of departure in his music. On occasion his melodies
take on twelve-tone contours, but always within the grip of a
tonality. In his first two symphonies the scoring attracts the attention. The moods are optimistic, the musical ideas fairly distinctive, the structures logical, and the climaxes rousing. Ward's greatest
recognition as a composer came with the premiere of his opera
The Crucible by the New York City Opera, in 1961. The libretto,

fashioned by Bernard Stambler, is based on Arthur Miller's stage play on the Salem witch trials of the late seventeenth century and humans ensnared in a tragic web woven by hysteria and sexual drives. For the most part the music comes across as unsentimental, yet fleshed out with virile emotions. Only a few arias are allowed the singers. Ward's musical idiom changes to accommodate the drama. At times the sound hews to the dignified simplicity of the eighteenth-century New England tunesmiths; or it resorts to the rich palette of late–nineteenth-century romanticism; or it jangles with the chromaticism and nervous rhythms of posttriadic modernism. Expressive recitative and arioso, sometimes interrupted with folklike melodic phrases, describe the nature of most of the singing. *The Crucible* represents one of the more notable and successful attempts at operatic composition by a composer of the postwar period.

Equally notable was Carlisle Floyd's opera *Susannah* (1954). Carlisle Floyd is often decribed as a Southern regionalist composer owing to the place of action in a few operas and to the musical Americanisms in his music. *Susannah*, Floyd's third opera, was his first and greatest success. Musically uncomplicated, direct in expression, in a language peculiarly American, and with action based on verism, it has been described as an outstanding example of folklike opera. Winthrop Sargeant, who in 1963 saw it along with a revival of another folklike opera, Douglas Moore's *The Ballad of Baby Doe*, wrote that both operas ran "counter to all the highbrow fashions of the past half century, as well as to a great deal of current fashion in the realm of music education." Both works were in "a basic language of music," which had not changed and remained valid, in spite of the teachings of modernists.[23]

Floyd wanted the language simple and colloquial, the characterization clear cut. In two short acts, the opera reinterprets the biblical story of Susannah and the elders, in a tale of false virtue, malevolence, and the corruption of innocence. The drama unfolds to the sounds of speech song, square dance, hymnody, and folk-inspired melody. In the highly effective second act, Susannah, lost in thought, sings a fetching aria, "Ain't It a Pretty Night?" A sharp contrast is the nonchalant "Jaybird" tune that follows. Then an emotion-filled revival meeting begins with a chorus singing a rousing hymn, followed by Reverend Blitch's harangue, calling

on Susannah to redeem herself from sin. Excitement mounts to
an immense climax. For relief, Susannah's lovely song "Come Back,
O Summer" is introduced. Such a sequence of musical events reveals awareness of the necessity for always catching the audience's
interest.

Floyd's other operas have not won the sustained interest accorded *Susannah*. It is, however, no small thing to have written
one American opera that has maintained its popularity with audiences over a period of thirty years.

One other opera that has had constant success wherever it has
been produced is *The Face on the Barroom Floor* (1978), by Henry
Mollicone. Folk, popular, and jazzlike tunes abound. Andrew Porter
of the *New Yorker* found the score and libretto skillfully written
and the music predictable but strangely powerful. He adds that
the audience was gripped by the work.[24] Since Porter was not
naturally inclined toward the opera's idiom, his surely is a reliable
reportage. Admittedly, nothing terribly original sounds, but pretense is absent. The story hinges on a triangular love relationship
both in the present and the past. The locale is Central City, Colorado. Honky-tonk piano music, snips from *La Traviata*, "Home
on the Range," an eloquent folklike ballad, "He Came to the West,"
and a trio, "He Paints a Portrait of His Love," sung as the artist
paints on the floor comprise the principal melodic interest of the
composition.

Mollicone and the other musical conservators mentioned in this
section have written immediately appealing and accessible compositions. What is more, American audiences have readily taken
them to heart. If for this reason alone, they deserve wider and
more frequent performance than they are now granted.

THE MEDIAL MAINSTREAM

The medial mainstream includes composers whose idiom is more
advanced than that of the musical conservators. Traditional procedures are modified by greater admixtures of dissonance, chromaticism, nontriadic harmony, tonal ambiguity, rhythmic unpredictability, or any combination of these. Values shared with the
past, like overall tonal control, perceptible harmonic direction,

traditional rhetorical devices, recognizable melody, and comprehensible motives and their equally comprehensible working out
are not discarded. Norman Dello Joio summarized the attitude
toward audiences of most composers making up the medial mainstream when he stated: "I do not go along with the esoteric approach—you know, 'the Philistine public be damned.' I think there
is a growing return to the idea that you take the trouble to put
notes on paper in order to communicate with somebody."[25]

Dello Joio's music displays vigor, clear melodic direction, contrapuntal vitality, carefully regulated sonorities, and aurally logical
structures. Influences include jazz, Verdi's and Puccini's operas,
the Catholic sacred music played by his father, a church musician,
and the compositions of his teacher Paul Hindemith. With his Sonata
for Piano No. 3 and his *Variations, Chaconne, and Finale* for orchestra, both written in 1947 he arrived at his mature style, one
giving prominence to variational procedures. Enjoyable instrumental works followed, including the *Serenade* for orchestra, the
Fantasia on the Gregorian Theme for violin and piano, the *New York
Profiles* for orchestra, the *Epigraph* "in memory of A. Lincoln Gil-
lespie, Jr.," and the deeply felt *Meditations on Ecclesiastes* for string
orchestra.

Dello Joio's opera *The Triumph of Joan* (1950), despite its excellent vocal writing (for example, Joan's monologue in the first scene
of Act I, and her exultant duet with the Dauphin in the coronation
scene), failed owing to the unfocused libretto, by Joseph Machlis,
and the reserved musical expression. The next year, the composer
refashioned music from the opera into a three-movement orchestral composition, titled *The Triumph of Saint Joan*. In a letter to
Robert Whitney, conductor of the Louisville Orchestra, Dello Joio
describes the first movement, "The Maid," as a set of variations
in 6/8 meter on a tune from the opera. He says that the second
movement, "The Warrior," is to start off briskly and relentlessly
mount to a climax, after which a more stately 4/4 section enters
to depict the coronation with a "blaze of glory." The last movement, "The Saint," is meant to make the orchestra sing before
ending on a note of triumphant serenity. Dello Joio closes the
letter by saying the work is his most ambitious attempt for orchestra.[26] At its premiere in December 1951, Martha Graham danced

while the Louisville Orchestra played. The music made an extraordinary impression on the audience. Applause was unstinting.[27]

Around 1943, Vincent Persichetti completed three compositions which won him recognition: the *Fables* for narrator and orchestra, the *Pastoral* for wind quintet, and the Sonata for Piano No. 3. Persichetti's style, more advanced than that of Dello Joio, is marked by sureness of touch and emotional restraint. Although discouraging to listeners addicted to full-blown romanticism, his music rewards those appreciative of subtle expressivity—the result of skillful handling of contrapuntal lines, multiple rhythms, and variable phrasings.

The *Pastoral*, for flute, oboe, clarinet, horn, and bassoon, delineates Persichetti's manner. The piece uses some triadic but mostly posttriadic harmony and normally maintains a five-part contrapuntal flow. Yet it is clearly in *A*-major, and its cheery melodiousness makes for pleasant listening. The Piano Sonata No. 4 (1949) boasts an expanded harmonic idiom, one fairly dissonant, much of it the result of seventh, ninth, and eleventh triadic chords from traditional practice but also polychords, chords constructed on seconds, fourths, and fifths alone, and, now and then, a tone cluster. Dignified, sonorous progressions, contrapuntal activity, and rhythmically tricky and jazzy passages are integrated into the music.

The Symphony No. 4 reveals a significant aspect of the composer—polished craft and laconic utterance in movements that are episodically constructed—and go from amiable melody to sprightly dance to fast and thrusting repartee. A similar compositional approach is found in the song cycle *Harmonium*, the Concerto for Piano Four-Hands, the Piano Quintet, the Piano Sonata No. 10, and the Serenade No. 10, for flute and harp.

He has another creative side where ingenuity and impersonality gives way to direct feeling. Episodic thinking is replaced with a smoother flow of ideas. A comprehensible initial idea undergoes constant transformation as it recurs in section after section. The result is easier communication with a general audience. An example is furnished by the *Symphony for Strings* (1953), a one-movement and four-sectioned composition. The intense and beautiful lamentation of the violas in section 1, slowly rising from a low *E* to the *C* over two-and-a-half octaves above and swelling from a dynamic of *p* to *fff*, gives the listener a different and very human view of Persichetti; the same is true of the high, diatonic, and expressive violin solo in section 3.

Persichetti's Symphony No. 9 (*"Janiculum"*) of 1970 transmutes individual feeling into universal expression. Heard at the beginning and end of the work is music derived from the chimes of the Chiesa de San Pietro sul Giancolo of Rome. The one–movement composition for full orchestra requires an augmented percussion section. The work is intended as a meditation on life's meaning. The ancient god Janus, after whom the Janiculum Hill is named, has two faces that look in opposite directions and represent the male-female, active-passive, comic-tragic principles of life. The ear hears little triadic harmony and no sentimentality. There is a feeling of disquiet throughout, much of it projected through the plaintive wail of solo instruments. The end strikes the ear less as an affirmation of life, more as a determination to endure. The work can reach concertgoers open to expressive music more complexly set forth than that of Flagello.

In 1973, Persichetti was at the center of a contretemps involving President Richard Nixon. The Republican Presidential Inaugural Committee asked the composer for a work to be played by the Philadelphia Orchestra at the Kennedy Center on 19 January. The result was *A Lincoln Address* for narrator and orchestra, to a text taken from Abraham Lincoln's second inaugural address. The words expressed a deep faith in humans and strong desire for peace. Without warning, however, the Republicans rejected the work, fearing to embarrass Nixon, owing to the continuing war in Vietnam. Persichetti refused to delete the Lincoln text in favor of (as the composer put it) "some pretty poem so that Charlton Heston can read it." An opposition concert was organized to take place at Washington Cathedral, with Leonard Bernstein as director. The premiere of the Persichetti work came on 24 Jaunary, when it was performed by Walter Susskind and the St. Louis Symphony, with William Warfield as narrator.

Persichetti has written some music that seems dry, fussy, or overly formal. On the other hand, at its best, his music strikes an

effective balance between lyricism and counterpoint, diatonicism
and chromaticism, emotion and intellect, and romanticism and
neoclassicism.

Far less balance is evident in the music of Leonard Bernstein (b.
1918), a composer who has also won international acclaim as an
orchestral conductor. In his music one hears wit, heat, conflict,
melody, theatricality, and, at times, extravagant exhibitionism.
Popular were his Broadway theater pieces: *Fancy Free*, *On the Town*,
Wonderful Town, *Candide*, and *West Side Story*; also the music to
the film *On the Waterfront*. His art combines a bewildering variety
of styles: Broadway, jazz, rock and roll, folk, Mahler, Stravinsky,
Shostakovich, Bartók, Copland, among them. When the synthesis
of these disparate elements is successful, his tunes and rhythms are
addictive. Even when most superficial and coarse, the music amuses
as it offends, fascinates as it infuriates. He loved and believed in
people and in himself. He said of Ravel's Piano Concerto in G:
"That's one piece I play better than anyone else in the world"; of
operatic composition: "I'm the logical man to write the Great
American Opera"; and poetizing: "No one can handle the sonnet
form like me and Millay."[28]

If one looks behind the immense ego, one finds human frailty
and uncertainty. He has said: "If I can write one real, moving
American opera that any American can understand (and one that
is, notwithstanding, a serious musical work), I shall be a happy
man." The only "durable art has been made by old-fashioned artists"; not by the "way-outest, the beatist, the sickest, the cli-
quest—all of which is to say the most dated." Old-fashioned artists are progressive extenders of tradition who are aware of their
roots, constantly measuring them against the future. They have a
social conscience but also humor. The beauty they wish to create
shows concern for the needs and limitations of others.[29]

Bernstein has spoken about the crisis in modern music, of young
composers no longer certain of what to write, of listeners no longer
interested in the music being written, of stylistic fashions strong
one day and passé the next, and of postwar decades when composers shun genuine melody. He asked: "Does anyone care any-
more—really care—if any one of us here ever writes another note?
You see, our crisis *is* different from the historical precedents: it is
concerned with human expressivity, the mirroring of our inner

lives in music. Are we still living in a world where an octave leap upward implies a sense of yearning, or reaching? Or has it become only an intervallic symbol? Do we still base our forms on the concept of struggle and resolution, or are we now condemned to reveal ourselves as forever unresolved?"[30]

His Symphony No. 1 (*"Jeremiah"*), completed in 1943, caught the notice of the art-music world. It is one of his most heartfelt works, free of dissimulation and in rapport with the general public's tastes. The first movement, "Prophecy," like the movements that follow, was intended to have emotional and not programmatic meaning. Here, the aim was to parallel in feeling the intensity of the prophet's pleas with his people. The principal musical idea, heard first in the horns, is from the Jewish liturgical service. The second movement, "Profanation," portrays the destruction and chaos attendant on pagan corruption. An Ashkenazic cantillation opens a movement that utilizes dance rhythms in a profane scherzo. It reaches a peak of intensity when horns vulgarly blare out the "Prophecy" theme in the midst of orgiastic commotion. The last movement, "Lamentation," is on the cry of Jeremiah mourning his beloved and ruined Jerusalem. Again, one hears Ashkenazic cantillation and, later, a reintroduction of the "Prophecy" music. The symphony's music employs nonfunctional dissonance, bitonality, and flexible rhythms. But the brilliant orchestration and the appealing melodies proved enjoyable at the premiere and have continued to please listeners in subsequent performances.

Less convincing works were the two symphonies that followed. Many of their passages were obvious derivations from other composers' styles. Little of Bernstein's integrative flair was evident. One, however, does not doubt Bernstein's seriousness of purpose in composing them. The Symphony No. 2 (*"Age of Anxiety"*) deals with existentialism. The Symphony No. 3 (*"Kaddish"*) is embarrassing in spots, especially when free rein is given to bad temper and God is shouted at.

A chamber opera, *Trouble in Tahiti*, libretto and music by Bernstein, came out in 1950. A satire on the suburban middle class, the composition, in forty-five minutes, tells a tragic tale about an American couple, Dinah and Sam. Ironic music parodies jazz and popular-song styles. Banal words capture the insipidity and sadness of the couple's usual activities. Neoclassic leanness of musical texture, fluent expression, and effective scoring are welded into a felicitous whole.

In 1954 he wrote the *Serenade* for solo violin, string orchestra, harp, and percussion, "after Plato's *Symposium*." Five unprogammatic episodes in praise of love share musical themes that undergo change from episode to episode. The work proves a rewarding experience for the listener. Equally rewarding is the *Chichester Psalms* for mixed chorus, boy soloist, and orchestra (1965), one of Bernstein's finest compositions.

Just as certainly, the *Mass*, a "theater piece for singers, players, and dancers," composed in 1971, is a much lesser work. Bernstein says that, like the *Kaddish* symphony, it brings up the problem of faith and is a questioning of God. Nevertheless, the ingredients of the *Mass*—the choral music, the ditties of the rock singer and band, the sounds of the marching band, and the accompaniments of the pit orchestra—refuse to mix. When it first came out, the composition seemed to capture the alienation of the times. As the years have passed, however, it seems more and more a dated *piece d'occasion*.

In 1983 Bernstein completed a new opera, *A Quiet Place*, intended as a sequel to *Trouble in Tahiti*. Depicted is the human struggle to appreciate, pardon the transgressions, and feel affection for one another. The music draws on the American vernacular and shares some musical themes with the earlier opera. Certainly, it is one of his most mature works.

Bernstein was not alone in the attempt to write the great American opera. Giannini, Ward, and Floyd, three composers already mentioned, have engaged in a similar endeavor. So also has Jack Beeson. His second musical drama, the chamber opera *Hello Out There* (1953), did demonstrate his gift for vocal melody and dramatic effect. The one-act composition is written for thirteen instrumentalists and three singers. The libretto, based on a story by William Saroyan, is built around a dialogue between a man imprisoned in a small-town jail and a lonely girl, just before he is unjustly hanged. The opening music does project a haunting atmosphere of solitariness in an uncaring world. A harmonium and trumpet repeatedly play a two-note skip upward of a fourth, after which the young man enters singing "Hello" on the same motive.

No lengthy arias follow but alternating snatches of melody, arioso, and recitative. A "Gambler's Song" contains effective musical echoes of the American West. Later, "The Girl's Song" heightens the emotional tone of the drama.

In 1956 Beeson completed a two-act opera, *The Sweet Bye and Bye*, libretto by Kenward Elmslie. Featured were a simple and straightforward plot, enjoyable lyricism, and a variety of mood changes—by means of songs, marches, dances and hymns. The audience enjoyed it; most reviewers reported on it favorably. Beeson, however, had to run the gauntlet of several influential reviewers who held to different aesthetic principles. Rockwell, for example, wrote that Beeson's operas, along with those of other American composers, among them Moore, Copland, Foss, Floyd, and Ward, had failed in freshness and originality. Beeson offered "the plodding, naturalistic conventions that afflict so many American operas. A setting between the seacoasts somewhere and a few folk tunes stuck like cloves into the ham of conservative composition do not a modern musical-theatrical experience make."[31]

In 1965 Beeson finished *Lizzie Borden*, an opera again with a libretto by Kenward Elmslie. The subject was the notorious hatchet murder that had taken place in Fall River, Massachusetts. Pretty tunes are absent; dissonance and passages verging on atonality abound. The music envelops the drama with an aura of evil, tortured grief, despondency, and horror. Some lyric and tonal moments occur in order to contrast the neurotic passages allotted to Lizzie. Although the music successfully accentuates the drama (and its cumulative effect is powerful), the audience discovers no big tune that it can take to heart and hum later. Tonal, decidedly tuneful, and therefore more accessible are three operas he wrote in the 1970s: a television opera based on a Saroyan play, *My Heart's in the Highlands*; a musical comedy, *Captain Jinks of the Horse Marines*; and an attractive chamber opera based on the Hawthorne story, *Dr. Heidegger's Fountain of Youth*. Also accessible are his instrumental compositions, the Piano Sonata No. 5 and the Symphony No. 1, for example. Surprising was the appreciation of the symphony by the otherwise modernistically inclined Alfred Frankenstein, in 1966, when he wrote: "The Symphony by Jack Beeson . . . is conservative in idiom, but warmhearted, beautifully shaped, superbly orchestrated, highly distinguished in thematic material and general feature, and many times worth the price of admission."[32]

Peter Mennin (1923–83), unlike Beeson, was not an opera composer. His compositional forte was mostly symphonic and chamber music. His music is precisely stated in carefully sculpted melodic lines that owe something to Mennin's Italian ancestry. An early Symphony No. 4 (*"The Cycle"*) for chorus and orchestra, written in 1947–48, grew out of the contributions of older American composers like Piston, Harris, Schuman, and Creston. Typical of Mennin's style, the symphony is remarkably lucid in structure, thematic development, and orchestration. It delineates man's deliverance from spiritual bondage through the eternally active processes of nature. The symphony sounds assured and, in many spots, quite individual.

The Symphony No. 5 and the String Quartet No. 2 travel along a similar pathway. Their music mixes tonality with bitonality, uncomplicated lyricism with energetic counterpoint, and straightforward meter with asymmetric rhythmic patterns. Despite the fact that melody tends to sound diatonic, it is sustained by unabashedly dissonant harmony. Add to this the rather abstracted and emotionally reticent nature of the expression, and we can understand why Mennin's compositions have not won over as wide a public as he would have liked.

Mennin's most memorable contribution to symphonic literature is perhaps the Symphony No. 7 (the *"Variation-Symphony"*) of 1963. Mennin speaks of "the emotional involvement with the content of musical ideas that created the urgency to make the work come into being."[33] The work is full of heroic rhetoric, poignant outcries, and mysterious lyricism but empty of sentimentality, melting melody, and opulent harmony. Each of its five sections grows in intensity to achieve a large climax, the largest coming at the end. The high coefficient of dissonance, the frequency of nontriadic harmony, and the obscuring of tonal feeling identify it as indisputably a twentieth-century work.

Like Mennin, Ned Rorem (b. 1923) avoids excessive emotionality. Unlike Mennin, Rorem's forte is art song, not instrumental composition. He developed an adolescent love for French music that continued into his adult years. Like Virgil Thomson, one of his teachers, he attempts an exact setting of words and desires a precise musical expression of word meanings. He believes that overplayed feeling detracts from a song's value. Depending on the mood Rorem wishes to evoke, the song may be entirely diatonic or chromatic, strophic or through composed, and artlessly folklike or eruditely sophisticated. On the whole, most songs are short. For example, Columbia MS 6561 contains thirty-two of his songs, all of them sung in fifty-seven minutes.

A description of two songs is helpful at this point. "For Poulenc," text by Frank O'Hara, describes an American's first day in Paris. The music suggests a modernized *gymnopédie*, composed by an admirer of Erik Satie. The ternary structure shapes a simple and pleasing diatonic melody that moves normally in quarter notes and with a gentle swing. Its key is *D*, but mostly in the Aeolian, and sometimes the Dorian, mode, rather than in the more orthodox major or minor. "The Tulip Tree," text by Paul Goodman, tells of a boy in a tree, tossing blossoms down to girls below and of boughs swaying in a wind that is bringing rain. Again, Rorem prefers simplicity and emotional restraint. A mostly diatonic lyric line moves above mildly dissonant triadic harmonies. No problem of idiom hinders the listener from enjoying the music.

Because Rorem's vocal music has always respected and maintained its connection with traditional practices, it has been prey to modernists' censures. These critics admit that many people like his songs, and that sometimes he writes posttertian sounds, though discreetly. But they also claim that other composers have made better settings of older poetry and that his idiom belongs too much in the past to do justice to contemporary poetry. On the other hand, significant numbers of singers and music lovers genuinely value Rorem's songs. Rorem himself is no shrinking violet and has given as good as he has taken from critics in his articles and books, among them *Critical Affairs* (1970), *Pure Contraption* (1974), and *Setting the Tone* (1983).

Rorem insists: "Art is clarity. The most complicated statement, if it is art, is the simplest form for that statement." Although he believes that profundity and deep emotion are not necessarily absent from his music, he also points out that nothing is "wrong with froth, light, charm. Emotional profundity is for sophomore bull sessions." He resents the attention given the Johnny-come-

latelies who, beginning with the late 1970s, claim to have redis-
covered tonal music, while he and others like him, who have always valued tonality, are ignored. When he asks himself the question: "For whom do I compose?" He answers: "For the listener
within me. Sure, I hope other listeners may find a sympathetic
point of contact, and I need those listeners. But I don't know who
they are. There are as many audiences as there are pieces, and the
audiences don't necessarily overlap."[34]

His instrumental music exhibits the same virtues and the same
avoidance of emotional excess as his songs. Worth hearing are the
Third Symphony, the *Eleven Studies for Eleven Players*, and *Sunday
Morning* for orchestra. Some chamber music gives the impression
of songs without words, for example, *Night Music* for violin and
piano and *Romeo and Juliet* for flute and guitar.

For emotion larger sized than that of Rorem, the listener must
turn to Benjamin Lees (b. 1924). Lees is predominently a composer of instrumental, not vocal, music. His style is bolder than
Rorem's. Though he abjures atonality, he clothes his works with
the harsher sounds of the posttertian composers. Yet his is a bold-
ness capable of winning the public's favor. Lees composes coher-
ent music that is idiomatic to the instruments employed. Structures are graspable. Contrasts—in instrumental coloration,
dynamics, and texture—please the ear. One hears chromaticism,
organum, and bitonal harmony when the expressive need arises.
Sharp, percussive, even primitivistic sections and other sections
that sound bizarre and idiosyncratic are balanced by aurally satisfying lyrical passages. Musical themes usually are striking, therefore easy to remember and recognize within the fabric of a work.
In short, Lees does worry over who is performing, how the music
will sound, and what a piece's effect will be on the listener. Several reviewers have reported on the enthusiastic ovations given his
music by audiences, including those made up of symphony subscribers.

Lees says that he wants to communicate, not play cerebral games.
For this reason, among others, he considers himself not to be a
modernist and avoids all current fashions. The contemporary musical world, he says, "goes in wild swings that are really swings
of desparation. . . . The fad today [this commentary was made
in 1982] is to quote 10 composers in a single piece or to write

very, very cerebral music with . . . voluminous program notes. It's all a game and really has very little to do with music."[35]

In his unpretentious First Piano Concerto (1955) and the Violin Concerto (1958), tonality is fluid and tension carefully regulated however explosive it becomes. Surprisingly ingratiating lyricism offsets passages of contrapuntal complexity. The Concerto for String Quartet and Orchestra, written ten years after the Piano Concerto, shows some reining in of emotion. At the same time, it strikes the ear as an original and personal work, with a hint now and again of Prokofiev's style. The likeness is especially evident in the energetic and brittle rhythms of the first and the last movements. The composer's technical skill and genius for inventing and developing consequential musical themes make it a winning work.

When I first heard the Symphony No. 3, it struck me as a tragic and moving composition. A flood of deep feeling continues from beginning to end. Lees's idiom employs simultaneous use of major and minor chords and melodies, bitonality, and parallel streams of jarring harmonies. The symphony, composed in 1968, when the war in Vietnam was at its height, captures the horror and despair of Americans at that time, sublimating them into acutely felt human experiences. Lees's richly dramatic and emotional style is also heard to good effect in chamber music, like the Violin Sonata No. 2 and the Cello Sonata. More recently, in September 1983, the Williams Trio of Williamstown, Massachusetts, premiered a commissioned Trio for Violin, Cello, and Piano. It is a brief composition in which Lees exposes one strikingly muscular motive and engages in its singleminded development for the several minutes the piece lasts. It proves that Lees still has vital things to say and can convey them in eloquent terms to his audience.

Romantic heat not always disciplined by logical neoclassic procedures marks the works of Lees. Logical neoclassic procedures never resorting to romantic excess marks the works of Robert Muczynski (b. 1929). Muczynski's style honors clarity, conciseness, and craftsmanship, above all. Prokofiev influenced his earlier compositions; but he built his musical foundation principally on a well-known American tradition already articulated by Walter Piston (with significant accretions from Samuel Barber). In response to a query I had sent him, Muczynski replied: "Samuel Barber was the *only* veteran American composer who took a stand and who was *not* intimidated by all the ballyhoo [of the avant-garde]. That took courage. In fact, if you would ask me, again, 'What does the word *music* mean to you,' I would answer—Samuel Barber."[36]

In Muczynski's compositions, harmony progresses functionally, though not necessarily in triadic configurations. At times triads are thickened with added seconds. At other times quartal harmony or free pandiatonicism replace the triads. Tonal centers are respected. Simultaneous use of major and minor, bitonality, polytonality, and chromaticism add piquancy to the sound. Melodic lines sing, though excessive sweetness and emotionalism are squeezed out. None of the avant-garde experimentation of the postwar period interested him. Indeed, he has been articulate about the problems of the traditional composer working in the hostile atmosphere of the postwar decades. He wrote, in 1981: "If you didn't embrace the favored trends of the day it was a virtual shutout—especially in university circles where theorists delighted and salivated over the 'new notation' via graphs, charts, and diagrams of every sort." Critics of modernist persuasion "refused to judge the music for what it *was* but rather what they felt it *ought* to be—and often this was very vague." He continues: "The most damning condemnation was 'sounds like. . . . ' If you employed too many consecutive fourths, it was Hindemith. If you were percussive, it was Bartók or Stravinsky. A bluesy phrase evoked Gershwin and a tender, lyrical statement was Barber. A folk-like tune was Copland, and so on. If you are a tonal composer (I am), there are only so many possibilities within that system." A composer, nevertheless, can achieve something unique with it, he claims.[37]

In a letter that Muczynski sent to me in 1983, he speaks of the quest for newness and originality that led postwar composers astray. Only recently, he states, have some of them begun to write in an intelligible musical language and to try coming to terms "with the age-old problem of communication with a non-elite concert-going public" in order to survive.

Even more than Lees, Muczynski has favored instrumental over vocal composition. His recordings of his own piano works give evidence of considerable pianistic ability. The Second Piano Sonata (1966), in four movements, is spare, controlled, clear in texture and layout, and romantic in content. A substantial composition is the Third Piano Sonata (1974). Evidenced in the work are the composer's penchant for laconic statement, ironic wit, and the opposition of a dry, dispassionate idea against an expressive, personal one. The *Twelve Maverick Pieces* for piano, written 1976–77, show another side of Muczynski. They are brief, independent compositions sporting a variety of moods, textures, and pianistic colorations. Broadway dance and ballad (the first and second piece, particularly) and jazz effects (the fifth piece, for example) break out in the music. The last piece, an Allegro con spirito, has a winsome French-like clarity to it.

In 1981 Paul Snook wrote an appreciation of Muczynski's piano compositions. He stated: "In the aftermath of the postwar tidal wave of anti-music unleashed by the likes of Babbitt, Carter, and Wuorinen—plus the not-so-innocuous buffoonaries perpetrated by John Cage . . . the legitimate claims of many talented and committed American composers whose individuality sought sustenance and fulfillment within a more traditionally tonal framework have been glaringly slighted. Except for special cases such as Rorem and Corigliano, many of these men have subsisted in an artistic limbo on the obscure margins of an increasingly atomized musical culture extended throughout the university systems of the Mid and Far West." Snook found in Muczynski a serious and distinctive composer who owed a debt to Prokofiev, but who was also unmistakably an American composing music that was natural and eloquent.[38]

A *Fantasy Trio* for clarinet, cello, and piano and an Alto Saxophone Sonata, both written 1969–70, are pieces to gladden the music lover. Melody is more to the fore and more sustained in all movements than is usually the case with Muczynski. Less weighty in substance are the three orchestral compositions that I have heard, *Dance Movements*, *Symphonic Dialogues*, and *A Serenade for Summer*. They are light entertainments designed to gratify an audience wishing to enjoy itself. For serious music worthy of thoughtful consideration, the Cello Sonata, the Second Piano Trio, and the Concerto for Alto Saxophone and Chamber Orchestra can be recommended. What the listener immediately notes in these last three compositions is the heightened and more open emotional content, when compared with most of the music already discussed. The

Trio, especially, has the virtue of making the listener wish that it could have gone on longer than the thirteen minutes it occupies on the disc.

Assuredly, Muczynski and the other composers taken up in this chapter have made vital contributions to art music. Not discussed, but composers who have also written excellent compositions belonging to the American mainstream, are Halsey Stevens, Morton Gould, Gail Kubik, Roger Goeb, Robert Palmer, William Bergsma, Alfred Read, Dominick Argento, Ray Luke, and David Amram. Works like Goeb's Fourth Symphony, Argento's opera *Postcard from Morocco*, and Luke's Second Symphony are creations about which any country can be proud. Listeners seeking meaningful music that has qualities of freshness and that honors cultural continuity will be recompensed when they experience the best musical efforts of these artists.

NOTES

1. Elie Siegmeister, "Modernism and Humanism," article in manuscript, 10–11.

2. I know of two people who advised Druckman about outstanding works by mainstream composers. He chose not to follow the advice.

3. Gregory Sandow, "The Great Unknowns," *Village Voice*, 7 June 1983, 70.

4. Elie Siegmeister, letter sent to me, dated 25 August 1983.

5. David Ewen, *American Composers: A Biographical Dictionary* (New York: Putnam's, 1982), s.v. "Gottlieb, Jack."

6. Walter Simmons, "Contemporary Music," *Fanfare* (May/June 1981): 22–23.

7. For a similar statement concerning art in the postwar period, see Barry Schwartz, *The New Humanism: Art in a Time of Change* (New York: Praeger, 1974), 22.

8. This is not a completely original observation. Leo Steinberg makes a similar one concerning twentieth-century art in *Other Criteria: Confrontations with Twentieth-Century Art* (New York: Oxford University Press, 1972), 295.

9. Garry E. Clarke, *Essays on American Music* (Westport, Conn.: Greenwood, 1977), 179–180.

10. Quoted in *Musical America* (July 1971), 32.

11. Ewen, *American Composers*, s.v. "Hoiby, Lee."

12. Bernard Holland, "Opera: Ensemble in 'Scarf' and 'Boor.' " *New York Times*, 6 November 1983, 84.

13. Richard Dyer, review of Hoiby's *The Scarf*, in *Boston Globe* (3 February 1983): 23.

14. Walter Cavalieri, "Lee Hoiby," *Music Journal* (December 1980): 11.

15. Martin Mayer, in *Musical America* (July 1972), 10.

16. Quotations from several such reviews were kindly supplied me by Walter Simmons in a letter dated 8 November 1983.

17. A copy of the review, in French, along with an English translation was supplied by Walter Simmons.

18. A First Symphony was composed in 1968.

19. Walter Simmons, *Fanfare* 5 (January/February 1982): 266–267.

20. Winthrop Sargeant, *New Yorker* (12 February 1972): 70.

21. Ewen, *American Composers*, s.v. "Pasatieri, Thomas."

22. John Harvey, in *Musical America* (January 1977): 21–22.

23. Winthrop Sargeant, in the *New Yorker* (11 May 1963): 151.

24. Porter is quoted in the liner notes to CRI SD 442.

25. Ewen, *American Composers*, s.v. "Dello Joio, Norman."

26. Belfy, ed., *The Louisville Orchestra*, p. 19.

27. William Mootz, "Commissioned Works Given in Louisville," *Musical America* (1 January 1952): 4.

28. Leonard Bernstein, *Findings* (New York: Simon & Schuster, 1982), 137–138; Allan Hughes, "Leonard Bernstein," *Musical America* (January 1961): 110.

29. Bernstein, *Findings*, 129, 170–72.

30. Ibid., 214.

31. John Rockwell, in *High Fidelity* 24 (August 1974): 84.

32. Alfred Frankenstein, review of CRI SD 196, in *High Fidelity* 16 (June 1966), p. 83.

33. See the remarks of the composer in the liner notes to CRI 399.

34. Ned Rorem, *Setting the Tone* (New York: Coward-McCann, 1983), 43–44, 64, 168, 193.

35. Steve Schneider, "Communicating with a Concerto," *New York Times*, 7 November 1982, sec. 21, 25.

36. Robert Muczynski, letter to the author, 14 May 1983.

37. Robert Muczynski, letter to *Fanfare* 5 (September/October 1981): 2.

38. Paul Snook, review of Laurel LR 114, *Fanfare* 5 (May/June 1981): 118–119.

7

Venturesome Composers of the Traditional Mainstream

The composers to be discussed have tried out a variety of creative procedures, from the concordant triadic conventions of the past to the atonalism, chance operations, and other dissentient usages of the modernists. Yet they have continued to regard themselves as belonging in the contemporary mainstream of the American humanistic tradition in music. They, like the composers mentioned in the last chapter, express an interest in reaching the general music public, seeing in it a microcosm of the greater human society, however much their music may diverge from traditional practices. Many of them view Americans as close to succumbing to the dictates of a strengthening technocracy empty of humane considerations. They believe that quite a few concertgoers yearn for bold compositions that speak of their harsh tribulations, aggressively assert their worth, and give vivid expression to that portion of their inner being where some nobility and sense of beauty abide.

The composers see themselves simply as musicians trying to create telling works by every resource at hand. If this means the writing of absolutely consonant sounds, so be it. If it means unsettling cacophony, then strident tones are called forth. They are not dogmatists, philosophers, theorists, scholastics, or scientific inquirers. Neither fashion, experimentation, nor originality is a primary consideration. Composing, they say, calls for thought and deliberation. Tones must be subjected to systematic planning so that they will form a cohesive unity.

The listener whom they hope to reach is not the incurious and conservative type, but one capable of excitement over fresh approaches to timeless subjects. Although some of these composers may claim to write for themselves first, they all take heed of the public's response to their music. Owing to the modernisms introduced into their works, more performances than those required for more conservative works are necessary for the listener to appraise the worth of their music. Yet they also agree, if a work is given exposure and after several years still cannot find adequate sponsorship, then the fault may well lie with the composer, not the listener. As the first composer to be discussed, Elie Siegmeister (b. 1909) says: "I am definitely *not* indifferent to the audience's reaction. I want them to enjoy and be moved by my music. Otherwise why write it? When some of my works laid eggs, I promptly withdrew them." Although he writes for the general and not a specialized audience, he makes certain distinctions: "A composer doesn't write the same way for a small chamber-music audience as for the broad symphony audience . . . whether it's Beethoven, Bartók, or Siegmeister."[1] His "musical thoughts often appear on different levels—from the rich textures of my Third Symphony to the C major of my children's pieces." Depending on the basic idea of a piece he may write "ferocious dissonances, atonality, tone cluster, glissandi, intricate polymeters and—sometimes even in the same work—long-line, sweeping, very tonal melodies. But beneath all the modern devices, I believe, is an absolutely classical structure."[2]

A NEW-FASHIONED TRADITIONALISM

Most of these composers had studied with academics who favored the musical styles associated with atonalism or serialism. All of them have tried to reconcile atonality or serialism to more traditional tonal practices. At times only a hairline divides some of their compositions from the late works of composers like Rochberg and Kirchner. Herein lies their problem—each must worry about his rapport with audiences.

By 1950, Siegmeister had ventured into several styles, from the dramatic and extremely dissonant *Strange Funeral at Braddock* (1933) to the tuneful and cowboy song–oriented *Western Suite* (1945). The first was a political leftist's protest over the suffering of economically deprived Americans. The second was an uninhibited exaltation of the American spirit.

He was born in Brooklyn and grew up to the sound of popular music and jazz. Later, he studied folk song and the idiosyncratic music of Charles Ives. By the 1950s, he was able to assume several manners. One of them is revealed in the simplicity and easy melodiousness of vocal music like *Two Songs of the City* (1951) and the song cycle *For My Daughters* (1952). These tonal, triadic, and consonant ballads successfully depict the dreams and feelings of ordinary men and women and the homely and unaffected dialogues between child and parent.

Another manner is beholden to jazz and blues, as in the Clarinet Concerto (1956). The concerto candidly looks back into Siegmeister's own urban background and the city sounds of his youth. The composer states that jazz has been a persistent strain in his music, not a fashion or plaything to be taken up for a while and then discarded. He points to the jazz fugue in his First String Quartet, the boogie in *American Sonata*, the persistent blues in *Sunday in Brooklyn*, the fugatos and riffs in Sextet for Brass and Percussion, and the rag and cool jazz in the Fourth Symphony and the Piano Concerto.

The Flute Concerto of 1960 is a cool, lyric piece that suggests jazz only in the closing movement. The slow movement is linked to Gershwin's Broadway through its harmonic progressions, inner chromaticism, and syncopated rhythmic inflections. The melodies sound lovely, but without Gershwin's sense of bittersweet emptiness over something lost.

A third manner, and one that became more and more dominant in Siegmeister's mature years, attempts to synthesize all facets of his writing. Sound grows harsher, less tonal, even "wilder," as he likes to put it. Americanisms become less obvious and are modified by introversion and an overflow of personal feeling. The Third Symphony (1957) represents a mature realization of his changed outlook. The work, in fantasylike variation form, is cast in one trisectioned movement. An introductory "Moderato" announces three embryonic motives, out of which the entire composition is evolved. Americanisms are employed subtly and, probably, unconsciously—for example, the introduction and allegro of the first section do show rhythms and motivic transformations that indicate kinship to the *Western Suite*. However, the extroversion of the earlier work is replaced by an emotionality that the composer powerfully feels and urgently wants to communicate.

The Fourth Symphony (1970) is highly expressive and made up of expert oppositions of declamatory and melodic passages. It is also surrounded by an off-putting atonal-dissonant environment, not unlike the sounds Charles Ives achieved in his more adventurous orchestral ventures. It gives an insight into Siegmeister's Americanism, which does not mean just referring to folk song or jazz, but also to the continuation of a more advanced musical tradition unique to America.

The five violin sonatas he composed between 1956 and 1972 established him as the American equivalent of Bartók, with their sublimated kernels of folk music, passionate declamation, vehement rhythmic energy, and intense inwardly turned melodiousness. The first sonata layers essentially diatonic melody onto chromatic harmony and remains tonal. By the fifth sonata, we are asked to share in an altered world—one of fluid tonality verging on atonality, of fragmented and disjointed motives, and of highly intricate construction. It presents the general listener with problems of understanding and enjoyment similar to those encountered in the Fourth Symphony.

The most overtly Bartókian of his compositions is the Second String Quartet (1960). In the liner notes to the CRI recording, Siegmeister states: "During the 1960's I developed a keener interest in tighter organic structures and more closely woven, subtler sonorities." Although "melody is still the core of" this music, "a kind of wildness" is also introduced "as a balancing force—a craggy, harsh feeling that appears in violent rhythms and biting harmonies. It becomes most intense in such works as the second Theme and Variations for piano, the Sextet for Brass and Percussion, and the Second Piano Sonata." The piano sonata, in particular, pushed exploration to the extreme, when he tried to capture the "sonorities of the modern piano, using hammered notes, tone clusters, plucked strings, harmonics, wild leaps, cross-rhythms, and others."

After studying the instrumental works written in the decade and a half after 1970, one detects several characteristic procedures, like the commencing of a melodic phrase with a wide skip upward, through two or three notes, and then a skipping downward, usually by a third, more rarely by a fourth or fifth. One also hears an intriguing dichotomy between a tonal melodic phrase (often diatonic) and its underlying posttertian harmonies—the former giving direction and unity to the latter. The style is flexible enough to encompass and capture a wide variety of moods and feelings.

Few Siegmeister compositions for voice employ extreme or constant dissonance and atonality. For example, the several selections from his opera *The Plough and the Stars* (1963, rev. 1969) that the composer sent to me are given tonal centers and triadic order. They represent a fascinating mix of folk, popular, and art music. Edward Mabley's libretto draws upon a Sean O'Casey play on the anti-British Irish uprising of 1916 and some of its tragic consequences. Critics have praised the composer's knowledge of theater, the music's rich variety, and the opera's power. The opera also experienced the rare honor of being mounted by a French opera company in the city of Bordeaux.

The streetwise instinct for survival amongst many black Americans is given expression in *Madam to You* (1964), a song cycle based on poetry by Langston Hughes. We find earthiness, a joy of life, and toughness touched with tenderness in the words and music. As might be expected, rollicking rhythms and jaunty jazz colorations abound. Less tonal and triadic and more difficult to assimilate are the settings of the Langston Hughes text *The Face of War*, the song cycle on William Blake's *Songs of Experience*, the *Five Cummings Songs*, and the song cycle *Ways of Love* on poems by various writers. Also consistently dissonant, in spite of frequent allusions to black music, is the telling cantata for baritone, chorus, and orchestra *I Have a Dream*, whose text is drawn from the words of Martin Luther King, Jr.

Some Siegmeister works have won immediate admiration from audiences; others have proved rewarding after repeated hearings. One or two works have presented knotty listening problems. Yet the music is invested with sincerity. The music lover may find listening to it worthwhile.

Michael Colgrass (b. 1932) started his professional life as a percussion player. Early attempts at musical composition embraced atonality and serialism. Then, in the middle of the 1960s, what he describes as a singular and psychically disordering experience forced a reappraisal of his life and music. Music for him, he decided, should no longer be an intellectual exercise in twelve-tone rationalism nor an attempt to reach only a narrow audience. Now more traditional melody, tonality, and other once-respected practices interested him.

Reflecting on what he had been, Colgrass states: "In general, we composers tend to think of ourselves as being on a plane with scientists—highly specialized intellectuals presenting our research to colleagues in closed session. We write our ideas in journals for our peers and consider the general public musically illiterate (mainly because they don't come to our concerts)." New York City, in particular, is a place where a composer is most likely to "be trapped in a tight intellectual circle," out of which he has to break out.[3]

He decided not to belong to any artistic circle or create in isolation: "I came from a world of music where you improvise, and have close contact with your audience, and the music is not intellectualized. . . . The great musicians of any given time communicated with an audience. So I started to say to myself, if you're really a good composer, then you should be able to contact people who are nonspecialists in your art."[4]

He did reach audiences with *As Quiet As*, an orchestral suite completed in 1966. Colgrass says that the several movements of the work illustrate the answers that certain fourth-grade pupils gave when their teacher asked them to complete the sentence: "Let's be as quiet as. . . . " The quietness suggested by the children is that of a leaf turning colors, a deserted creek, an ant walking, children asleep, time passing, a soft rainfall, and the first star coming out. The leaf is described in very soft, overlapping long tones. Mood is stressed, not melody. The creek is rendered in two- and three-note figures; a high-up line whispers over a low bass; a tremendous hollowness of silence remains between. The ant is a faint, scratchy scramble of violin and percussion tones, with many a twitter heard before the movement ends. The dreaming children sleep to murmuring tones. Of this movement and the movements that follow, Colgrass states: "Following light breathing and heartbeats, a sonatina written by Beethoven as a child appears through a montage of 'sleeping sound,' and then reappears fragmentarily in musical styles from 1800 to the present. . . . 'A Soft Rainfall' and 'The First Star Coming Out' are the spring and summer counterparts of" the first two similes, "and are related musically as well."[5] The entire composition breathes peace, serenity, and dreamlike musing. Its innocent charm captures the child's view of the life around and within him. It also shows Colgrass's new direction was toward neoimpressionism, a projection in sound of hazy, evanescent, and dreamlike images. Audiences took to the music, making the composer nationally known in concert music circles.

The successful song cycle *New People*, for mezzo-soprano, viola, and piano, came out in 1969. A talent for tune writing, not fully evidenced in the previous work, comes to the fore here. The music combines melody "with a sardonic realism suggesting a modern Mussorgsky."[6] The text is Colgrass's own. Images of nature are given urban significance: a bird auditioning for Broadway, trees growing into skyscrapers, stars observing the strange behavior of earthlings. Tonal and atonal sounds, commonplace jazz, and strange serial passages depict the city dweller's sense of estrangement from modern society. The singer recalls feelings of tenderness in a baby's eyes; she finds her life a prison where she has no shadow; she satirizes friends, who are new people living like computers; she sympathizes with people who experience a sense of falling; she cries out for someone to communicate with her; she asks why she should sing if nobody is listening, and answers that spring is listening; and she closes with a ray of hope, when, as if talking to herself, she bids a thankful goodnight to the day and promises to return at the same time next year.

From the general listener's point of view, *Concert Masters* for three violins and orchestra (1975) is not nearly as pleasing as the previous two compositions. The work shows Colgrass's admiration for Vivaldi and interest in serial techniques. It mixes conventional with dissonant practices—producing a hybrid of styles: eighteenth century, romantic, impressionistic, and post-Webern. The work begins with dissonant, almost atonal, music, in what remains the prevalent style of the entire piece.

On a commission from the New York Philharmonic, Colgrass wrote *Déjá Vù* in 1977. The piece is for orchestra, with the percussion section given prominence. The title indicates something already experienced and, apparently in this composition, refers a bit obscurely to Colgrass's musical past and to Western music's historical past, if one goes by the several hints at different styles. On balance, it is music one listens to with a pleasure not produced by *Concert Masters*.

John Harbison (b. 1938), in his early pieces, sounds atonal, polyphonic, and academic. Here and there, a different sound (jazz, for one) finds itself in alien surroundings. For the most part, the style was Central European in its persistent dissonance, phrase fragmentation, melodic angularity, and expressionistic gestures. By the mid-seventies, Harbison had reconsidered his creative stance and modified his artistic viewpoint. Soon he could state: "I am simply not interested in the projection of personal *angst*. . . . Lately the expression of personality seems to be leading to mannerism and empty gesture. As far as I'm concerned, this exposure of the psychological, overtly personal is just an unexamined inheritance from Viennese Expressionism."[7] Dissonance and atonality did not permanently disappear. However, he relieved these with jazz, American popular song and dance, and references to the compositions of past composers. Unhappily, the conglomerate of sound usually failed to fuse into a whole.

Harbison's first opera, *Winter's Tale* (1974), shows the changes he was attempting. Schoenberg's and Webern's ideas are in abeyance; Haydn's, Brahms's, and even Verdi's are allowed some ascendancy. Harmony begins to make sense. Simple and fairly attractive pastoral songs are heard. "Dumb Shows," pantomimes designed to add colorful contrast yet move an audience, appear within the drama. In this composition, Harbison is still feeling his way toward an individual style.

Two years later, he wrote *The Flower-Fed Buffaloes*, for baritone, chorus, and seven instrumentalists, including a percussionist performing on a jazz set of drums, cymbals, vibraphone, and anvil. The published score, in holograph, contains the following performance note: "The performers should strive to infuse *all* the music with *both* 'classical' and 'nonclassical' (jazz or popular) feeling," a request hard to execute.

The text pursues two subjects: one, the dualistic and paradoxical nature of America, from the generous to the selfish; and, two, the American's involvement with the frontier, once physical and now spiritual. The music often sounds atonal or rather bitonal and even tritonal. Care is taken so that the audience can clearly hear the words. The *Preamble* replicates the fourths and fifths of ancient organum. In the movements that follow, the first produces a jazz ambience, especially by means of an effective riff; the second features fragmented and angular instrumental motion against the long tones of the baritone singer; the third gives an impressionistic interpretation of American songs, including "I'll Be Loving You, Always," and "America, the Beautiful"; the fourth has a pianist and percussionist back the baritone, who now performs in Schoenbergian speech song; the final movement contains a great deal of veiled homophonic singing by a chorus.

Ritualism, mysticism, trance-states make their appearance in *Diotoma* for orchestra, and *Full Moon in March*, a one-act opera based on a subject from Yeats.

The aim in the Piano Concerto of 1978 is to join advanced techniques to old-fashioned romanticism. The first movement starts off with hints of atonality and smears of clashing sounds. Everything, however, is toned down, so that the music will not arouse strong hostility. When the main melody arrives, its composer seems to yearn to turn it into a full-blown romantic tune. Tonal feeling is held in check by the mildly atonal surroundings. The next movement commences like a march derived from a popular tune. Nervous, asymmetrical rhythms and irregular eruptions of sound enter. Next, a canzona intervenes, which Harbison could have changed into a jazz ballad if he had abated the astringency of its accompaniment. Nevertheless, the dissonance is not obtrusive and the melody generates a pleasant warmness. Later a syncopated, jazz-oriented tune starts up in the piano and proceeds in the tempo of a foxtrot.

Similar comments could be made about his Violin Concerto of 1980. Andrew Porter writes that this concerto is "like all his music, hard to categorize and easy to enjoy. It pleases the mind but is composed with a freedom properly called 'romantic.' Harbison is a poetic, civilized, courteous composer. His fancy ranges, but he doesn't shout and stamp."[8]

The Symphony and the *Motetti di Montale*, which followed soon after the Violin Concerto, show further amelioration of his modern idiom. About the accessibility of Harbison's music, little doubt now remained. Richard Dyer, critic for the *Boston Globe*, wrote of the latter work: "A major work by a major musician who has found his own voice; these songs sound like no other music in the world, except when Harbison wants them to."[9]

On 30 January 1984, I heard his *Marabai Songs*, for soprano, harp, bass clarinet, flute, strings, and percussion, performed and came away convinced that it was an individual and communicative work. The text comprises ecstatic religious poetry to Krishna, the Dark One, written in sixteenth-century India by Marabai, who sang her poetry as she danced on the streets. The six songs are unapologetically romantic and glow with burning heat. Madrigalisms are introduced with fine effect, as in the second song, "All I Was Doing Was Breathing," where on the words "Dancing Energy" an infectious dance rhythm sets in. Sections like this and entire movements, like the fast dance song "Why Mira Can't Go Back to Her Old House" (No. 3), serve as wonderful foils to the slow, rhythmically subdued parts of the work, like the contemplative "Where Did You Go?" (No. 4) and to the passionately pleading "Don't Go, Don't Go" (No. 6). Harbison has written a composition of the first order.

Other composers whose styles are similar to the ones just discussed and whose works have a worth beyond the ordinary are Hall Overton, Robert Starer, Ezra Landerman, William Mayer, and Ellen Taaffe Zwilich, who is most accessible when not sounding like Sessions, as in her Chamber Symphony and Symphony No. 1.

THE ARTISTIC MAVERICKS

Among the composers active in the postwar years were some nonconformists who marked off individual creative courses that defied classification within any stylistic group. The music they wrote drew on the past but, as importantly, also looked to the future and indicated some directions the mainstream might take.

The first of the mavericks, David Del Tredici (b. 1937), had studied with Seymour Shifrin, Andrew Imbrie, and Roger Sessions. Even as he attended Princeton, he showed inclinations toward romanticism. An early work written in 1964, *I Hear an Army*, for soprano and string quartet, is based on a James Joyce poem. It is in many ways a product of his training, however creatively resourceful Del Tredici proves himself to be. The composer states that the composition depicts a frightened sleeper awakening from a nightmare, to find despair and loneliness but no relief. A long, agitated introduction for the strings depicts fearful sleep by means of evanescent and incomplete motives. The postlude allows the frightening dream to sink away, but one single, insistent note *B* lingers on, "a symbol of the sleeper's poignant, unrelenting loneliness, which remains undimmed to the end." The piece is atonal and employs serial procedures. The voice part makes the expected angular leaps and steep descents characteristic of atonalism. Yet imaginative passages give point to an expressionistic psychodrama.

Though also set to Joyce's verse and also atonal, *Night Conjure-Verse* for soprano, mezzo-soprano, woodwind septet, and string quartet, completed two years later, shows a softening of Del Tredici's advanced idiom. The voices move more frequently in conjunct motion, and long tones help the piece cohere better. A second work written in the same year, *Syzygy*, for amplified soprano, French horn, tubular bells, and chamber orchestra, demonstrates a further softening of the atonal idiom.

In 1968 Del Tredici launched his series of works based on Lewis Carroll's *Alice* writings, with *Pot-Pourri* for amplified soprano, rock music group, chorus, and orchestra. Successive numbers in the series tended more and more toward consonance and traditional practices. Popular idioms increasingly found their way into the scores. With *Adventures Underground* of 1971, a different sort of sound took shape.

Del Tredici's most impressive work of the series is *Final Alice*, composed in 1976 as a bicentennial commission. The required musical forces include an amplified soprano narrator, a solo concertante folk instrument group, and a large orchestra. The hour-long "opera written in concert form" generated a great deal of excitement in audiences during the first year, but, soon after, conductors and orchestras began to ignore it. Del Tredici states that he composed "elaborate arias interspersed by dramatic episodes from the last two chapters of *Alice's Adventures in Wonderland*," where the absurd trial and Alice's return to "dull reality" take place. Added are new poems, especially a parody of the poem "Alice Gray," by the nineteenth-century poet William Mee, and a closing Apotheosis, taken from *Through the Looking Glass*. Two stories are told: "The bizarre Wonderland happenings, and the implied love story—the human side of Carroll." Simple harmonies of the tonic, dominant, and subdominant, and genuinely pleasing melodies are heard. Yet Del Tredici uses them as if they were newly minted. The lyricism and orchestral colors stem from late–nineteenth-century styles. Only in the "growing" music of the beginning and the bedlam during the trial scene does atonality occur. A final dissonant stroke warns us that all that has happened was a dream and this is "dull reality."[10]

One critic remarks on how truly up to date all of this was: "Del Tredici stakes his claim to modernity first through his very decision to write such unashamed tonality: by now consonance itself sounds strange and fresh. In addition, his almost obsessive repetition of a few tunes and variants of them casts an hypnotic spell very different from the theme and counter-theme, contrapuntal developments and resolution of the typical nineteenth-century orchestral piece. And the use of the 'folk group' and other popsy touches lend the enterprise an insouciant contemporary spirit."[11]

The composer states that he was afraid his modernist colleagues would think he had gone insane. They saw the success of *Final Alice* as a threat to them and the use of consonance as a way of catering to the public. However, he had not wanted just to write tonally and win over a huge audience; what he did was also instinctual. He decided that if an audience really liked a piece at first hearing, it did not necessarily mean the music was vulgar and terrible. He asked: "Why are we writing music except to move people and to be expressive? To have what has moved us move somebody else? Everything is reversed today. If a piece appeals immediately, sensuously, if an audience likes it: all those are 'bad things.' It is really very *Alice in Wonderland*."[12]

Another success with audiences was *In Memory of a Summer Day*. It recalls a day when Carroll and the real Alice rowed on the Thames. What Del Tredici especially wanted to depict were "the interior landscapes" of child and adult. On the one hand is the child's innocent joy; on the other, the adult's feeling of pleasure coupled with regret. A "chord of rapture and regret"—which is

Tristan und Isolde–like in its evocation of longing—conveys this dual essence of the piece. The song "Simple Alice" states the main tune in unadorned major form, except for an excursion into the minor during the singing of the fourth verse. The song closes on Carroll's painful realization that: "We are but older children, dear, / Who fret to find our bedtime near." Motivic developments, march music, variations on the "Alice" melody follow each other. The "chord of rapture and regret" returns. Then comes "Ecstatic Alice," a dense, chromatic, and passionate reworking of the Alice melody, whose climax arrives on the words: "The magic words shall hold thee fast: / Thou shalt not heed the raving blast." Finally, serenity slowly permeates the music and, along with it, sorrow and nostalgia for a past that will never again return.

No other work by Del Tredici has met with the enthusiasm accorded *Final Alice* and *In Memory of a Summer Day*. It remains to be seen if future performances of the two works will make a similar impact on listeners.

Frederic Rzewski (b. 1938), like Del Tredici, commenced as a modernist. Despite the fact that he studied with Milton Babbitt, Rzewski would experiment with a variety of styles, not just serialism: indeterminacy, multimedia, electronics, and minimalism. He developed a social and political awareness that had considerable influence on several of the compositions he would write. For example, his concern over the Attica prisoners' uprising of September 1971 caused him to compose *Coming Together* and *Attica*. Declamation of prisoners' words against an aggressive, repetitive, and percussive instrumental accompaniment guaranteed a favorable reception from an avant-garde audience.

The *Song and Dance* of 1977, for flute, clarinet and bass clarinet, contrabass, and vibraphone, mixed jazz and minimalist idioms and also introduced some indeterminacy. Along with the expected repetitions of short rhythmo-melodic figures, the music comprised a dreamlike song and a bustling jazz-edged dance, easy to listen to but without memorable melodies.

During the 1970s, Rzewski had also turned to a musical style which he claimed embodied "humanist realism." The result was accessible music, usually for piano, based on solid tonal melody and incisive rhythm. Peter Davis, in a 1981 article, cites the *Four Pieces* and Ballad No. 3 ("Whose Side Are You On?") as examples. Davis states that almost every phase of Rzewski's career has produced "something of interest and perhaps his current preoccupations are yielding the richest results. This 'fusion' music freely incorporates 19th-century keyboard techniques, Schoenbergian structures, jazz rhythms, folk or protest song material, and experimental sonorities."[13]

The mightiest musical example of Rzewski's "humanist realism" is certainly *The People United Will Never Be Defeated! 36 Variations on a Chilean Song* for piano, composed in 1975. The event inspiring the composition was the deposition of the Allende government. The song's lovely melody was written by Sergio Ortega and Quilapayun and had come to be identified with Chilean resistance to the dictatorship imposed after Allende's defeat. Within a carefully planned structure occur variations going from heaven-storming grandiloquence to delicate reticence. Variations are at one moment unlyrical and dissonant, at another effervescent and jazz-like, at still another hypnotic and rhythmic, or on occasion seemingly aleatoric and unplanned. Some fifty minutes of breathtaking pianistic virtuosity are required for the composition's performance. The listener has no problem enjoying it from beginning to end.

Rzewski also wrote *Four North American Ballads* for piano. Titles indicate extramusical meanings: "Winnsboro Cotton Mill Blues," "Dreadful Memories," "Down by the Riverside," and "Which Side Are You On?" Virtuosity, sophistication, and directness of expression characterize the music. They have been described as "people's rhapsodies" and "almost Lisztian" in the conduct of their tunes. Colorful passages include the "dynamistic growl-and-pound painting" of the first ballad, the "polytonal and sometimes free-atonal treatments" of the second ballad, and the "hardly less exhilarating" remaining music.[14]

Like the *Alice* pieces of Del Tredici, Rzewski's musical contributions to "humanist realism" take on the appearance of overly specialized music, focusing on a specific doctrine and realized in a restrictive style, in which lie both their attractiveness and limitations.

Too busily eclectic to specialize in any one idiom, John Corigliano (b. 1938) has used a number of procedures, traditional and modernist, to achieve his ends. He saw no purpose in stylistic conformity, saying that a composer should do anything he feels is appropriate to a piece. He was a pragmatist—if some usage might work in performance and stimulate an audience, use it. The important thing was not to be tied to a theory about how music should be composed. Early in his career, he decided that too many contemporary composers wrote bookish and not aural music, and few tried to reach the general audience. Why shouldn't music stir the viscera as well as the intellect, he wondered? Why didn't composers take pains to write clearly? "An interviewer recently [c. December 1981] said to me that I wasn't cerebral," comments Corigliano. "That infuriated me. I think and work my butt off for a year of my life to give an audience 30 minutes of comprehensibility."[15] He angrily disagreed with the Babbitt claim that audiences were too musically illiterate and lazy to understand any meaningful music. In fact, he stated, as have other mainstream composers, that the audience was under no obligation to hear and understand new music: "Audiences pay money to see or hear something that will move them, excite them, interest them or in some form involve them. If a composer has something important to say, it is his obligation to find a way of saying it that fulfills these basic requirements without compromising his standards in any way.[16] He considered the quest for originality to be "a leftover of that horrible 19th-century originality complex."[17]

His debut as a composer came with *Kaleidoscope* for two pianos and *Fernhill* for mezzo-soprano, chorus, and orchestra, composed to a Dylan Thomas text. Wider recognition ensued when his Sonata for Violin and Piano, composed in 1963, won first prize in a Spoleto Festival chamber music competition. The sonata is tonal, though with some nontonal and polytonal sections. Rhythms vary constantly; meter changes in almost every measure. Virtuosity adds spice to a basically optimistic work.

Five years later came the Piano Concerto, in a language that one moment is restrained and another, agitated. The first movement opens on a perky, staccato theme and brilliant orchestral colors. Suddenly, the theme ceases and a quiet romantic tune is heard. The rest of the movement stresses the contrast between the two moods. The second movement, a brief, playful scherzo, hints at jazz. The slow movement (like that of the Violin Sonata) makes a big, intense arialike statement. And the last movement goes at a pell-mell pace, building excitement until a tremendous climax is achieved. As with many of Corigliano's compositions, and not unlike the music of Bernstein, the listener senses theatrical drama behind every note of the concerto. The work was a striking success when first performed.

When writing a piece featuring a soloist, Corigliano imagined him as the protagonist in a play, whose personality is defined by the nature of his instrument, and who interacts with other instrumental actors. For example, when he was composing the Concerto for Oboe and Orchestra, he kept in mind not only the musical ideas but also the oboe's character, both being one and the same. "In the Oboe Concerto," states Corigliano, his themes "had to do with what exactly an oboe is—the instrument has certain unique qualities, such as its lower range being the most forceful, and I used them as building blocks."[18]

In five movements, the Oboe Concerto begins with the oboe helping the orchestra to tune. Gradually, the random tones make sense, and the first movement is on its bumptious way, only again to be stopped as the instruments are made to untune themselves. The slow movement, as is usual with Corigliano, is completely songlike. The Scherzo movement abruptly interrupts the song with a loud percussive stroke. Then an oboe (which at times sounds like a kazoo) and percussion chase after each other. The Trio of the Scherzo, scored for vibraphone, celeste, and harp, evokes the eighteenth century by means of extremely soft, delicate, and tinkling sounds. The "Aria" that comes next is designed to bring out the dramatic, coloratura qualities of the oboe. With the Finale arrives a Moroccan dance, the oboe made to sound raw, open, and woody. Audiences found much they could enjoy in the concerto.

The exploitation of dramatic contrast has been mentioned as integral to Corigliano's thinking. In 1977 after he had completed his Clarinet Concerto, Corigliano stated: "Contrast is one of the most important elements in music. A score should be balanced: I make sure that mine have both lighthearted parts and more serious parts. For instance, in the Clarinet Concerto, I think of the first two movements as being terribly serious and the last as a kind of festival for all players."[19]

When premiered, the Clarinet Concerto received a standing

ovation from a New York Philharmonic audience assumed to be timid about liking anything new. The music exposes a variety of styles—from conventional harmony, tonal passages, and regular metric divisions, to tone clusters, twelve-tone rows, violent syncopations, and garish coloristic effects. Virtuosic, stimulating, theatrical, and sure-handed are words that come to mind when the concerto is heard.

Like Corigliano, Joseph Schwantner (b. 1943) employs whatever musical procedures seem appropriate to a work. The compositions of both composers contain an accessible modernism that has grown out of a contemporary aesthetic viewpoint and contemporary sound experimentation. Schwantner's style, however, is unlike Corigliano's. The music sounds less intense, less exciting, and more impersonal. Non-Western musics have made contributions to his style. Major and minor scales mix with ancient modes or scales of his own invention. Some passages sound minimalist; others the result of indeterminacy. At one moment, harmonies resonate richly; at another, they have no existence apart from the individual lines that accidentally bring them to notice. David Owens, writing in the *Christian Science Monitor*, has denominated Schwantner to be an accessible composer, but not a romantic or minimalist. Schwantner often rouses the gentler feelings and creates a "rarified, other worldly atmosphere," Owens says, or a "moody atmospheric music."[20]

Through the 1960s, Schwantner favored serialism. In the 1970s, his interest in tonality increased and his experiments with novel resonances, textures, and procedures, including indeterminacy, also increased. Works like *Consortium I* and *II* show him turning away from serialism. *Caelestis (Consortium III)*, composed in 1972, contains subtle sound effects similar to those in George Crumb's compositions. The music is constantly calm and abstracted, with Eastern-like metallic clangs and shimmery long tones. Toward the end, an extensive flute solo makes other worldly sounds against a percussive accompaniment. Then ten sonorities are heard, Schwantner leaving it to the conductor to decide the duration and intensity of each sonority.

He continued moving toward greater lyricism and less rigid construction. The congeniality of his style to that of George Crumb also continued. *Elixir (Consortium VIII)* is a miniature concerto for flute and five players. In it are unorthodox sonorities—produced by striking or bowing on antique cymbals, by fingering crystal glasses, and by whistling. *Wild Angels of the Open Hills* for soprano, flute, and harp sets the strange visions of science-fiction writer Ursula Le Guin to music. Mysterious harp arpeggios, delicately tinkling bells, whispered effects, and bird warbling create a fantastic atmosphere for the words. *Sparrows*, whose text is fifteen Japanese *haikus* by Issa, asks for a soprano backed by eight players. Lyricism is more evident. Harmony is lusher. Short, recognizable motives recur. In and out of these tiny musical pictures float snatches of Renaissance dance and baroque counterpoint. At times, the instrumentalists are asked to sing quietly. The sung tunes are haunting, making *Sparrows* one of the most communicative of Schwantner's compositions. Of his turning to tonality, the composer says: "Well, I guess I'm on the bandwagon. I don't think it's important. It's a new way of looking at something you haven't looked at for a long time."[21]

Aftertones of Infinity, composed in 1978, was an ambitious attempt to carry over the idiom refined under chamber music conditions into his orchestral music. The expected ethereality and carefully wrought instrumental effects are all in place. A "celestial choir," whose voices are those of the orchestral players is also heard. Yet the work lacks the tonal focus and attractive melodies of *Sparrows*.

By 1980 when he composed *Wind, Willow, Whisper* for five players, his style was becoming predictable. A few phrases show some exuberance; most are quiet, with instructions like "delicate little bells" for repeated high notes in the piano, and "ethereal" for lyrical fragments played by one or another of the instruments. The players' whistling is normal for a Schwantner piece, as is the "haunted" effect created by the pianist when he keeps the damper pedal depressed for the entire work.

New Morning for the World ("Daybreak of Freedom") was completed in 1982. For narrator and orchestra, its words are those of Martin Luther King, Jr. Its sequence of fanciful "events" are what we have come to expect from Schwantner. The music is mostly pretty and sometimes poignant. In much of the work, lyrical snippets, no big tunes, are heard. On occasion, he piles up an orchestral resonance, at the last moment adding the thunder of percussion, until the full orchestra achieves a moment of power and drama. The work is pleasing to experience, yet when one comes away from hearing it, one feels as if something insubstantial had been presented.

When we attempt to evalute contemporary works like those of Del Tredici, Rzweski, Corigliano, and Schwantner, the old question of surface and substance comes to the fore. The exteriors of the best compositions by these four composers offer great attractions to the general music public. The textures are skillfully calculated. The "events" follow each other with attention to psychological and dramatic rightness. The sheer sound seduces the senses. The surface promises an abundance of substance beneath. Nevertheless, after prolonged exposure to these composers' offerings, we feel compelled to rethink our experiences. We wonder if, at times, the music is too eclectic, whether the compositional manner is too facile or the tones contain much sustenance. This is not to say that nothing of intrinsic value is present, simply that we are not sure how much genuineness exists. A musical drama is enacted. Performers feign the grander emotions. Is it merely the staged activity and the impressive gesticulations of the musicians that we admire, or is it the insights into universal human experience (which should be residuals of any encounter with artistic productions)? In short, we have appreciated the sound and fury, but we hope they signify something.

NOTES

1. Elie Siegmeister, letter to the author dated 21 July 1983.

2. Gus Freedman, "Elie Siegmeister," *Music Journal* 35 (April 1977): 7.

3. Michael Colgrass, "Then I Stood on My Head," *New York Times*, 28 May 1972, sec. 2, 11.

4. David Ewen, *American Composers: A Biographical Dictionary* (New York: Putnam's, 1982), s.v. "Colgrass, Michael Charles."

5. See the composer's explanation in the liner notes to RCA LSC 3001.

6. Siegmeister, "Humanism and Modernism," *Keynote* (January 1984): 9.

7. Janet Tassel, "A Homecoming for John Harbison," *Boston Globe Magazine*, 26 February 1984, 46.

8. Andrew Porter, "Tumult of Mighty Harmonies," *New Yorker* (20 June 1983): 88.

9. Richard Dyer, "Keeping Time," *Boston Globe*, 17 May 1983, 56.

10. See Del Tredici's explanation in the liner notes to London LDR 71018.

11. John Rockwell, *All American Music* (New York: Knopf, 1983), 74.

12. Ibid., 82–83.

13. Davis, "Pianos Still Stir Composers' Souls," 23.

14. Peter Frank, *Fanfare* 4 (July/August 1981): 214.

15. Bernard Holland, "Highbrow Music to Hum," *New York Times Magazine*, 31 January 1982, 25.

16. Ibid., 70.

17. Allan Kozinn, "The 'Unfashionable Romantic' Music of John Corigliano," *New York Times*, 27 April 1980, sec. 2, 24.

18. Phillip Ramey, "A Talk with John Corigliano," liner notes to New World Records NW 309.

19. Ibid.

20. David Owens, *Christian Science Monitor*, 4 January 1983, 20.

21. David Patrick Stearns, "Joseph Schwantner," *Musical America* (December 1979): 7.

8
Reconciliations

When the United States entered the twentieth century, most Americans saw no reason to reject the culture they had inherited. Tinker with it and improve it, yes; but not total rejection. Only a few people expected the breakdown of the beliefs, values, and cultural forms that then existed. Soon came savage wars, industrial regimentation, genocidal hatreds, economic depression, and dictatorships. Millions of people starved, suffered, and died—soldiers and civilians, adults and children alike.

During and after World War II, an American minority wondered about themselves and the patterns of their lives, which seemed to have disintegrated. The minority included intellectuals, writers, and creative people working in the arts. They discussed influential books, like Oswald Spengler's *The Decline of the West* (1918–22), which stated that every civilization and culture lived through a life cycle, from childhood to old age and death, and that Western civilization and culture had reached the death point, with no deliverance possible. They memorized and quoted large portions of Thomas Eliot's poetry, especially *Prufrock* (1917) and *The Waste Land* (1922), which delineated the anguish and hollowness of twentieth-century life, the anomie of the individual, and the bankruptcy of love. Many felt they should talk about James Joyce's *Finnegan's Wake* (1939), though few understood the novel. Joyce expressed a modern reality through radical arrangements and displacements of words to produce a complex of recondite meanings.

In painting, Pablo Picasso's *Les Demoiselles d'Avignon* (1907) had tossed traditional ways of viewing to one side in favor of forms that were fractionalized or twisted out of their normal shapes. His *Guernica* (1937), though centered on a horrifying incident of the Spanish Civil War, was taken as the definitive representation of the inhumanity, desolation, and agony investing modern living, a representation impossible to achieve through traditional means. In architecture, the influential Le Corbusier claimed his pillars, use of reinforced concrete, and preference for industrial rather than humane designs were honest expressions of contemporaneousness. In music, Stravinsky and Schoenberg originated new approaches to sound, which featured secundal harmony, irregular or indefinable rhythm, suppressed melodic references of the traditional sort, and atonality.

After World War II came the age of the nuclear bomb and the wars in Korea and Vietnam. By 1960, the experiences of this recent history, along with the cultural expressions they called forth, caused the notion of civilization's breakdown to flood our unconsciousness, then our consciousness, according to John Lukacs.[1] He continued by saying that up until around 1950, modernity in the arts often had the appeal of freshness and novelty, "a welcome breakaway" from Victorian tastes. However, by 1970, "modern" had become "far less attractive; its appeal" had decayed, "while its former antonym 'old-fashioned,' " had "risen in our estimation." We were entering a transitional period to another age.[2]

Increasing numbers of compositions written in the 1970s and 1980s by former avant-gardists have demonstrated a looking back. Moreover, the mainstream composers have become less despised by those addicted to modernism. To hear Barber and Menotti praised in 1984 by two composers, one once a devotee of serialism and another a post-Messiaenite, was quite a jolt to me.

THE MODERN COMPOSER IN A PERIOD OF TRANSITION

Apologists for modern composers claim that without the composer's contributions, music would not exist. Therefore, the composers active in the postwar decades must receive financial support and performances of their music. Unfortunately, the general music public finds most of the postwar directions taken by composers not to its taste. At the same time, it has a tremendous backlog of masterly works from the past to which it strongly relates. As far as the public is concerned, no need for the contemporary composer's productions exists. Only a residual romanticism about the dues owed the artist, which still lingers from the last century, remains in the public's mind—and this is now dwindling. Crisis mounts. Rebuilding a liaison between composer and public must have top priority.

The point is rapidly being reached where no composer can continue to function if only a miniscule audience exists for his music. Now that so many radical departures from traditional music have taken place and fantastical experiments have been claimed to have artistic value, no shock remains. Avant-gardism has lost its power to intimidate, to convince us that originality is in itself a good. Permanency leads a fleeting existence in today's art music world.

Yet many American composers have dedicated their lives to their music. They have sincerely tried to give of their best and, though fair-sized audiences may never be found for them, have contributed major works that mirrored significant aspects of today's civilization: Babbitt's *Philomel*, Carter's String Quartet No. 2, Feldman's *Rothko Chapel*, Subotnick's *The Wild Bull*, and the like. How painful it must be for them when the general audience rejects their compositions.

Composers, however mightily they labor, need to preserve the goodwill of more than a handful of people. Pulitzer prizes and other critical awards seem the result of in-house competitions and mean little to listeners. Private patronage, never large, now begins to look for a public mandate for the music it sponsors. Public, corporate, and foundation funds for the arts become less abundant. The people in charge of programming performances and the directors of publishing houses and record companies increasingly look askance at the inability of most composers to break out of their creative ghettos.

Indicative of a myopia still prevalent amongst composers is a report, published in the *New York Times* on 24 June 1984, which printed the opinions given by musicians selected by the *Times* as knowledgeable about the contemporary scene.[3] No members of the traditional mainstream were considered worth interviewing.

Spoken to were Wuorinen, Feldman, Subotnick, Anderson, and Anthony Davis. The first three composers, representative of older avant-gardisms, showed no modification of the views from the 1960s. Anderson seemed incapable of much verbalization, dwelt in her own private world, and was mostly out of it. Davis predictably was pro-black, pro-jazz, and pro–non-Western music.

Feldman still could assert: "The 19th century was overrated. Beethoven died in 1827, and then you had a lot of junk [Schumann? Chopin? Brahms? Mussorgsky? Verdi?]. . . . The 20th century is absolutely, very, very strong." Wuorinen chimed in with: "I agree about the 19th century, which for the most part is a pretty dull wasteland, and about the 20th, which in a single century serves almost to sum up what had been done in Western music in the preceding several hundred years." Anderson said nothing.

These composers still believed that they had to pull down most of the structures from the past, discard the dross of the present, and create something uncontaminated by American civilization and the American people. Asked if composers owed the public anything, Feldman said he had long ago stopped thinking about the audience. Subotnick never really answered, stating instead something about a composer's responsibility "not to lie and not to mislead people on purpose." Anderson failed to indicate whether she had any thoughts on the subject.

Writers like Marshall Berman, concerned over the problems of twentieth-century society, contradict the opinions just expressed. In the 1970s, Berman states, the power to blow away the past was lost: "Modernity could no longer afford to throw itself into 'action lightened of all previous experience' (as De Man put it). . . . The moderns of the 1970s couldn't afford to annihilate the past and present in order to create a new world *ex nihilo*; they had to learn to come to terms with the world they had, and work from there." Like the economy, the whole concept of modernity collapsed: "At a moment when modern society seemed to lose the capacity to create a brave new future, modernism was under intense pressure to discover new sources of life through imaginative encounters with the past."[4]

Needed was a reestablishment of symbolic continuity with the past. Needed was the use of sounds imbedded in a symbol system shared by composer and the larger audience he required in order for his art to survive. Because music defies exact definition and complete elucidation, this symbolism had to penetrate beneath the listener's consciousness and lead to significations incomprehensible to reason. When Carl Jung, for example, contemplated the wider possibilities of a common symbology, he spoke of the indefinable but exalted states to which it could lead, even to the concept of a "divine" being—whom reason and intellectualization are incompetent to define.[5]

Modernism as a distinctive manner of composing and as a standard of excellence, with the composer in each subsequent work reinventing a new symbol system from scratch, prevents such penetrations from happening. The promised remedies to Victorian rigidity have turned out to be as bad as the disease, because the needs of the twentieth-century audience were neglected. In an insightful article, published in the *Times* on 8 July 1984, a week after the published interview with the composers mentioned earlier, Will Crutchfield suggests that right after Mozart, music began to mean something beyond its immediate function. Composers began to think in terms of writing for the ages and got into trouble. "Several generations of heroic composers fought to win an audience for their ever richer, ever more complex, ever more idiosyncratic and personal musical visions." Some individuals won out, most lost.[6] The problem was to strike Mozart's balance between functional directness on the surface and multilayered substance underneath, which composers "consciously sought when they have felt a special need for intimate communication with their hearers."[7]

Complexity and individuality meant less carryover of meaning from work to work. Acquaintanceship with one work of a composer did not always permit the understanding of another of his works. Besides, relentless dissonance unrelieved by consonance and the difficulty of telling the direction of a movement produced first confusion, then revulsion in the general listener. From Mozart on, a growing number of people opted themselves out of the audience for contemporary music. With Schoenberg and Webern, only a small minority remained. Composers began to console themselves with "the lag theory of catching up." However, nothing suggests that this will ever happen: "It may be that the acceptance-lag has reached or passed the length of an entire listening lifetime, in which case it might as well be infinite." To expect otherwise is unreal-istic.[8] This conclusion I accept with deep regret, since I genuinely like many compositions that have evoked only limited interest.

Most performers and listeners have neither the time, patience, or desire to master avant-garde music. With even the best will in the world, they sometimes find it a hopeless task. Crutchfield tells of trying his utmost to understand Carter's *Night Fantasies*, a lengthy, convoluted, rhythmically intricate piano composition. He talked to its interpreter, the pianist Paul Jacobs. He studied its score, read articles and analyses of it, played some of it at the keyboard, and listened repeatedly to a recording by Jacobs over a long period of time. Though he began to recognize certain pas-sages, he added: "To this day I find a good deal of it unintelligi-ble, and still like best the brief snippets that suggest tonal music— the bits that (accidentally?) evoke music responses common to a larger community. I still cannot drop the needle and be confident of knowing immediately where in the piece it has landed, as I could without a second thought in a Mozart concerto I have heard only a third as often." The piece was too self-referential. "I no longer feel curious to hear it more."[9]

More voices than ever before were raised in the 1980s against incomprehensibility and the license to write anything one pleased and call it music. Some asked why excellence could not be found in works that enlarge upon the language that already is in place? They spoke in praise of the generation of Copland, Barber, and Creston, and younger composers of the traditional mainstream who believed in change growing out of continuity and in a constantly expanding tradition.[10] Besides, as Leonard Meyer wrote in 1967, contemporary American music has reached the point where what-ever its novel idioms and methods, it can no longer displace pre-viously existing ones: "The gamut of possibilities—from com-pletely pre-planned order to total chance, from teleological structuring to goalless meandering, from syntactic formalism to subjective psychologism, from the explicitly analytic to the essen-tially mystic—has all but reached its limit. New idioms and meth-ods will involve the combination, mixture, and modification of existing means rather than the development of radically new ones."[11]

To combine, mix, and modify extant sound, however, is not

enough to win over alienated listeners. We must ask what are the other necessary but missing factors that will produce greater confidence in the contemporary composer and greater affection for his music? First, the composer must feel, and make his audience feel, that he creates in and for an American society capable of remedying its failings, a society in which the composer has faith, and a society made up of imperfect human beings who, despite their faults, also aspire to nobility. These people's and the composer's inner imperfections and aspirations together can be fit matter for artistic works. Furthermore, the composer must believe that however defective in application, a set of enduring principles does guide his society, can justify its existence, will strengthen its future course, and is able to inspire artistic expression.

Second, the modern composer must cease his isolation. Incredible is the extent to which the avant-garde obsessively disdains or is alarmed by the general music public. The division of people into highbrow, middlebrow, and lowbrow is a convenient way to prove one's artistic superiority, but the actuality is never so clear cut.[12] The avant-garde was fortunate indeed that the Americans, in the three decades after World War II, continued to tolerate music they hated.

Third, the modern composer must reconsider the use and function of his music. A. L. Kroeber defines function as an activity that is natural, proper, or characteristic (a broom's function is to sweep the floor).[13] When we examine a composition, say Samuel Barber's *Adagio for Strings*, an arrangement of the slow movement of his string quartet made in 1937, we perceive a well-defined form articulated through the logical flow of a single melody, an intelligible rhythmic direction, and harmony that contributes to the maintenance of an integrated structure. The composition has taken on shared meaning and associations, agreed upon by performers and listeners alike, which are emotional and expressive of sorrow, frequently for some person or event since past. The piece has a use: it is performed privately to signal the passing of a loved one and publicly to memorialize the death of a prominent person. It is heard in the home, broadcast over the air, during church services, and at public commemorations. The piece has a function: it assuages grief; it unites people by furthering common feelings of reverence and appreciation of our mortality; and, at the same time, it excites aesthetic pleasure. Kroeber states that although meaning is subjective in music, widespread agreement exists on the meaning of certain compositions (like the *Adagio for Strings*), despite the fact that many cannot recall all of a given piece. Therefore, we can ascertain the meaning of these compositions objectively, as well as subjectively.[14]

Needed in compositions is perceptible form given coherence through internal relationships that, however individual they seem, are integrated with a society's prevalent cultural patterns. Only within this context can novelty take on meaning—meaning that entails the assent of a culture.[15] In 1983 Edward Rothstein recognized that avant-garde compositions had not won this assent and had no function. The staging of the "Horizons '83" festival in New York and the interest in neoromanticism, he said, was a major acknowledgment of this: "Compositional styles once considered clichéd and retrograde were back in favor. While once the use of a tonic-dominant harmonic progression would have been considered heretical, it is now nearly common practice. While three decades ago, the European Darmstadt school of serial composition ruled with a severe, serial hand, now, there is freedom to indulge in sentiment."[16]

Fourth, the composer must again achieve a sense of community with his society. Several composers are already discovering that the feeling of belonging to a society, which they had given up, is indeed to be cherished. As Yankelovich suggests: "Although difficult to define abstractly, the idea of community evokes in the individual the feeling that; 'Here is where I belong, these are my people, I care for them, they care for me, I am part of them, I know what they expect from me and I from them, they share my concerns, I know this place, I am on familiar ground, I am at home.' This is a powerful emotion, and its absence is experienced as an aching loss, a void, a sense of homelessness. The symptoms of its absence are feelings of isolation, falseness, instability and impoverishment of spirit."[17]

Witness Michael Colgrass's excitement about feeling he had come home. He had been invited to become artist in residence for one month in Fort Wayne, through funds provided by the Fine Arts Foundation of that city. Ralph Kohlhoff, the director of the foundation, was well aware of how often in the past similar attempts had failed because composers, though physically present, failed to reach a community. Colgrass quotes him as saying: "We need to integrate artists in the mainstream of American life in cities like Fort Wayne, instead of having them all go to culture centers [like New York City] or become teachers training more artists for non-employment." Colgrass took up residence and rehearsed choruses and other local performing groups, from those in public schools to professional ensembles, and commenced "rapping with almost everybody in town." The new experience of having a community reach out to include him in its life and of leaving his "cubbyhole with a piano," thrilled him. "I found myself asking, Is it possible that a creative artist could actually become functional in a community, be hired to live there and do his work?" He states: "Many composers I talk to are dissatisfied with the restricted lives they lead. They are bored by the parochial audience for new music and feel stifled by the university. They express a need for at least an occasional contact with people outside music who talk plain language; they need the inspiration of having their music utilized the way Bach's and Beethoven's was; they long to be put to work composing for a purpose or function. In other words, they are tired of the romantic view of the artists—misunderstood, suffering, alone—and feel the real challenge of composing is to communicate to a diverse body of people on one's own terms and get a response."[18]

People will listen to music that they find likeable, whether traditional or experimental, art oriented or a fusion of art and popular. Only convince them that what you write can be liked. This done, the composer will feel the elation that comes with the conviction that he at last is writing to some purpose.

Last, the composer must not spurn tradition. If his innovations have vitality, they will modify tradition, not merely offer alternatives to it. Besides, tradition cannot be wiped out. Culture always is received from the past. Even when change and innovation are most extreme, "several times as many items of culture" are being "transmitted from the past as there are being newly devised."[19] In the 1980s, the pronouncement of anathema against traditional values no longer sounds as loudly as it did. "We composers begin again to talk about 'morality' in music or 'uplifting experiences,' " admits Druckman. "We begin once again to use the word 'beautiful.' "[20]

The search is on for a meaningful style, and for creative roots. As already noted, beginning in the 1970s, some former modernists did begin to make changes that gave a different orientation to their music. At times it was direct quotation from the past, or an imitation of an older style. More frequently it meant overlaying music from the past with modern sounds—a Beethoven tune imbedded within an atonal texture, a Mozartian harmonic progression bombarded with secundal intervals. Though usually the mixture of musics failed to acculturate, composers like Rochberg, Crumb, and Druckman are to be commended for trying. In addition, whatever is ultimately decided about the worth of Glass's and Reich's music, at least it has brought about an awareness of the untouched possibilities of basic triads wedded to invigorating rhythms. What is more, their music has made connection with a large audience.

With artistic intolerance now abating, the noteworthy mainstream composers and compositions discussed in the previous two chapters should be revived in order to offer the public additional alternatives to the older music it already cherishes. The premiere-only-then-oblivion syndrome afflicting this and other contemporary music must give way to repeated presentations of our strongest compositions in our several major cultural centers in order to familiarize listeners with them and encourage greater interest in contemporary creativity. The chasm between new music and audience is bridgeable.

THE NATURE OF THE GENERAL AUDIENCE

Important to remember is one fact: The great majority of American men and women are indifferent to art music in its entirety. Various writers have given conflicting figures on the size of the audience for art music. Although the figure is at best an estimate, perhaps some twelve million Americans comprise the core public for art music. These twelve million, in turn, exhibit specific tastes: for orchestral, chamber, soloistic-recital, or operatic music; for Renaissance, Baroque, Classical, or Romantic music; or any combination of these.

What of contemporary music? Most twentieth-century music savored by listeners was composed in the first half of the century. It includes the less adventurous compositions of European composers, like Stravinsky, Bartók, Britten, Hindemith, Prokofiev, and Shostakovich; and of American composers, like Copland, Thomson, Barber, and, of course, Gershwin. The more tonal the work, the more likely is it to attract listeners. In all probability, no more than 100,000 people pay any real attention to American music of the postwar period, and, of these, less than half are seriously interested in the avant-garde's efforts, attending its concerts, and purchasing its recordings—or less than a quarter of 1 percent of the population. Assuredly the avant-garde audience can be a loyal and cohesive entity. However, it, in turn, divides into tiny subgroups, each faithful to a particular experimental style. Much as some composers would wish this information were otherwise, they must live with it.

Although the figures cited on the size of the several types of audience are disputable, they are approximately correct. At the least, they put into perspective what is meant by the general audience—which includes all listeners except those who have their attention engaged by the avant-garde—and the way this general audience divides into several special-listener groups. Better education and an enriched cultural environment can enlarge this audience, but it is difficult to believe that, with the most sustained effort of governmental agencies, foundations, democratic performance groups, and music educators, the number will ever amount to anything approximating even a third of the population. Such an effort, moreover, is not in the cards.

What all of this discussion leads to is the realization that, at best, art music has only a tenuous hold on the population. At any moment, demagoguery and application of the majority-rule principle can vitiate what hold there is. Thus, the danger to music, and particularly to contemporary music, is the cultural elitism of the avant-garde. In the fall of 1984, a much-touted New York concert of serial music had an embarrassingly poor attendance, and another given by Cage and his friends saw more than half the audience flee the premises before it was half through. Obviously, people are not coming around to accepting either sort of music.

We can understand why the swing toward moderation and caution, which began in the 1970s, was needed. Gathering strength was one aspect of American culture that posed a real threat to integrity—the imposition of crass, material values and conformity as a test for artistic creations. The threat must certainly become a reality if modern music continues recalcitrant to accommodation and adaptation. There are indeed mendacious public figures, political and otherwise, ready to play on the prejudices, and make capital of the ignorance, of the millions of cultural illiterates who regard high culture as superfluous. The only sizeable strength for art music has always resided in the American minority whom the avant-garde has been alienating.

Hilton Kramer in 1976 noted the moderating trend and the need for balance in all of the arts and worried about the danger of philistinism, saying: "The appetite for outrage and innovation, for shock and squalor, for assaults on the audience and on the medium, has clearly diminished where it has not completely disappeared. The taste now is for clarity and coherence, for the beautiful and the recognizable, for narrative, melody, pathos, glamour, romance and the instantly comprehensible, for empathy rather than entropy—for art that is a pleasure rather than a moral contest."[21]

The music lovers who are not enamored of postwar innovative sounds are not necessarily pigs satisfied, unthinkingly or lazily accepting only what music they are used to and only when this music is thinned to the consistency of pabulum. More than a few of them are dissatisfied with their worldly fate and long for a richer inner life that belies the ordinariness ready to engulf them. Art music that wins its way into this audience's affection does not simply entertain but transfigures personal being by augmenting and ameliorating it. Music takes on depth depending on its insight into people's emotional and aesthetic requirements, and the thoroughness with which it embodies this insight. Depth is further measured by the extent to which numbers of men and women from various walks of life, inhabiting different places, and born into different generations conceive a music to be united to them in spirit.

Earlier, Subotnick was quoted as saying that it was the composer's duty "not to lie and not to mislead people." Here we should like to paraphrase a comment that Mario Vargas Llosa made about the novel and the role of fiction—for a musical composition "to tell the truth" means to make the listener experience something nonexistent in normal reality, and "to lie" means an inability to bring about this illusion. Furthermore, truth and falsehood are to be perceived as aesthetic concepts.[22] As Keats once said: " 'Beauty is truth, truth beauty,' that is all / Ye know on earth, and all ye need to know." From this perspective, by repeatedly denying listeners the experience of beauty, a beauty that does not exist in normal reality, many a composition has lied.

Continuing our paraphrase of Llosa, people want to be moved and awed. They want music to metamorphose them into "bewitched beings." This accomplished, "the asphyxiating constriction of our lives opens up and we sally forth . . . to have vicarious experiences which [music] converts into our own."[23]

Dogmas do not interest music lovers. If men and women are moved and awed, they do not particularly care what technical or expressive means have been used to achieve the result. Consistency of style, intellectual control over or the limitation of expression, restriction of musical means—in short, the restraints imposed by modernists—have no validity as far as listeners are concerned. If a composer wishes to draw from folk or popular music, or from that of a non-Western culture, they may do so, as long as the purpose and the result is to touch people's feelings. Moreover, this is exactly what more and more composers in the 1980s are trying to achieve as they try to integrate various already available techniques and styles and apply them to new compositions.

In 1983 the trend to enjoyable music was sufficiently pronounced to require recognition. That Druckman did when he announced the discovery of a "new romanticism" in music and put it on display in the New York festival called "Horizons 1983." Overall attendance at the concerts was an unheard of 70 percent of available seats. Owing to the vigorous promotion of the festival, people believed it would contain enjoyable music. The concerts, however, were a mixed bag of available and inaccessible music. "At first, the complicated music gang seemed to make all the noise, booing anything with a tune. But by June 10 all that had changed. Now the civilians (as a friend of mine called them) were noisy too," booing anything without a tune.[24]

A "civilian" that I spoke with, who had attended three of the

concerts was angry about his being taken in by the promises in
the advertisements. He said the aims of these "so-called neoro-
mantics" were the same as the avant-gardes of serialism and atonality and of the post-Cageian composers, "who did everything
they could to annihilate what was human in music. They gave us
nothing instead, because they had nothing to offer," he added.
"All this business about bringing back melody and harmony and
older music," he went on, "that's a way of covering up emptiness, with little else there. You want to know why the triumph
of older music? It's because this music gives listeners a self-inclu-
sive cosmos. There's order in it. Most of these modern composers
I heard gave out boredom, or a feeling of worry and insecurity,
or they just created plain, simple bedlam."

What is unconscionable about "Horizons 1983" was the fooling
of the music public into believing that its kind of music would be
heard. What is encouraging was the demonstration that if it is
promised sounds it can relate to, the public will turn out. What is
inferable is that the public is made up of incurable romantics. This
last point was brought up by Guy Friedman, when he asked the
shrewd conductor Erich Leinsdorf whether he agreed with a statement of Harold Schoenberg about our entering a neoromantic period. Leinsdorf replied: "The enormous success of Del Tredici
would certainly bear this out. I would go one step further, I don't
think that the public has ever left its predilection for Romanticism, in spite of a number of very vocal and eloquent composers
and critics exhorting the public to change its attitude to music.
But to argue with the public is a pretty hopeless endeavor and I
don't believe that the public has ever changed. I do think that now
the composers are changing and this is perhaps what Harold meant
by his 'reentering.' "[25]

The "turning around" is best observed in areas outside New
York City, among composers less adamant about their own importance than are their New York counterparts. In 1983 Frank
Peters, music editor of the St. Louis Post-Dispatch, reported on the
results of the Friedheim Competition, saying of the eighty works
submitted, there were only traces of serialism and analytical clas-
sicism and plenty of triads and diatonic melodies. He said this was
a manifestation of "the Postmodern or anti-Modern currents that
have been building in all the arts since the middle 1960s—a delib-

erate turning away from aesthetic directions taken in the first two-thirds of our century. Call it reactionary, nostalgic, whimsical, Camp, whatever fits—Postmodernism is a fact, and some of our most competent people in art, architecture, and music are working in its spirit." [26]

A few months later, James Chute wrote about Florida State University's Festival of New Music in Tallahassee. "Gimmickry," he said, "is out, melody is in." Thirty-six works were performed. None had electronic tape or synthesized sounds; one work stressed theatrical effects; only one was a multimedia piece. The 400 works submitted were more conservative than those submitted in 1980. None were by composers "from the Northeastern schools and establishment." Noticeable were increased consonance, a return to melody, and a reintroduction of recognizable development and repetition. [27]

Most composers in the 1980s are groping toward a style that reconciles whatever is usable from all of the musics that have existed and synthesizes them into an expression that balances ease of communication with profound content. We must continue to believe with Donal Henahan, "that a serious composer with a genuine, unquenchable melodic gift will one day come along and show us what has been missing in so much contemporary music of the last 30 years. The works of this new Schubert will speak directly and deeply to our emotional and intellectual needs in ways that neither academic nor popular music do today. We won't have to be told when this bright new star appears, either. The applause from all·sides will be deafening." [28]

Art music is generally acknowledged as essential to our democratic civilization, by thoughtful men and women who have a concern for the quality and health of American society. In 1963 after considering the artistic babble that surrounded him, August Heckscher suggested that the greatest ages have been distinguished by a common style, where affinities exist between various forms of art and where clear connections exist between artistic achievements and those of leaders in other fields. The United States, he said, was increasingly an urban civilization, yet one whose greatness would be defined by how the arts make city life entertaining and ennobling. "A city without a brilliant cultural life must always be a dreary spectacle." [29]

What is hopeful in the 1980s is the search for a common style that can entertain and ennoble. Two years after the Heckscher statement was made, Peter Drucker showed similar concern over the cultural confusion in the United States and spoke of the importance of a truly educated society in order to ensure our future survival. He spoke of the need to prepare every American for the demands of his personal life and also spoke of the danger in downgrading experience that is direct, immediate, and not verbal. He feared "that 80 per cent of Man that is not verbal intelligence but capacity to do, capacity to create, capacity to sense," was withering away "out of sheer intellectual arrogance." In order not to destroy our society, he said, there must be a "commitment to communicate intelligibly" with "the layman." The catering of artistic specialists exclusively to special groups has gone on too long.[30]

In a democracy, all citizens have a right to be introduced to those creations of the human mind that represent their civilization at its best. Composers in a democracy have the responsibility not to deny citizens this right. If they have something to say musically, they should try to say it with less obfuscation, with less worry about individuality and consistency of style. Such an approach can eventually result in a style that is natural and effective. We must remember Voltaire's assertion that "*Tous les genres sont bons hors le genre ennuyeux*" (All styles are good except for the boring kind). In return, if composers do sincerely try to live up to their obligations to communicate, they also must be treated honestly and fairly by the public and by political and economic leaders.

We hope that art music will again have a function in society. The days are numbered for the continuance of meaningless musical babble. All that is asked is to let us find sense in our new music and to let new music make sense in our inner lives.

NOTES

1. John Lukacs, *The Passing of the Modern Age* (New York: Harper & Row, 1972), 4–5.

2. Ibid., 13.

3. "Where Is 20th-Century Music Now?" *New York Times*, 24 June 1984, sec. 2, 1, 28.

4. Marshall Berman, *All That Is Solid Melts into Air: Experience of Modernity* (New York: Simon & Schuster, 1982), 332.

5. Carl G. Jung, et al., *Man and His Symbols* (New York: Dell, 1968), 3.

6. Will Crutchfield, "Did Music Hit Its Peak with Mozart?" *New York Times*, 8 July 1984, sec. 2, 1.

7. Ibid., 17.

8. Ibid.

9. Ibid.

10. John Gardner, *Self-Renewal* (New York: Harper & Row, 1965), 6–7; Tim Page, "The New-Music Schism," *Musical America* (December 1982): 21.

11. Leonard Meyer, *Music, the Arts, and Ideas* (Chicago: University of Chicago Press, 1967), 209.

12. See Lukacs, *The Passing of the Modern Age*, 115, on this subject.

13. A. L. Kroeber, *Anthropology: Cultural Patterns & Processes* (New York: Harcourt Brace Jovanovich, 1963), 112.

14. Ibid., 114. For a discussion of musical form, meaning, use, and function, see ibid., 112–18.

15. Ibid., 119, 170.

16. Edward Rothstein, "The Musical Avant-Garde: An Idea Whose Time May Have Gone," *New York Times*, 26 June 1983, sec. 2, 1.

17. Daniel Yankelovich, *New Rules: Searching for Self-Fulfillment in a World Turned Upside Down* (New York: Bantam, 1982), 224.

18. Michael Colgrass, "Then I Stood on My Head," *New York Times*, 28 May 1972, sec. 2, 11.

19. Kroeber, *Anthropology: Cultural Patterns & Processes*, 64.

20. David Ewen, *American Composers: A Biographical Dictionary* (New York: Putnam's, 1982), s.v. "Druckman, Jacob Raphael."

21. Hilton Kramer, "A Yearning for 'Normalcy'—The Current Backlash in the Arts," *New York Times*, 23 May 1976, sec. 2, 1.

22. Mario Vargas Llosa, "Is Fiction the Art of Lying?" trans. Toby Talbot, *New York Times Book Review*, 7 October 1984, 40.

23. Ibid.

24. Gregory Sandow, "Music of Its Time," *Village Voice*, 28 June 1983, 93.

25. The interview with Erich Leinsdorf was published in the *Music Journal* 35 (May 1977): 8.

26. Frank Peters, letter in *Musical America* (April 1983): 2.

27. James Chute, "Florida State's Festival of New Music," *Musical America* (August 1983): 30–31.

28. Donal Henahan, "One Tiresome Extreme May Breed Another," *New York Times*, 22 January 1984, sec. 2, 19.

29. August Heckscher, "Government and the Arts," *Music Journal* 21 (March 1963): 17, 82.

30. Peter F. Drucker, in *The Revolutionary Theme in Contemporary America*, ed. Thomas R. Ford (Lexington: University of Kentucky Press, 1965), 93–94.

Discography of Works Referred to in Chapters 3 through 7

I. SERIAL AND QUASI-SERIAL COMPOSITIONS: THE OLDER GENERATION

Finney, Ross Lee (1906–   )

Piano Quartet (1953)	Columbia ML-5477
Symphony No. 1 (1942)	Louisville 652
Symphony No. 2 (1958)	Louisville 625
Symphony No. 3 (1960)	Louisville 672

Perle, George (1915–   )

String Quartet No. 5 (1960, rev. 1967)	Nonesuch 71280
String Quartet No. 7 (1973)	CRI 387
String Quintet (1958)	CRI 148
Three Movements for Orchestra (1963)	CRI 331

Weber, Ben (1916–79)

Concerto for Piano and Orchestra (1961)	CRI 239
Sonata da Camera (1950)	New World NW 281

II. SERIAL AND QUASI-SERIAL COMPOSITIONS: THE MIDDLE GENERATION

Babbitt, Milton (1916–   )

Composition for 4 Instruments (1948)	CRI 138
Philomel, for soprano and synthesizer (1964)	New World NW 307
String Quartet No. 2 (1954)	Nonesuch 71280

Schuller, Gunther (1925–   )

Seven Studies on Themes of Paul Klee (1959)	Mercury SRI 75116
Symphony for Brass and Percussion (1950)	Argo ZRG 731

Shapey, Ralph (1921–   )

The Covenant, for soprano, ensemble, and tapes (1977)	CRI 435
Fromm Variations, for piano (1973)	CRI 428
Praise, an oratorio (1971)	CRI 355
Rituals for Orchestra (1959); *String Quartet No. 6* (1963)	CRI 275

III. SERIAL AND QUASI-SERIAL COMPOSITIONS: ONE OF THE YOUNGER GENERATION

Wuorinen, Charles (1938–   )

Arabia Felix, for 6 players (1973)	CRI 463
Chamber Concerto for Cello and 10 Players (1963)	Nonesuch 71263
Chamber Concerto for Flute and 10 Players (1964)	CRI 230
Percussion Symphony (1976)	Nonesuch 71353
Piano Concerto (1966)	CRI 239
Time's Encomium (1969)	Nonesuch 71225

IV. MUSIC WITH AFFINITIES TO SERIALISM

Bassett, Leslie (1923–   )

Echoes from an Invisible World (1975)	CRI 429
Trio for Clarinet, Viola, and Piano (1953)	CRI 148
Variations for Orchestra (1963)	CRI 203

Carter, Elliott (1908–   )

Cello Sonata (1948); *Sonata for Flute, Oboe, Cello, and Harpsichord* (1952)	Nonesuch 71234
Concerto for Orchestra (1970)	CRI 469
Double Concerto for Harpsichord, Piano, and 2 Chamber Orchestras (1961); *Duo for Violin and Piano* (1974)	Nonesuch 71314
A Mirror on which to Dwell, song cycle (1976)	CBS M 35171
String Quarter No. 1 (1951) and *2* (1959)	Nonesuch 71249
String Quarter No. 2 (1959) and *3* (1972)	CBS M 32738
A Symphony of Three Orchestras (1977)	CBS M 35171
Syringa, for mezzo-soprano and 11 players (1978)	CRI 469

Druckman, Jacob (1928–   )

Animus II, for mezzo-soprano, percussion, and tape (1968)	CRI 255
Animus III, for clarinet and tapes (1969)	Nonesuch 71253
Aureole (1979)	New World NW 318
Lamia, for soprano and orchestra (1975)	Louisville 764
Windows, for orchestra (1972)	CRI 457

Imbrie, Andrew (1921–   )

Legend, for orchestra (1959)	CRI 152
Serenade for Flute, Viola, and Piano (1952); *Cello Sonata* (1966); *String Quartet No. 4* (1969)	New World NW 212

V. TOWARD A MORE BENIGN ATONALITY

Kirchner, Leon (1919–   )

Piano Concerto (1953)	New World NW 286
Sonata Concertante for Violin and Piano (1952)	Desto 7151
String Quartet No. 1 (1948)	CRI 395

Rochberg, George (1918–   )

La Bocca della Verita, for oboe and piano (1959)	CRI 423

Music for the Magic Theater (1967); *Chamber Symphony for 9 Instruments* (1953)	Desto 6444
Serenata d'Estate (1955)	Nonesuch 71220
String Quartet No. 1 (1952); *Duo Concertante* (1959); *Ricordanza*, for cello and piano (1972)	CRI 337
String Quartet No. 3 (1972)	Nonesuch 71283
String Quartet Nos. 4, 5, and 6 (1977, 1978, 1978)	RCA ARL2-4198
Symphony No. 1 (1949)	Louisville 634
Symphony No. 2 (1956)	CRI 492
Violin Concerto (1974)	CBS M 35149

Tower, Joan (1938–)

Petroushskates, for flute, clarinet, violin, cello, and piano (1980)	CRI 441

Westergaard, Peter (1931–)

Mr. and Mrs. Discobbolos (1966)	CRI 271

VI. MUSICAL COUNTERCURRENTS

Ashley, Robert (1930–)

Perfect Lives (Private Parts)	Lovely LML 1001, VR 4908

Brown, Earle (1926–)

Time Five (1963); *Octet I* (1953); *December 1952*; *Novarra*	CRI 330

Cage, John (1912–)

Fontana Mix (1958)	Turnabout TV 34046
	Columbia M 7139
Music of Changes (1951)	New World NW 214
The Seasons (1947)	CRI 410
Sonata and Interludes for Prepared Piano (1946–48)	CRI 199
String Quartet in 4 Parts (1950)	Vox SVBX 5306
Third Construction, for percussion quartet (1941)	New World NW 319

Feldman, Morton (1926–   )

Durations (1961)	Time 58007
Projections (1950–53)	CRI 276
Rothko Chapel, for soloists, chorus, viola, celesta, and percussion (1972)	Odyssey Y 34138
Structures, for string quartet (1951)	Vox SVBX 5306

Foss, Lukas (1922–   )

Baroque Variations, for orchestra (1967)	Nonesuch 71202
The Prairie, cantata for soloists, chorus, and orchestra (1943)	Turnabout 34649
Song of Songs, cantata for soprano and orchestra (1947)	CRI 284
String Quartet No. 3 (1976); *Music for Six* (1977)	CRI 413
Thirteen Ways of Looking at a Blackbird, for mezzo-soprano, piano, and percussion (1978)	CRI 442
Time Cycle, for soprano and orchestra (1960)	Columbia CMS 6280

Gaburo, Kenneth (1926–   )

Linqua II: Maledetto, for 7 virtuoso speakers (1969)	CRI 316

Penn, William (1943–   )

Fantasy for Harpsichord (1973, rev. 1975)	CRI 367

VII. MODERN MUSIC, VISIONARY CONNECTIONS

Crumb, George (1929–   )

Ancient Voices of Children (1970)	Nonesuch 71255
Black Angels, for electric string quartet (1970)	Vox SVBX 5306
Echoes of Time and the River (1967)	Louisville 711
Eleven Echoes of Autumn, 1965	CRI 233
Night Music I (1963)	CRI 218

Harrison, Lou (1917–   )

Main Bersama-Sama (1978); *Threnody for Carlos Chavez* (1978); *Serenade*, for gamelan and suling (1978); *String Quartet Set* (1979)	CRI 455
Symphony on G (1954, 1966)	CRI 236

Glass, Philip (1937–   )

Einstein on the Beach, excerpts (1976)	Tomato TOM 4-2901
Music in 12 Parts (1974)	Virgin CA 2010

Hovhaness, Alan (1911–   )

And God Created Great Whales, for orchestra and tape (1969)	CBS M 34537
Symphony No. 2 ("Mysterious Mountain") (1955)	RCA LSC 2251
Symphony No. 9 ("Saint Vartan") (1951)	Poseidon 1013
Songs	Poseidon 1008/9

Partch, Harry (1901–74)

Castor and Pollux (1952); *The Letter* (1944); *Windsong* (1958); *Cloud-Chamber Music* (1950); *The Bewitched* (1955)	CRI 193

Reich, Steve (1936–   )

Come Out (1966)	Odyssey 32160160
Drumming (1971); *Six Pianos* (1973); *Music for Mallet Instruments, Voices, and Organ* (1973)	Deutsche Grammophon 2750106
Music for 18 Musicians (1976)	ECM/Warner 1129
Music for a Large Ensemble (1978); *Octet* (1979); *Violin Phase* (1967)	ECM/Warner 1168
Tehillim (1981)	ECM/Warner 1215

Riley, Terry (1935–   )

In C (1964)	CBS MS 7178
Shri Camel (1976)	CBS MS 35164

Subotnick, Morton (1933–   )

Ascent into Air (1981); *A Fluttering of Wings* (1981)	Nonesuch 78020-1
Silver Apples of the Moon (1967)	Nonesuch 71174
Wild Bull (1967)	Nonesuch 71208

VIII. THE MUSICAL CONSERVATORS

Baksa, Robert (1938–   )

Oboe Quintet (1972); *Six Bagatelles*, for   Mus. Heritage Society MHS 4895
piano (1974); *Three Bagatelles*, for
piano (1975)

Flagello, Nicolas (1928–   )

Concerto for String Orchestra (1959); *Piano*   Serenus 12002
Sonata (1962)
Contemplazioni di Michelangelo (1964);   Serenus 12005
Islands in the Moon (1964)
Odyssey, for symphonic band (1981)   Cornell C.U.W.E. 29
Symphony of the Winds, for symphonic   Cornell C.U.W.E. 23
band (1970)

Giannini, Vittorio (1903–66)

The Taming of the Shrew (1950)   CRI 272

Hoiby, Lee (1926–   )

After Eden, ballet (1966)   Desto DC 6434
"Anatomy Lesson," from *Summer and*   New World NW 305
Smoke (1971)
Piano Concerto No. 1 (1958)   CRI 214

La Montaine, John (1920–   )

Piano Concerto (1958)   CRI 166
Wilderness Journal, for bass-baritone, or-   Fredonia FD 9,11
gan, and orchestra (1972); *Sonata for*
Flute Solo; *Come into My Garden* and
Conversations for Flute and Piano

Mollicone, Henry (1946–   )

The Face on the Barroom Floor (1978)   CRI 442

Pasatieri, Thomas (1945–   )

Three Poems of James Agee (1973)   Owl 28

Rosner, Arnold (1945–   )

French Horn Sonata (1979)   Opus One 91

Ward, Robert (1917–   )

The Crucible (1961)	CRI 238
Symphony No. 1 (1941)	Desto DST 6405
Symphony No. 2 (1947)	CRI 127

IX. THE MEDIAL MAINSTREAM

Beeson, Jack (1921–   )

Captain Jinks of the Horse Marines (1975)	RCA ARL 2-1727
Dr. Heidegger's Fountain of Youth (1978)	CRI 406
Hello Out There (1954)	Desto 6451
Lizzie Borden (1965)	Desto 6455/7
The Sweet Bye and Bye (1965)	Desto 7179/80
Piano Sonata No. 5 (1951)	CRI 464
Symphony No. 1 in A (1959)	CRI 196

Bernstein, Leonard (1918–   )

Serenade, for violin, strings, harp, and percussion (1954)	Deutsche Grammophon 2531196
Symphony No. 1 ("Jeremiah") (1943); *No. 2 ("The Age of Anxiety")* (1949); *No. 3 ("Kaddish")* (1963); *Chichester Psalms*, for chorus and orchestra (1965)	Deutsche Grammophon 2709077

Dello Joio, Norman (1913–   )

Meditations on Ecclesiastes, for strings (1956)	CRI 110
New York Profiles, for orchestra (1949)	CRI 209
Serenade, for orchestra (1948)	Desto 6413/4E
Triumph of St. Joan, for orchestra (1951)	CRI AML 4615

Lees, Benjamin (1924–   )

Cello Sonata (1981)	Spectrum 158
Concerto for String Quartet and Orchestra (1965)	CRI 451
Symphony No. 3 (1968)	Louisville 752
Violin Concerto (1958)	Turnabout 34692
Violin Sonata No. 2 (1973)	Desto 7174

Mennin, Peter (1923–83)

Symphony No. 4 ("The Cycle") (1948)	Desto 7149

Symphony No. 5 (1950)   Mercury 90379
Symphony No. 7 ("Variation-Sym-   CRI 399
phony") (1964); *Piano Concerto* (1958)

Muczynski, Robert (1929–)

Flute Sonata (1961); *Piano Sonata No. 2*   Coronet 3004
(1966); *Fantasy Trio for Clarinet, Cello,*
and Piano (1969); *Alto-Saxophone Son-*
ata (1970)
Muczynski Plays Muczynski: Six Preludes   Laurel LR 114
for Piano (1953); *Piano Sonata Nos. 1*
and 3 (1958, 1974); *Twelve Maverick*
Pieces, for piano (1976)
Piano Trio No. 2 (1975)   Laurel LR 106

Persichetti, Vincent (1915–)

Piano Sonata No. 10 (1955)   SPF 41203
Serenade No. 10, for flute and harp (1957) Desto 7134
Symphony No. 9 ("Janiculum") (1970)   RCA LSC 3212

Rorem, Ned (1923–)

Eleven Studies for Eleven Players (1960) Louisville 644
Night Music, for violin and piano (1972) Desto 7174
Romeo and Juliet, for flute and guitar   CRI 394
(1977)
Songs   Columbia MS 6561
Symphony No. 3 (1958)   Turnabout 34447

X. THE VENTURESOME COMPOSERS OF THE MAINSTREAM

Colgrass, Michael (1932–)

As Quiet As, for orchestra (1966)   RCA LSC 3001
Concerto Masters, for 3 violins and or- Turnabout 34704
chestra (1975)
Déjá Vù, for orchestra (1977)   New World NW 318
New People, song cycle for mezzo-so-   Grenadilla GS 1010
prano, viola, and piano (1969)

Harbison, John (1938–   )

The Flower-Fed Buffaloes, for baritone, chorus, and chamber ensemble (1976)	Nonesuch 71366
Piano Concerto (1978)	CRI 440

Siegmeister, Elie (1909–   )

Clarinet Concerto (1956); *Flute Concerto* (1960)	Turnabout 34640
String Quartet No. 2 (1960)	CRI 176E
Violin Sonata Nos. 1 and 5 (1956, 1972)	Grenadilla 1024
Song Cycles: *Madam to You* (1964), *The Face of War* (1960); *String Quartet No. 3* (1973)	CRI 416
Symphony No. 3 (1957)	CRI 185
Western Suite (1945)	Turnabout 34459

XI. THE ARTISTIC MAVERICKS

Corigliano, John (1938–   )

Clarinet Concerto (1977)	New World NW 309
Oboe Concerto (1975); *Poem in October*, for tenor and chamber ensemble (1970)	RCA ARL 1-2534
Piano Concerto (1968)	Mercury 75118
Violin Sonata (1963)	CRI 215

Del Tredici, David (1937–   )

Final Alice (1976)	London LDR 71018
I Hear an Army, for soprano and string quartet (1964)	CRI 294
In Memory of a Summer Day (1980)	Nonesuch 79043
Night Conjure-Verse, for 2 vocalists and chamber ensemble (1966)	CRI 492

Rzewski, Frederic (1938–   )

Four North American Ballads, for piano (1979)	Nonesuch 79006
The People United Will Never Be Defeated! 36 Variations on a Chilean Song for Piano (1975)	Vanguard 71248

Schwantner, Joseph (1943–   )

Aftertones of Infinity, for orchestra (1978) Mercury 75141

Exilir (Consortium VIII), for flute and 5 players (1976); *Sparrows*, for soprano and 8 players (1979) Smithsonian Collection 22

New Morning for the World, for speaker and orchestra (1982) Mercury 411031-1

Wind, Willow, Whisper, for flute, clarinet, violin, cello, and piano (1980) CRI 441

A Selective Bibliography
of Works Consulted

Abraham, Gerald. *The Tradition of Western Music*. Berkeley: University of California Press, 1974.

Agena, Kathleen. "The Return of Enchantment." *New York Times Magazine*, 27 November 1983, 66, 68, 72, 74, 76, 79–80.

Amram, David. *Vibrations*. New York: Macmillan, 1968.

Anderson, Garland. "The Music of Ned Rorem." *Music Journal* 21 (April 1963): 34, 71–72.

Appleton, Jon H. "Electronic Music: Questions of Style and Compositional Technique." *Musical Quarterly* 65 (1979): 103–10.

——. "New Role for the Composer." *Music Journal* 27 (March 1969): 28, 59–61.

Ardoin, John. "The American Composer: Underdog of American Orchestras." *Musical America* (June 1961): 12–13, 58–59.

——. "Leonard Bernstein at Sixty." *High Fidelity* 28 (August 1978): 53–58.

Babbitt, Milton. "The Composer as Specialist." In *Esthetics Contemporary*, ed. Richard Kostelanetz. Buffalo, N.Y.: Prometheus, 1978, pp. 280–87. Reprint of "Who Cares if You Listen." *High Fidelity* 8 (February 1958): 39ff.

Bacon, Ernst. *Words on Music*. Syracuse, N.Y.: Syracuse University Press, 1960.

Barri, Richard. "Opera for the People." *Music Journal* 30 (October 1972): 16–17, 72.

264 Selective Bibliography

Barzun, Jacques. *Critical Questions.* Ed. Bea Friedland. Chicago: University of Chicago Press, 1982.

Battcock, Gregory, ed. *Breaking the Sound Barrier: A Critical Anthology of the New Music.* New York: Dutton, 1981.

Bennett, Myron. "Music as Furniture." *High Fidelity* 22 (February 1972): 64–66.

Berman, Marshall. *All That Is Solid Melts into Air: The Experience of Modernity.* New York: Simon & Schuster, 1982.

Bernstein, Leonard. *Findings.* New York: Simon & Schuster, 1982.

Bither, David. "Philip Glass." *Horizon* (March 1980): 39–43.

Boretz, Benjamin, and Edward T. Cone, eds. *Perspectives on American Composers.* New York: Norton, 1971.

Botstein, Leon. "The Tragedy of Leonard Bernstein." *Harper's* (May 1983): 38–40, 57–62.

Briggs, John. *Leonard Bernstein.* Cleveland: World, 1961.

Brown, Royal S. "Leon Kirchner." *Musical America* (April 1977): 6–7, 39.

Burton, Stephen Douglas. "The Emperor's New Clothes, or, Contemporary Music Revisited." *Symphony Magazine* 34 (June/July 1983): 59–63.

Cage, John. *Empty Words.* Middletown, Conn.: Wesleyan University Press, 1979.

———. *For the Birds.* Boston: Boyars, 1981.

———. "The Future of Music." *Music Journal* 20 (January 1962): 45–46, 80–83.

———. *John Cage.* Edited by Richard Kostelanetz. London: Allen Lane Penguin, 1971.

———. *M.* Middletown, Conn.: Wesleyan University Press, 1973.

———. *Silence.* Cambridge: M.I.T. Press, 1966.

———. *A Year from Monday.* Middletown, Conn.: Wesleyan University Press, 1967.

Calinescu, Matei. *Faces of Modernity.* Bloomington: Indiana University Press, 1977.

Carrington, Mark. "6 Orchestras Adopt a Composer." *Symphony Magazine* 34 (February/March 1983): 24–26, 62–63.

Carter, Elliott. *The Writings of Elliott Carter.* Ed. Else Stone and Kurt Stone. Bloomington: Indiana University Press, 1977.

Cavalieri, Walter. "Lee Hoiby." *Music Journal* 38 (December 1980): 10–12.

Chancellor, John. "Melodic Lines and Bottom Lines." *Symphony Magazine* 34 (August/September 1983): 19–22.

Chase, Gilbert, ed. *The American Composer Speaks*. Baton Rouge: Louisiana State University Press, 1966.

Chasins, Abram. *Music at the Crossroads*. New York: Macmillan, 1972.

Clarke, Garry E. *Essays on American Music*. Westport, Conn.: Greenwood, 1977.

Coe, Robert. "Philip Glass Breaks Through." *New York Times Magazine*, 25 October 1981, 68, 70, 72, 74, 76, 78, 80, 90.

Coker, Wilson. *Music and Meaning*. New York: Free Press, 1972.

Colgrass, Michael. "Then I Stood on My Head." *New York Times*, 28 May 1972: sec. 2, 11, 14.

Cope, David H. *New Directions in Music*. 2d ed. Dubuque, Iowa: Brown, 1976.

Copland, Aaron. "Is the University too Much with Us?" *New York Times*, 26 July 1970, sec. 2, 13.

————. *The New Music, 1900–1960*. Rev. ed. New York: Norton, 1968.

Crutchfield, Will. "Did Music Hit Its Peak with Mozart?" *New York Times*, 8 July 1984, sec. 2, 1, 17.

Cumming, Robert. "Total War." *Music Journal Annual* 20 (1962): 9, 74–75.

Curtin, Phyllis. "Pioneering for New Music." *Music Journal* 19 (October 1961): 53–55, 86–87.

Davies, John Booth. *The Psychology of Music*. Stanford, Calif.: Stanford University Press, 1978.

Davis, Peter G. "Electronic Music on Records." *High Fidelity* (October 1967): 108–10.

De Lio, Thomas. "Structural Pluralism: Some Observations on the Nature of Open Structures on the Music and Visual Arts of the Twentieth Century." *Musical Quarterly* 67 (1981): 527–43.

De Mott, Benjamin. *Surviving the 70's*. New York: Dutton, 1971.

Deutschman, Ben. "Music from Mathematics." *Music Journal* 22 (October 1964): 54, 56.

Dickstein, Morris. *Gates of Eden: American Culture in the Sixties*. New York: Basic Books, 1977.

Dorian, Frederick. *Commitment to Culture*. Pittsburgh: University of Pittsburgh Press, 1964.

Downes, Edward. "The Music of Norman Dello Joio." *Musical Quarterly* 48 (1962): 149–72.

Druckman, Jacob. "Stating the Case for the 'New Romanticism.' " *Ovations* 3 (June 1983): 6, 44.

Edelman, Richard. "New Directions for Opera." *Music Journal* 24 (June 1966): 29–30, 56.

English, John W. *Criticizing the Critics*. New York: Hastings House, 1979.

Ericson, Raymond. "The Pick of Modern American Music." *New York Times*, 25 August 1974, sec. 2, 13, 18.

Ewen, David. *American Composers: A Biographical Dictionary*. New York: Putnam's, 1982.

Farnsworth, Paul R. *The Social Psychology of Music*. New York: Dryden, 1958.

Fischer, Irwin. "Contemporary Music—A Problem Child." *Music Journal* 24 (March 1966): 60, 117–19.

Fisher, Charles M. "The Performing Arts in Akademia." *Music Journal* 26 (April 1968): 36–37, 66–67.

Fleming, Shirley. "Donald Martino." *Musical America* (September 1974): 8–9, 40.

———. "Jacob Druckman." *Musical America* (August 1972): 4–5.

———. "Thomas Pasatieri." *Musical America* (March 1972): 4.

Ford, Thomas R., ed. *The Revolutionary Theme in Contemporary America*. Lexington: University of Kentucky Press, 1965.

Frank, Peter. "Electronic Music." *Fanfare* 3 (July/August 1980): 16–35.

———. "E(xcellence) = CP^2." *Fanfare* 4 (November/December 1981): 70–73.

Frankenstein, Alfred. "Andrew Imbrie's 'Angle of Repose.' " *Musical America* (March 1977): 30–31, 36.

———. "In Retrospect—The Music of John Cage." *High Fidelity* 10 (April 1960): 63–64.

Freedman, Guy. "Elie Siegmeister." *Music Journal* 35 (April 1977): 6–7, 53.

———. "Metamorphosis of a 20th Century Composer." *Music Journal* 34 (March 1976): 12–13, 38.

Frith, Simon. *Sound Effects*. New York: Pantheon, 1981.

Fromm, Paul. "The Princeton Seminar—Its Purpose and Promise." *Musical Quarterly* 46 (1960): 155–58.

Gagne, Cole, and Tracy Caras. *Soundpieces: Interviews with American Composers*. Metuchen, N.J.: Scarecrow, 1982.

Gardner, John. *Self-Renewal*. New York: Harper & Row, 1965.

Garland, David. "Philip Glass: Theater of Glass." *Downbeat* 50 (December 1983): 16–18.

Gerberding, William P., and Duane E. Smith, eds. *The Radical Left*. Boston: Houghton Mifflin, 1970.

Gordon, Suzanne. *Lonely in America*. New York: Simon & Schuster, 1976.

Gottfried, Martin. *A Theater Divided*. Boston: Little, Brown, 1969.

Gottlieb, Carla. *Beyond Modern Art*. New York: Dutton, 1976.

Greckel, W. C. "Music Misses the Majority." *Music Journal* 30 (December 1972): 20–21, 32, 51, 53, 55, 67, 70, 72.

Green, Harris. "That Subscription Crowd Must Go!" *New York Times*, 7 June 1970, sec. 2, 13.

Griffiths, Paul. *Modern Music: The Avant-Garde Since 1945*. London: Dent, 1981.

Gutman, John. "Why Do You Go to the Opera?" *Musical America* (February 1952): 24, 158.

Hamilton, David. "A Synoptic View of the New Music." *High Fidelity* 18 (September 1968): 44–61.

———. "The Unique Imagination of Elliott Carter." *High Fidelity* 24 (July 1974): 73–75.

Hamm, Charles. *Music in the New World*. New York: Norton, 1983.

Hanson, Howard. "Cultural Challenge." *Music Journal* 19 (January 1961): 4–5, 69.

———. "The Music of 1967." *Music Journal Annual* 25 (1967): 26–28, 52.

Hanson, Howard, and Walter Sheppard. "Music in Our Age." *Music Journal Annual* 23 (1965): 50–51, 111–14.

Harris, Marvin. *America Now: The Anthropology of a Changing Culture*. New York: Simon & Schuster, 1981.

Hart, Jeffrey. *When the Going Was Good: American Life in the Fifties*. New York: Crown, 1982.

Hart, Philip. "Art Surveys: To See Ourselves." *Musical America* (August 1974): 15–17.

———. *Orpheus in the New World*. New York: Norton, 1973.

Heckscher, August. "Government and the Arts." *Music Journal* 21 (March 1963): 17, 82–83.

Hemming, Roy. "The Serious Side of Morton Gould." *Ovation* 3 (November 1982): 8, 10–11, 35.

Henahan, Donal. "Crumb, the Tone Poet." *New York Times Magazine*, 11 May 1975, 16–17, 50, 54–59, 66–67.

———. "John Cage, Elfin Enigma, at 64." *New York Times*, 22 October 1976, sec. C, 1, 7.

———. "Music Has Lost Ground in Modern Operas." *New York Times*, 23 October 1983, sec. 2, 21, 24.

———. "Music: Philharmonic Concludes 'Horizons '83.'" *New York Times*, 17 June 1983, sec. C, 12.

Heylbut, Rose. "Brainwash or Back Talk?" *Music Journal Annual* 25 (1967): 36–37, 58, 62, 65.

Heyworth, Peter. "Modern Opera in a Muddle." *High Fidelity* 11 (November 1961): 54–56, 138–39.

Hiemenz, Jack. "Jan De Gaetani." *Musical America* (April 1974): 6–7.

Hines, Robert Stephen, ed. *The Orchestral Composer's Point of View.* Norman: University of Oklahoma Press, 1970.

Hirschfeld, Jeffrey G. "Milton Babbitt: A Not-so-Sanguine Interview." *Musical America* (June 1982): 16–18, 40.

Hitchcock, H. Wiley. *Music in the United States.* 2d ed. Englewood Cliffs, N.J.: Prentice-Hall, 1974.

Holland, Bernard. "Highbrow Music to Hum." *New York Times Magazine*, 31 January 1982, 24–25, 56–57, 65, 67, 70.

Howe, Irving, and Michael Harrington, eds. *The Seventies.* New York: Harper & Row, 1972.

Hughes, Allen. "Leonard Bernstein." *Musical America* (January 1961): 15, 110, 114.

Husarik, Stephen. "John Cage and LeJaren Hiller: HPSCHD, 1969." *American Music* 1 (1983): 1–21.

Jacobs, Norman, ed. *Culture for the Millions?* Boston: Beacon, 1964.

Jacobson, Bernard. "The Composer on Campus—How Does He Fare?" *Musical America* (September 1968): 8–11.

Janiec, Henry. "The Festival and New Music." *Music Journal* 22 (May 1964): 30–31, 50–51.

"John Cage and Roger Reynolds: A Conversation." *Musical Quarterly* 65 (1979): 573–94.

Johnson, Ellen H., ed. *American Artists on Art from 1940 to 1980.* New York: Harper & Row, 1982.

Johnson, Tom. "In Their 'Dream House,' Music Becomes a Means of Meditation." *New York Times*, 28 April 1974, sec. 2, 13.

Johnston, Edgar G., ed. *Preserving Human Values in an Age of Technology.* Detroit: Wayne State University Press, 1961.

Kaplan, Max. "Music and Mass Culture." *Music Journal* 18 (March 1960): 20–21, 150.

———. "Sociology of the Musical Audience." *Music Journal* 19 (January 1961): 60–61, 110.

Keller, Anthony. "Composers on Campus." *High Fidelity* 16 (October 1966): 104–7.

Kellner, Robert Scott. "Avant-Garde Meatballs: Are They Edible?" *Music Journal* 31 (March 1973): 16, 51–52.

Kenyan, Nicholas. "Musical Events: Puzzles." *New Yorker* (15 February 1982): 120–23.

Kerr, Walter. *The Decline of Pleasure.* New York: Simon & Schuster, 1962.

Keyes, Ralph. *We, the Lonely People.* New York: Harper & Row, 1973.

Kingman, Daniel. *American Music.* New York: Schirmer, 1979.

Koplewitz, Laura. "From Pen to Podium with New Music." *Symphony Magazine* 33 (February/March 1982): 9–13, 64–65.

———. "Joan Tower: Building Bridges for New Music." *Symphony Magazine* 33 (June/July 1983): 36–40.

Kostelanetz, Richard. "The Astounding Success of Elliott Carter." *High Fidelity* 18 (May 1968): 41–45.

———., ed. *Esthetics Contemporary*. Buffalo, N.Y.: Prometheus, 1978.

Kouwenhoven, John A. *Half a Truth Is Better Than None*. Chicago: University of Chicago Press, 1982.

Kozinn, Allan. "The American Composers Orchestra." *Symphony Magazine* 34 (June/July 1983): 23–27.

———. "Is There Life After Premieres for New Works?" *New York Times*, 27 December 1981, 19–20.

———. "Philip Glass." *Ovation* 5 (February 1984): 13–16.

———. "The 'Unfashionable Romantic' Music of John Corigliano." *New York Times*, 27 April 1980, sec. 2, 19, 24.

Kozma, Tibor. "Music vs. the Majority." *Music Journal* 21 (March 1963): 50, 86, 101.

Kraft, William. "The Wuorinen Hassle." *Musical America* (August 1975): 3–4.

Kramer, Hans, and Shulamith Kreitler. *Psychology of the Arts*. Durham, N.C.: Duke University Press, 1972.

Kramer, Hilton. "A Yearning for 'Normalcy'—The Current Backlash in the Arts." *New York Times*, 23 May 1976, sec. 2, 1, 25.

Kupferberg, Herbert. "The Concord Quartet Embarks upon Its Second Decade." *Ovation* 3 (December 1982): 12–13, 36.

La Barbara, Joan. " 'Concerts by Composers' Illuminates Downtown School." *Musical America* (May 1982): 13–14.

———. " 'New Music, New York' at The Kitchen." *Musical America* (September 1979): 12–13, 17.

Lamb, Hubert. "The Avant-Gardists." *Music Journal* 22 (January 1964): 22–23, 98–100.

Lang, Paul Henry. "Music at Columbia Will Endure even without Wuorinen." *New York Times*, 29 August 1971, sec. 2, 11.

———., ed. *Problems of Modern Music*. New York: Norton, 1962.

Lasch, Christopher. *The Culture of Narcissism*. New York: Warner, 1979.

Lees, Benjamin. "The American Composer, His Audience and Critics." *Music Journal* 26 (March 1968): 37, 85–86.

Leinsdorf, Erich. *Cadenza*. Boston: Houghton Mifflin, 1976.

Lenneberg, Hans. "The Myth of the Unappreciated Genius." *Musical Quarterly* 66 (1980)): 219–31.

Levey, Joseph. "Is Serialism Art?" *Music Journal Annual* 21 (1963): 22–24.

Lipman, Samuel. *The House of Music.* Boston: Godine, 1984.

———. *Music after Modernism.* New York: Basic Books, 1979.

Lowenthal, Jerome. "Pianist's Diary: Birth of a Concerto." *Music Journal* 29 (January 1971): 23, 43.

Luening, Otto. *The Odyssey of an American Composer.* New York: Scribner's Sons, 1980.

Lukacs, John. *The Passing of the Modern Age.* New York: Harper & Row, 1972.

Lundin, Robert W. *An Objective Psychology of Music.* 2d ed. New York: Ronald, 1967.

McMullen, Roy. *Art, Affluence, and Alienation: The Fine Arts Today.* New York: Praeger, 1968.

Mahoney, Margaret, ed. *The Arts on Campus: The Necessity for Change.* Greenwich, Conn.: New York Graphic Society, 1970.

Mann, Dennis Alan, ed. *The Arts in a Democratic Society.* Bowling Green, Ohio: Bowling Green University Popular Press, 1977.

Mayer, Alfred. "Electronics Music, Like It or Not." *Music Journal* 31 (April 1973): 17, 36–37.

Mayer, William. "Live Composers, Dead Audiences." *New York Times Magazine,* 2 February 1975, 12, 34–38, 42.

Mellers, Wilfred. *Music in a New Found Land.* New York: Knopf, 1965.

Meyer, Leonard B. *Music, the Arts, and Ideas.* Chicago: University of Chicago Press, 1967.

Miller, Douglas T., and Marion Nowak. *The Fifties.* Garden City, N.Y.: Doubleday, 1977.

Morgan, Robert P. "The New Pluralism." *High Fidelity* 31 (March 1981): 56–60.

Nash, Dennison. "The Role of the Composer (Part I)." *Ethnomusicology* 5 (1961): 81–94. "(Part II)." Ibid., 187–201.

Neil, J. Meredith. *Toward a National Taste.* Honolulu: University Press of Hawaii, 1975.

Norton, Richard. "The Vision of Morton Subotnick." *Music Journal* 28 (January 1970): 35, 48–51.

O'Grady, Terence J. "Aesthetic Value in Indeterminate Music." *Musical Quarterly* 67 (1981): 366–81.

Owens, David. " 'Avant-Garde': What Does It Mean Today?" *Christian Science Monitor,* 24 August 1983, 20.

———. "Inside 20th-Century Music." *Christian Science Monitor,* 13 December 1982, 21.

Page, Tim. "The New-Music Schism." *Musical America* (December 1982): 20–21.

Partch, Harry. *Genesis of a Music*. New York: Da Capo, 1974.

Pasatieri, Thomas. "The American Singer." *Music Journal* 32 (January 1974): 15, 30.

Pavlakis, Christopher. "Symposium: Tradition and Experiment, Are They Compatible?" *Music Journal* 35 (March 1977): 12–14.

Peckham, Morse. *Man's Rage for Chaos: Biology, Behavior, and the Arts*. Philadelphia: Chilton, 1965.

Peyser, Joan. *Boulez*. New York: Schirmer, 1976.

———. "Harbison's Continuing Ascent." *New York Times*, 16 August 1981, sec. 2, 17, 20.

Phillips, Harvey E. "The American Composers Orchestra." *Musical America* (February 1981): 32–33.

Pirie, Peter J. "A Reprieve for Romanticism." *High Fidelity* 10 (October 1960): 48–50, 130–31.

Porter, Andrew. *Music of Three Seasons: 1974–1977*. New York: Farrar Straus Giroux, 1978.

———. "Musical Events: Babbitt on Broadway." *New Yorker* (15 March 1982): 126, 129–33.

———. *A Musical Season*. New York: Viking, 1974.

Powell, Mel. "The Debasement of New Music." *Musical America* (September 1970): 14–15.

Read, Gardner. "The Year of the Artist-in-Residence, Part I." *Music Journal Annual* 25 (1967): 34, 56–57.

Reardon, John. "The Challenges of Modern Opera." *Music Journal* 29 (April 1971): 28–30, 50–51, 64.

Reyer, Carolyn. "Why Perform American Music?" *Music Journal* 27 (April 1969): 28, 70.

Riesman, David, in collaboration with Reuel Denney and Nathan Glazer. *The Lonely Crowd*. New Haven, Conn.: Yale University Press, 1950.

Ringer, Alexander L. "The Music of George Rochberg." *Musical Quarterly* 52 (1966): 409–30.

Risenhoover, Morris, and Robert T. Blackburn. *Artists as Professors*. Urbana: University of Illinois Press, 1976.

Rochberg, George. "Contemporary Music in an Affluent Society." *Music Journal* 26 (February 1968): 54, 71–72.

Rockwell, John. *All American Music*. New York: Knopf, 1983.

———. "Electronic Music Takes a New Turn." *New York Times*, 6 April 1980, sec. 2, 21, 26.

———. "Which Works of the 70's Were Significant?" *New York Times*, 27 July 1980, sec. 2, 19, 22.

Rorem, Ned. *An Absolute Gift*. New York: Simon & Schuster, 1978.

———. *Critical Affairs*. New York: Braziller, 1970.

———. *Pure Contraption*. New York: Holt, Rinehart & Winston, 1974.

———. *Setting the Tone*. New York: Coward-McCann, 1983.

Rosenberg, Bernard, and David Manning White, eds. *Mass Culture Revisited*. New York: Van Nostrand Reinhold, 1971.

Rosenberg, Harold. *The Anxious Object: Art Today and Its Audience*. New York: Horizon, 1964.

Rothstein, Edward. "The Musical Avant-Garde: An Idea Whose Time May Have Gone." *New York Times*, 26 June 1983, sec. 2, 1, 14.

Rothstein, Joel. "Terry Riley." *Downbeat* 48 (May 1981): 26–28, 63.

Russcol, Herbert. *The Liberation of Sound*. Englewood Cliffs, N.J.: Prentice-Hall, 1972.

Sabin, Robert. "Norman Dello Joio." *Musical America* (1 December 1950): 9, 30.

Safane, Clifford Jay. "An Interview with Ralph Shapey." *Music Journal* 37 (May/June 1979): 23–25.

Salzman, Eric. "From Composer to Magnetron to You." *High Fidelity* 10 (August 1960): 40–42, 90–91.

———. "Music from the Electronic Universe." *High Fidelity* 14 (August 1964): 54–57.

———. *Twentieth-Century Music: An Introduction*. Englewood Cliffs, N.J.: Prentice-Hall, 1967.

Sandow, Gregory. "The Complicated Music Gang." *Village Voice*, 10 May 1983, 76–77.

———. "From the Other World." *Village Voice*, 25 January 1983, 76, 78.

———. "The Great Unknowns." *Village Voice*, 7 June 1983, 67, 70–71.

———. "Lost Generation." *Village Voice*, 24 January 1984, 78–79.

Sargeant, Winthrop. "Musical Events: The Dead Hand of the Present." *New Yorker* (27 August 1966): 116–18.

———. "Musical Events: Huckleberry Hash." *New Yorker* (29 May 1971): 57–59.

———. "Musical Events: Lost in a New Found Land." *New Yorker* (23 April 1966): 186–91.

———. "Musical Events: Whither?" *New Yorker* (4 December 1965): 200–2.

Schiff, David. *The Music of Elliott Carter*. London: Eulenberg, 1983.

Schonberg, Harold C. "Can Composers Regain Their Audiences?" *New York Times*, 4 December 1977, sec. 2, 1, 15.

———. "Carter, Cage, Reich . . . Speak to Me." *New York Times*, 4 February 1973, sec. 2, 15.

———. "A Critic Reflects on 44 Years in the Business." *New York Times*, 6 July 1980, sec. 2, 13–14.

———. *Facing the Music*. New York: Summit, 1981.

————. "Neo-Romantic Music Warms a Public Chilled by the Avant-Garde." *New York Times*, 20 March 1977, sec. 2, 1, 17.

Schuller, Gunther. "Can Composer Divorce Public?" *New York Times*, 18 June 1967, sec. 2, 17.

Schwartz, Barry. *The New Humanism: Art in a Time of Change*. New York: Praeger, 1974.

Schwartz, Elliott. *Electronic Music*. Rev. ed. New York: Praeger, 1975.

Schwartz, Elliott, and Barney Childs, eds. *Contemporary Composers on Contemporary Music*. New York: Holt, Rinehart & Winston, 1967.

Siegmeister, Elie. "Beyond the Avant-Garde." *Musical America* (December 1971): 13–14, 32.

————. "Humanism and Modernism." *Keynote* (January 1984): 6–11.

————. "A New Day Is Dawning for American Composers." *New York Times*, 23 January 1977, sec. 2, 15, 20.

Silbermann, Alphons. *The Sociology of Music*. Trans. Corbet Stewart. London: Routledge & Kegan Paul, 1963.

Simmons, Walter. "An Atrophy of Musical Creation in Our Time?" *Fanfare* (May/June 1981): 10–12, 203.

————. "Contemporary Music." *Fanfare* 4 (May/June 1981): 22–23.

————. "Persichetti: Concerto for Piano. Piano Sonata No. 9. Sonata for Two Pianos. Mennin: Symphony No. 7. Barber: Concerto for Violin and Orchestra." *Fanfare* 6 (January/February 1983): 226–28.

Slater, Philip. *The Pursuit of Loneliness*. Boston: Beacon, 1976.

Soria, Darle J. "Steve Reich." *Musical America* (December 1982): 6–8, 40.

Southern, Eileen. *The Music of Black Americans*. New York: Norton, 1971.

Stearns, David Patrick. "Joseph Schwantner." *Musical America* (December 1979): 6–7.

Steele, Mike. "Dominick Argento." *Musical America* (September 1975): 8–9, 40.

Steinberg, Michael. "Tradition and Responsibility." *Perspectives of New Music* (Fall 1962): 154–59.

Tassel, Janet. "A Homecoming for John Harbison." *Boston Globe Magazine*, 26 February 1984, 14, 38, 40, 42, 44, 46, 48.

Taylor, Fannie. "Audiences—What's Happened to Them?" *Musical America* (December 1970): 10–12, 31.

Temianka, Henri. *Facing the Music*. New York: McKay, 1973.

Terry, Kenneth, "Charles Wuorinen, Atonal Tonalities." *Downbeat* 48 (February 1981): 16–18.

Thomson, Virgil. *American Music Since 1910*. New York: Holt, Rinehart & Winston, 1971.

————. "Music in the 1950's." *Music Journal* 19 (January 1961): 12–13, 100–2.

Toffler, Alvin. *The Culture Consumers*. New York: Random House, 1973.

Trilling, Lionel. *Beyond Culture*. New York: Viking, 1964.

Vinton, John, ed. *Dictionary of Contemporary Music*. New York: Dutton, 1974.

Von Gunden, Heidi. *The Music of Pauline Oliveros*. Metuchen, N.J.: Scarecrow, 1983.

Weber, William. *Music and the Middle Class*. New York: Holmes & Meier, 1975.

Westbrook, Peter. "Alan Hovhaness, Angelic Cycles." *Downbeat* 49 (March 1982): 27–29.

Whipple, Harold W. "Beasts and Butterflies: Morton Subotnick's Ghost Scores." *Musical Quarterly* 64 (1983): 425–41.

Wolfe, Tom. *The Painted Word*. New York: Bantam, 1976.

———. *The Purple Decades*. New York: Farrar, Straus & Giroux, 1982.

Wuorinen, Charles. "Are the Arts Doomed on Campus?" *New York Times*, 8 August 1971, sec. 2, 11.

———. "The Composer and the Outside World." *New York Times*, 5 March 1967, sec. 2, 28.

———. "We Spit on the Dead." *Musical America* (December 1974): 16–17.

Yankelovich, Daniel. *New Rules: Searching for Self-Fulfillment in a World Turned Upside Down*. New York: Bantam, 1982.

Index

About the Author

NICHOLAS E. TAWA is Professor of Music at the University of Massachusetts in Boston. He is the author of *Sweet Songs for Gentle Americans: The Parlor Song in America, 1790–1860, A Sound of Strangers: Musical Culture, Acculturation, and the Post-Civil War Ethnic American, A Music for the Millions: Antebellum Democratic Attitudes and the Birth of American Popular Song, Serenading the Reluctant Eagle: American Musical Life, 1925–1945,* and *Art Music in the American Society: The Condition of Art Music in the Late Twentieth Century* (forthcoming).